D0152730

Culture and Customs of Honduras

Honduras. Courtesy of Bookcomp, Inc.

Culture and Customs of Honduras

JANET N. GOLD

Culture and Customs of Latin America and the Caribbean
Peter Standish, Series Editor

GREENWOOD PRESS
Westport, Connecticut • London

Library of Congress Cataloging-in-Publication Data

Gold, Janet N.
  Culture and customs of Honduras / Janet N. Gold.
    p. cm.—(Culture and customs of Latin America and the Caribbean, ISSN 1521–8856)
  Includes bibliographical references and index.
  ISBN 978–0–313–34179–3 (alk. paper)
  1. Honduras—Social life and customs.   I. Title.
  F1503.8.G65   2009
  306.097283–dc22   2008047697

British Library Cataloguing in Publication Data is available.

Copyright © 2009 by Janet N. Gold

All rights reserved. No portion of this book may be
reproduced, by any process or technique, without the
express written consent of the publisher.

Library of Congress Catalog Card Number: 2008047697
ISBN: 978–0–313–34179–3
ISSN: 1521–8856

First published in 2009

Greenwood Press, 88 Post Road West, Westport, CT 06881
An imprint of Greenwood Publishing Group, Inc.
www.greenwood.com

Printed in the United States of America

The paper used in this book complies with the
Permanent Paper Standard issued by the National
Information Standards Organization (Z39.48–1984).

10 9 8 7 6 5 4 3 2 1

To Irma Leticia de Oyuela, "Doña Lety,"
grande dame of Honduran culture
and to Roberto Castillo,
author, philosopher and friend,
In memoriam.

Contents

CONTENTS

Series Foreword

CULTURE IS A problematic word. In everyday language we tend to use it in at least two senses. On the one hand, we speak of cultured people and places full of culture—uses that imply a knowledge or presence of certain forms of behavior or of artistic expression that are socially prestigious. In this sense, large cities and prosperous people tend to be seen as the most cultured. On the other hand, there is an interpretation of culture that is broader and more anthropological; culture in this broader sense refers to whatever traditions, beliefs, customs, and creative activities characterize a given community—in short, it refers to what makes that community different from others. In this second sense, everyone has culture; indeed, it is impossible to be without culture. The problems associated with the idea of culture have been exacerbated in recent years by two trends: less respectful use of language and a greater blurring of cultural differences. Nowadays, culture often means little more than behavior, attitude, or atmosphere. We hear about the culture of the boardroom, of the football team, of the marketplace; there are books with titles like *The Culture of War* by Richard Gabriel (1990) or *The Culture of Narcissism* by Christopher Lasch (1979). In fact, as Christopher Clausen points out in an article published in the *American Scholar* (Summer 1996), we have got ourselves into trouble by using the term so sloppily. People who study culture generally assume that culture (in the anthropological sense) is learned, not genetically determined. Another general assumption made in these days of multiculturalism has been that cultural differences should be respected rather than put under pressure to change. But these assumptions, too, have sometimes proved to be problematic. Multiculturalism is a fine ideal, but in practice it is not always easy to reconcile with the beliefs of the very people who advocate it—for example, is female circumcision an issue of human rights or just a different cultural practice? The blurring of cultural differences is a process that began with the steamship, increased with radio, and is now racing ahead with the Internet. We are becoming globally homogenized. Since the English-speaking world (and the United States in particular) is the dominant force behind this process of homogenization, it behooves us to make efforts to understand the sensibilities of members of other cultures. This series of books, a contribution toward that greater understanding, deals with the neighbors of the United States, with people who have just as much right to call themselves Americans. What are the historical, institutional, religious, and artistic features that make up the modern culture of such peoples as the Haitians, the Chileans, the Jamaicans, and the Guatemalans? How are their habits and assumptions different from our own? What can we learn from them? As we familiarize ourselves with the ways of other countries, we come to see our own from a new perspective. Each volume in the series focuses on a single country. With slight variations to accommodate national differences, each begins by outlining the historical, political, ethnic, geographical, and linguistic context, as well as the religious and social customs, and then proceeds to a discussion of a variety of artistic activities, including the media, cinema, literature, and the visual and performing arts. The authors are all intimately acquainted with the countries concerned; some were born or brought up in them, and each has a professional commitment to enhancing the understanding of the culture in question. We are inclined to suppose that our ways of thinking and behaving are normal. And so they are ... for us. We all need to realize that ours is only one culture among many, and that it is hard to establish by any rational criteria that ours as a whole is any better (or worse) than any other. As individual members of our immediate community, we know that we must learn to respect our differences from one another. Respect for differences between cultures is no less vital. This is particularly true of the United States, a nation of immigrants, but one that sometimes seems to be bent on destroying variety at home and, worse still, on having others follow suit. By learning about other people's cultures, we come to understand and respect them; we earn their respect for us; and, not least, we see ourselves in a new light.

Peter Standish
East Carolina Universtiy

Preface

In this, the first decade of the new millennium, a multiplicity of signs points to the demise of nation-states. The forces of globalization are legion: mass migrations, instantaneous communication, the dissolution of international trade barriers, and media access to news and information around the world. It has become a commonplace to declare that these forces are having a profound effect on local and regional cultures. Many observers, in fact, declare that culture as we have known it is rapidly disappearing. In the case of Honduras, those forces that have played such an important role in the creation of its cultures, such as climate and topography, the exploitation of its natural resources, regionalism, foreign intervention, land ownership, and religion, continue to shape its cultural expressions today, although in ways that reflect the influence of the aforementioned forces of globalization.

Honduras has repeatedly been described as an impoverished country with a long and lamentable history of exploitation by foreign powers. Variously, it has been seen by outsiders as a sleepy cultural backwater; the quintessential banana republic; an impoverished Central American country, exploited by the United States for its own political and military purposes in the region; and most recently as a violent country where youth gangs terrorize the population. Economists have declared that Honduras is rich in natural resources but has been unable to harness those resources to its own collective benefit.

To some degree, all of this is or has been true. Yes, Honduras is one of the poorest nations in the Western Hemisphere. According to a 2008 report by the U.S. State Department, the average annual income is $1,600, second only to Haiti. And yes, Honduras encompasses within its approximately 43,000 square miles, an area slightly smaller than the state of Virginia, enviable natural resources: virgin hardwood forests, fertile agricultural plains, grasslands for grazing, pine-covered mountains, and tropical beaches. Its mineral wealth was exploited by the Spanish during the colonial period; its agricultural land has been exploited by U.S. fruit companies; and the U.S. military has a base just outside Comayagua. The ironies and injustices of these Honduran realities have intrigued social scientists and a considerable amount has been written about the economic, political, military, and social conditions of the country.[1] Indeed, most scholarship in English about Honduras has concerned itself with the history and nature of U.S.–Honduran relations, particularly in the areas of economics and military diplomacy, which may in part explain the prevalent images of violence, poverty, and exploitation.

But these images represent only a partial picture and do not do justice to the complex reality of Honduras, nor do they illuminate the rich cultural expression of the country. Because few scholars outside of Honduras have turned their attention to the country's cultural production, very little information about Honduran arts and literature is available in English. Hondurans themselves, on the other hand, have always had a keen interest in their country; they have studied their reality with great care and have eloquently described and analyzed it in many books and essays and there is ample information available in Spanish. Unfortunately, most Honduran writing has not been translated, leaving the English-speaking reader with limited resources with which to understand our neighbor to the south.

Today, in addition to traditional works of scholarship, we also have the wide world of the Web at our disposal to both post and find information. Evangelical missionaries, international nonprofit aid organizations, and all manner of businesses offering goods and services from escorts to real estate to traditional crafts have Web sites where they offer images of Honduras. Travelers of all ages post descriptions of their experiences in Honduras on their blogs, along with countless photos.

In the preparation of this book I consulted the range of this variety of resources, in print and electronic, in English and in Spanish; I conducted personal interviews and exchanged e-mail correspondence with numerous artists, writers, and other acquaintances in Honduras. I have included information about individuals and areas of achievement not easily accessible in English and, because most non-Hondurans are unfamiliar with the various visual and performing arts of Honduras, these areas have been described with care.

Conversely, I have devoted less attention and space to some topics that are certainly of interest but that have been extensively documented elsewhere in English. One example is the much-studied Mayan civilization that flourished

at Copán in western Honduras. Copán is possibly the most thoroughly studied Mayan archaeological site in Mesoamerica and the interested reader can
quickly find copious information in libraries and on the Web.

As recently as the 1980s, most Hondurans, if asked to define or name their
cultural identity, would most likely have responded that Honduras is a *mestizo*
country. The commonly accepted official story regarding the nation's cultural
heritage was that the indigenous populations that inhabited the territory that
was to become Honduras at the time of the Spanish conquest, were killed,
died from imported diseases, or were enslaved; those who did not suffer this
fate were absorbed into the newly dominant Spanish culture. There was little
specific knowledge of these indigenous groups. When international scholarly
interest turned its attention to the Mayan ruins at Copán in the late nineteenth century and an awareness of the impressive cultural and intellectual
accomplishments of the Maya was popularized, a sense of pride began to grow
in the national consciousness. Honduran historian Darío Euraque, who currently holds the position of director of the Honduran Institute of Anthropology and History and has written extensively on the evolution of Honduran
national identity, has asserted that a "mayanization" occurred in official discourse in the early decades of the twentieth century that essentially erased the
actual diversity of Honduras' ethnic and racial past and adopted in its place a
mestizo identity, but one that foregrounded the Mayan heritage.[2]

A number of other Honduran scholars such as Leticia de Oyuela and Marvin Barahona have contributed to exploring the forces that have shaped Honduran national and cultural identity throughout its history. Much important
work is also being done by linguists, anthropologists, and social scientists who
are not only reconstructing Honduras' indigenous and African past but also
documenting these cultures in the present and in some cases have become
actively involved in supporting the efforts of indigenous groups to keep alive
or revive their cultural heritage. Consequently, increasing numbers of Hondurans are becoming more aware of their diverse cultural heritage and are re-
alizing that, rather than a single, homogeneous culture with a chronologically
traceable history, Honduras has various cultures. To reflect this contemporary
consciousness, a discussion of Honduras's regional and linguistic diversity is
followed by sections on the country's indigenous groups.

The chapter on religion goes beyond the long unquestioned assumption
that Honduras is a Catholic country. Although it may be true that a majority
of Hondurans embrace the Catholic faith, evangelical Protestant churches are
being "planted" at an astonishing rate and this phenomenon is discussed.

One sometimes hears Hondurans themselves complain that there is little
culture in their country, perhaps because Honduran cultural expression does
not always conform to prevailing U.S. or European standards. A high rate of

illiteracy certainly contributes to this perception, yet the oral tradition is alive and well in Honduras and is an integral piece of the cultural mosaic. In a similar fashion, the skill and imagination evident in Honduran handcrafts add color, texture, and functionality to Honduran art. In recognition of the diversity of cultural expression of Honduras, sections are devoted to oral literature and handcrafts.

What then, does characterize Honduran culture? What makes a song or a poem or a ritual identifiably Honduran? Some would say that there is no such thing as a cultural essence or personality. Honduran author Roberto Castillo once said that there is *cercanía* or feeling of closeness within Honduran culture that is its most valuable treasure. He added that this feeling is a great unknown and that its rich possibilities have yet to be explored.[3] I believe that this closeness, real yet elusive, has its origin in a deep love for and attachment to the Honduran land, to a shared history of invasion, exploitation and resistance, and to a shared struggle against poverty. Castillo, like countless other Honduran writers and artists, made it his life's work to explore the rich possibilities of this heritage. It is my hope that this book contributes to that exploration.

NOTES

1. A sampling of these studies might include Peckenham, Nancy and Street, Annie, Eds., *Honduras: Portrait of a Captive Nation,* New York: Praeger, 1985; Schulz, Donald E. and Sundloff Schulz, Deborah, *The U.S., Honduras and the Crisis in Central America,* Boulder, CO: Westview Press, 1994; Euraque, Darío. *Reinterpreting the Banana Republic: Region and State in Honduras.* Chapel Hill, NC: UNC Press, 1996.

2. Euraque, Darío A. *Conversaciones históricas con el mestizaje y su identidad nacional en Honduras.* San Pedro Sula: Centro Editorial, 2004.

3. Castillo, who died in January 2008, was fascinated with the cultural personality of his country. The author enjoyed many hours conversing with him about everything from Honduran religion and politics to architecture and poetry.

Acknowledgments

NUMEROUS FRIENDS, COLLEAGUES, and acquaintances in Honduras have assisted me as I searched for information and puzzled over the complexities of their country's culture. Some helped me long distance; others kept me company on my travels around Tegucigalpa and other parts of Honduras. Amanda Castro and Rebeca Becerra shared manuscripts, put me on cultural e-mail lists and generally kept me up to date on cultural happenings. Guillermo Yuscarán, Jorge Federico Travieso, Isabel Pérez, Leslie Jiménez, Regina Zelaya, Mirian Sevilla Rojas, and Blanca Guifarro were gracious hosts and thoughtful interlocutors. América Mejía and Bayardo Blandón of Mujeres en las Artes provided me with useful information and insights. My long-term thanks to so many people who have taught me about Honduran culture over the years, among them Ada Luz Pineda, Aída Sabonge, Delia Fajardo, Rafael Murillo Selva, Helen Umaña, Isolda Arita, Roberto Sosa, Roberto Quesada, Rigoberto Paredes, María Eugenia Ramos, Anarella Vélez, Juan Almendares, and María Elena Sánchez. Although I have never met Wendy Griffin, her work on Honduran culture has been invaluable. I especially appreciate her informative and very readable articles in *Honduras This Week*. Leticia de Oyuela and Roberto Castillo have been generous friends and colleagues over the years. I have learned so much about Honduras from them and have enjoyed our conversations and correspondence. I miss them both.

I appreciate the assistance of Deb Watson and the other reference librarians at Dimond Library of the University of New Hampshire and am grateful for the permission to purchase numerous books on Honduran culture for the library collection during a visit to Honduras in 2007. In spring 2008 I taught a class at the University of New Hampshire on the cultures of Central America. I would like to express my appreciation to all the students in that class for their enthusiasm and inspiration. I learned a great deal from them as we studied the indigenous cultures of Honduras together. A special thank you to graduate student Joseph Dunn, whose research findings and thoughtful ideas for an independent study on Honduran cultural identity were very useful and informative. And I thank Beth Derby, who provided generous assistance with skill and good humor as I struggled with the technology of transforming photographs into usable illustrations and my editor at Greenwood Press, Kaitlin Ciarmiello, for her ongoing assistance and encouragement.

Chronology

1642	British take Roatán Island
1796	British reoccupy Bay Islands, bring in "Black Caribs" from St. Vincent
1812	First Central American Constitution
1822	Central America joins Agustín Iturbide's Mexican Empire
1823	Central America declares independence and forms the United Provinces of Central America
1829	Honduras becomes an independent state with its own constitution
1830	*Gaceta del gobierno* published on Honduras' first printing press
1838	Dissolution of Central American union
1839	John Lloyd Stephens and Frederick Catherwood explore and purchase, for $50US, the Mayan ruins at Copán
1842	Francisco Morazán executed after unsuccessful attempt to reestablish Central American union
1845	Academia Literaria de Tegucigalpa founded; becomes National University in 1881
1850	Clayton-Bulwer Treaty between the United States and Great Britain signed, agreeing that neither country will attempt to exercise exclusive control over any part of Central America
1860	William Walker executed near Trujillo
1870–1890	Period of Liberal reform in Honduras
1871	Miner Cooper Keith begins construction of rail line in Costa Rica that signals the beginning of the vast rail, banana, and coffee empire that extended along the north coast of Honduras
1880	Tegucigalpa becomes capital of Honduras
1893	Lucila Gamero de Medina publishes first Honduran novel
1899	United Fruit Company formed
1924	U.S. Marines occupy Tegucigalpa
1930	First edition of *Corazón sangrante* by Clementina Suárez, first book of poetry published by a woman in Honduras
1932–1948	Tiburcio Carías Andino president and dictator of Honduras
1954	Honduras' first general labor strike (begins May 1 among banana company workers on North Coast, supported by industrial workers throughout country; on July 12, strikers' demands are met)

1955	Honduran women win the right to vote
1957–1963	Ramón Villeda Morales wins a free election and initiates progressive reforms
1960	Completion of Honduran portion of the Pan-American Highway
1963–1971	Military removes Villeda Morales and Conservatives return to power
1969	War between Honduras and El Salvador
1974	Hurricane Fifi nearly destroys North Coast banana plantings
1980–1990	Honduras a safe haven for anti-Sandinista Contras; "dirty war" results in approximately 180 assassinations or disappearances of government critics; dramatic increase in rural to urban migration
1982	A new constitution is approved and a freely elected civilian government comes into power
1982–2006	Seven consecutive democratic elections
1983–1984	Expansion of U.S. military presence in Honduras
1990s	Expansion of *maquiladoras* (more than 100,000 workers in at least 150 factories)
1998	Hurricane Mitch devastates Honduras, killing approximately 5,600 people, leaving 1.5 million displaced and causing more than $3 billion in damage
2008	President Mel Zelaya joins ALBA (Bolivarian Alternative for the Americas)

1

National Identity and Cultural Diversity

THE CONTEXT: A COUNTRY PROFILE

HONDURAS, LOCATED IN the center of the Central American isthmus, has one of the largest landmasses of the seven Central American countries, smaller only than neighboring Nicaragua. Its population of more than 7.6 million is unevenly distributed throughout its approximately 43,000 square miles.[1] The largest concentrations are in the central highlands in and around the capital city, Tegucigalpa and in the northwestern Ulúa Valley where the industrial, commercial, and residential centers of San Pedro Sula and El Progresso are located. Bordered on the south by Nicaragua and to the east by Guatemala and El Salvador, Honduras has a long and beautiful Caribbean coast on the north and a much smaller Pacific coast to the south in the Gulf of Fonseca, which it shares with Nicaragua and El Salvador. Choluteca is the largest city in this southern region and serves as the commercial center for its shrimp, meat, and dairy products. The region known as La Mosquitia comprises the northeastern region of the country. It is sparsely populated and commercially underdeveloped, with no highways and only minimal infrastructure. The shores of its many rivers are home to small communities of mostly indigenous heritage. The Bay Islands, off the northern, Caribbean coast, are a cluster of small, beautiful islands that are being developed for the tourist industry.

The terrain of Honduras is generally mountainous in the interior with narrow coastal plains, creating climate zones that are subtropical in the coastal lowlands and temperate in the interior highlands. The country's highest peak is Cerro Las Minas with an elevation of 9,416 feet. Although Honduras is subject to frequent but mild earthquakes, it has never experienced a devastating earthquake like its neighbors Guatemala, El Salvador, and Nicaragua and boasts of some of the oldest churches in Central America due to the fact that Tegucigalpa and Comayagua, its major centers of population during colonial times, were never destroyed by earthquakes. Hurricanes, on the other hand, have caused great destruction throughout the country, more so in recent times as a result of deforestation caused by logging and land clearing for farming and cattle grazing and the overbuilding on unsuitable terrain due to a rapidly expanding urban population. Hurricanes Fifi in 1974 and Mitch in 1998 were particularly devastating and exacerbated the already high incidence of poverty and social inequity. But tragedies sometimes generate change and various national and international aid and development organizations are designing and implementing a range of poverty reduction strategies, many of which have significant cultural components and are discussed throughout this book.

Honduras is a democratic constitutional republic, having won independence from Spain in 1821. The National Congress and the Supreme Court are located in Tegucigalpa. The president appoints governors for the eighteen political divisions of the republic, called *departamentos* (departments). They include Colón, Atlántida, Cortés, Yoro, Olancho, El Paraíso, Francisco Morazán, Choluteca, Valle, La Paz, Comayagua, Intibucá, Lempira, Ocotepeque, Copán, Santa Bárbara, Comayagua, and the Bay Islands. Although as an independent republic it has experienced a degree of political instability caused by a numbers of factors such as foreign interventions, the corruption of political leaders, and individual as well as regional political rivalries, its recent history has been characterized by democratic elections and the peaceful handing over of office. Throughout the twentieth century, Honduras' presidents have generally supported U.S. policies and collaborated politically and militarily with U.S. interests in their country. However, the current president, Manuel Zelaya, popularly called "Mel," who took office in 2006, has made news by aligning his government with Hugo Chávez, the controversial president of Venezuela and by joining ALBA, the Bolivarian Alternative for the Americas.

For most of its history, Honduras was primarily an agricultural and rural society. Tegucigalpa, the capital, was the center of political and cultural life, whereas small cities such as Comayagua, Danlí, Trujillo, and San Pedro Sula were regional centers of commerce and culture. This picture has changed dramatically in recent decades, however, and it is possible that the population of Honduras will soon be more urban than rural. Another factor in this changing portrait is the large numbers of Hondurans who leave their country to live and work abroad. Hondurans have migrated to other Central American countries, to Europe, and to the United States. Many of these individuals send money home on a regular basis, thereby contributing to the local economy and to the well-being of their families. Although some emigrants stay in their new homes, others return to Honduras to visit or to stay. Their influence inevitably contributes to the internationalization of Honduran culture.

Spanish is the official language of Honduras, but English has long been important and is increasingly so due to the influence of the media, the Internet, and Honduran migration to the United States. English instruction is offered in public schools but often is inadequate. There are many private schools in Honduras; most of them are bilingual and students receive instruction in Spanish as well as English or to a lesser degree French or another second language. Some Hondurans of indigenous heritage continue to speak their traditional language, often in addition to Spanish.

REGIONAL DIVERSITY

The diverse cultures of Honduras are to a large extent delimited by its geography. In some geographic areas, such as La Mosquitia and parts of Olancho, the natural environment still largely determines the activities of daily life and moderates the pace of social and cultural change. The large cities, in contrast, such as San Pedro Sula and Tegucigalpa, have attracted growing numbers of previously rural residents in search of education and economic opportunity, for whom the urban experience promises the possibility of independence from the vagaries of a life tied to the earth and the seasons. The following regional divisions reflect geographic as well as historic and cultural determinants.

Tegucigalpa and Environs

The culture of the southern and central region is dominated by Tegucigalpa and to a lesser extent Comayagua. Gold and silver in the hills around Tegucigalpa and fertile farming and extensive grazing land around Comayagua produced the material wealth that attracted the interest and intervention first of Spain and later the United States. It is the area of the country most imbued with Spanish culture. Among the strongest and most enduring cultural traits that can be traced to the Spanish influence are a patriarchal family organization that is reflected in broader social and political structures; the Catholic religion; the importance of honor; and the family as the single most important social unit. Also because of its ties to Europe, this is the region that has paid the most attention to cultivating the various arts according to European and North American models. Accordingly, in Tegucigalpa one can attend a concert of Baroque classical music, a performance of a Tchaikovsky ballet, or an English-language production of a Eugene O'Neill play by an amateur theater troupe. The main campus of the National University is in Tegucigalpa as are the National Library, the National Archives, the National Institute of Anthropology and History, and numerous other public and private institutions of higher education, as well as the National Art Gallery and various museums and private art galleries. As the national capital, Tegucigalpa is also the center of government and home to the National Congress. Consequently, the political culture of Tegucigalpa has an air of prestige and traditional formality. The historic center of the city is a crowded labyrinth of narrow cobblestone streets, small parks and plazas, street vendors, and a colorful mingling of commercial, residential, and government buildings.

Tegucigalpa is also a rapidly growing city with wide commercial boulevards, an active nightlife and a modern youth culture. Notwithstanding the influences of global culture, there are still many endearingly old-fashioned customs prevalent in this region. It is not uncommon, for example, to receive an elegantly printed invitation to a lecture or a book presentation, hand-delivered by a messenger to your office or place of residence. Indeed, there are still residents of Tegucigalpa who will not attend a public lecture if they are not personally and formally invited. Even in our fast-paced world of multitasking and days taken up with a series of appointments and meetings that punctually follow one after the other, it is likely that your Honduran friend will call at 2 P.M. as you sit wondering what is keeping her from your 1 P.M. lunch date, to say that she's running late and could you make it the day after tomorrow instead. It is just as likely that another Honduran acquaintance will spend hours driving you around the city, preparing *nacatamales* for your visit and introducing you to his extended family.

Some say that the name Tegucigalpa was derived from an indigenous phrase translated as "Hill of Silver." Whether or not that was the case, there is no question that mineral riches in the surrounding hills played a central role in the importance of the region. Around Tegucigalpa are numerous small towns tucked into hillsides and valleys that have seen mining companies come and go. Most of the ore extracted from the mines first by the Spanish and later by North American companies was exported. While the companies operated and the mines produced, boomtowns flourished. San Juancito, headquarters of the Rosario Mining Co., boasted a Pepsi-Cola bottling plant and claims to have shown the first movie ever screened in Honduras. There were jobs and money. When the mining company ceased operations in 1954 it left empty buildings and open mine shafts. Today, Honduran artist Regina Aguilar oversees metalworking, glass art, a handmade paper workshop, a school for children, and an annual arts festival in this historic town nestled in the hills on the edge of La Tigra National Park.

Like San Juancito, most of these towns saw periods of economic boom that quickly dissipated when the foreign interests left. Santa Lucía, Valle de Angeles, Ojojona and San Juancito are examples of communities that have managed to survive or even prosper by encouraging a revival of traditional crafts, supporting cultural centers or simply being quiet, charming towns where residents of Tegucigalpa go for weekends and holidays or perhaps have second homes. Santa Lucía in fact is quickly becoming a bedroom community for people who work in the capital but prefer to live in a quieter and less polluted environment.

Farther to the east is Danlí, fifty-seven miles from the capital, close enough to allow relatively easy access but far enough to have an independent cultural life. Located in the Department of El Paraíso in a vast valley graced by seven hills, Danlí proudly calls itself "The Cradle of Culture" (La Cuna de la Cultura) because several important figures in Honduran culture were born there, including Lucila Gamero de Medina and Manuel Adalid y Gamero. The flat, fertile valley has become known for its excellent cigars, which are sold around the world.

Also in this region of hot, dry valleys and cool pine-forested hills are the towns of San Antonio de Oriente and Yuscarán. San Antonio de Oriente is a small, quiet town made famous by the artist José Antonio Velásquez, who painted the town's people, houses, churches, and hills in a charming, folkloric style. Yuscarán, the capital of the Department of El Paraíso, was founded in 1730 when gold, silver, and other minerals were discovered in the area.

For some Hondurans, this region and its typical cultural symbols represent the essence of Honduran identity: the white stucco buildings with terra cotta ceramic tile roofs; the small towns with their central plaza with its Catholic church and kiosk where local bands play Sunday concerts; pine-covered hills; red clay soil; soccer matches and painted ceramic roosters. This may well be the region where *mestizaje* or the blending of Spanish and indigenous cultures has been most pervasive. The spirit and culture of the Lenca indigenous people, who were the most numerous and powerful group living in Honduras at the time of the arrival of the Spanish, are now an integral and indivisible part of the cultural personality of southern and central Honduras.

The North Coast

The North Coast (unlike the south coast) is typically written using capital letters, thereby indicating that it is thought of as a distinct place with a proper name and not merely a geographical direction. Beginning near the Guatemalan border and proceeding east, the towns of Puerto Cortés, Tela, La Ceiba, and Trujillo on the Caribbean coast along with the city of San Pedro

Sula approximately thirty-six miles south of Puerto Cortés form the major centers of population in this region. This was where the Spanish first arrived in Central America, and where the first battles between the indigenous people and the Spanish and among the Spanish themselves were fought. Trujillo was the site of the first capital of Honduras and the important fort at Omoa was built in 1778 to protect Spanish interests against the English. But the Spanish did not put serious effort into establishing settlements in this part of the country, perhaps because they found the hot, humid climate enervating, perhaps because their interests lie in exploiting more immediate sources of wealth, such as the gold and silver in the hills in the south central region. The proximity of the North Coast and the Bay Islands off the coast to the English islands of the Caribbean and to the southern coast of the United States brought the influence of the English language and culture, commerce with such ports as Miami and New Orleans, and the settlement of the Garífuna people. The wide fertile plains around San Pedro Sula and to the east attracted the North American companies that built railroads and banana plantations that have dominated the economy of the region since the beginning of the twentieth century.

San Pedro Sula, with 15 percent of the country's population, is the second largest city in Honduras and the agricultural, industrial, and commercial hub of the country, producing 60 percent of its gross national product. Culturally and ethnically, San Pedro Sula is a city of immigrants. In 1866, when the first non-Spanish newcomers arrived, a group from New Orleans fleeing post-Civil War reconstruction, San Pedro Sula was a village with no priest, no school, and rustic one-story wattle and daub (*bahareque*) architecture with thatched palm roofs. Successive waves of immigration since then have made it an ethnically diverse and economically vibrant city with a mix of French, English, Spanish, Italian, German, Arab, and Jewish populations. Transplants from other regions of Honduras, particularly Olancho, have added their own local flavor to the mix. The early immigrants came to build a railroad, to farm, to log, and to trade. Most recently, newcomers from other parts of the country hoping to secure employment in the assembly plants and factories known as *maquiladoras* have been drawn to the region. *Maquiladoras* now employ well over 100,000 workers, the majority of whom—some estimates are as high as 80 percent to 85 percent—are young women between the ages of fourteen and thirty.

Observers agree that the culture of San Pedro Sula is different from that of Tegucigalpa. It is a culture of commerce and trade, of hard work that earns one higher wages than in other parts of the country, and of taking pleasure in the material side of life. Sampedranos, as the residents of San Pedro Sula are called, pride themselves on being *igualados* or having an egalitarian social consciousness, although there are of course significant differences in lifestyle depending on one's economic status. Families of Middle Eastern heritage tend to socialize together in private clubs and the wealthy look to Miami to purchase the latest fashions and the newest technology and tend to educate their children in bilingual private schools. As people in search of jobs and better wages continue to migrate to the region, the poorly serviced neighborhoods on the periphery have become increasingly violent as gangs of youth, known as *maras*, extend their operations into these areas.

Perhaps because of Tegucigalpa's long-standing reputation as the "Athens of Honduras," the center of high culture where circles of writers and artists formed, where books were published, and international touring companies performed, the arts have not flourished in San Pedro Sula in the proportion one would expect given the city's population and resources. It has been suggested that cultural events there are sponsored and attended more for their social and entertainment value than for their contribution to cultural growth. Although this may have been the case in the past, a sense of cultural independence and ownership has grown and taken root among artists and writers in San Pedro Sula, La Ceiba, and the North Coast in general. Writers such as Julio Escoto, Juan Ramón Saravia, Mario Gallardo, and Marta Susana Prieto and Honduras' foremost literary critic, Helen Umaña all live in San Pedro Sula. And Honduras' best-loved musical artist, Guillermo Anderson, proudly hails from La Ceiba.

Just as Honduras as a country can no longer unequivocally assert that it is a *mestizo* nation, Tegucigalpa can no longer claim hegemonic control of Honduran culture.

The Bay Islands

A group of islands in the Caribbean, approximately thirty miles north of mainland Honduras, known collectively as the Bay Islands or Islas de la Bahía, share some of the cultural characteristics of the North Coast but their location, history, and ethnic make-up all contribute to their unique role in the colorful mosaic of contemporary Honduran culture. Roatán, Utila, and Guanaja are the main inhabited islands; smaller islands include Barbareta, Santa Elena, and Morat. Farther removed from the main group are the Islas Santillanas, formerly known as Swan Islands and two clusters of cays, Cayos Zapotillos and Cayos Cochinos.

Columbus landed on the island of Bonacca (Guanaja) in 1502 and records from that voyage mention the presence of indigenous groups. Further exploration and settlement by Europeans did not begin until well over 100 years later and even then it was sparse and intermittent. Because of its designs on the north coast of the mainland, where it established a fort at Trujillo, Spain wished to control the islands offshore as well. Britain was also interested in establishing a trading presence in the region. The first European settlement on the islands was short-lived, when settlers sponsored by the British Provident Company of Massachusetts relocated to the island of Roatán in 1638 after being forced from their settlements on the Mosquito Shore by the Spanish. In 1642 the Spanish drove them from Roatán as well. Britain retaliated by destroying the Spanish fort at Trujillo and for the next 100 years Spain paid little attention to the islands or the north coast and British traders and pirates, particularly woodcutters interested in dyewood, which was used in the European textile industry, found the islands to be an attractive option, with their combination of accessible open harbors and numerous mangrove-lined coves where contraband could be safely hidden. As Britain's presence in the Caribbean increased and as African slaves were imported to work on the sugar plantations, Anglo-Antilleans and Afro-Antilleans made their way to the islands. They came as traders, seamen, escaped slaves, and settlers. In 1797, hundreds of Black Caribs, people of mixed African, Arawak, and European descent, were shipped to Roatán from the island of St. Vincent, where they presented a problem to British interests because of their alliances with the French. Known as Garífuna or Garinagu, they settled in Punta Gorda on the north shore of the island, where some of their descendents still live.

Spain and Britain continued to compete for control of the Caribbean coast of Central America until the Wyke-Cruz Treaty between Honduras and Britain in 1859, when the Bay Islands became part of the then independent Republic of Honduras. This treaty was agreed on by the two governments without consulting the local residents, who by this time were a diverse population, numbering approximately 1,800, consisting of Black Caribs and the descendents of Scottish, Irish, and English traders and settlers from various British Caribbean islands, especially Jamaica and the Cayman Islands. (The Spanish had forcibly removed the indigenous population earlier in the nineteenth century because they were reported to be assisting the British.) When news of the treaty reached the islanders the general reaction was one of outrage, as the vast majority considered themselves citizens of the British Empire. They were primarily Protestant English speakers and in fact, until the 1990s, English was the dominant language in the islands.

The Bay Islands, with their tropical climate, beautiful beaches, and excellent diving on the nearby barrier reef, have recently become known as attractive destinations for tourists and an international clientele in search of vacation homes and investment opportunities. The accelerated, some say overheated, pace of development has brought job opportunities and the inevitable influx of Spanish-speaking Hondurans from the mainland. In just fifteen years, Roatán has gone from being a quiet, undeveloped, sparsely populated

English-speaking island with a single dive resort, to one of the major dive destinations in the world. The beachfront town of West End has more than one dozen dive shops; the pristine white sand beach at West Bay is lined with expensive resorts and condos and trash disposal has become an urgent concern. Island natives are now a minority and Spanish has become prevalent, although many residents are bilingual.

Northeastern Honduras

Northeastern Honduras encompasses the area shared with Nicaragua known as La Mosquitia and also the Department of Olancho and the eastern part of the Department of Colón. The coastal area of this region has sweeping sandy beaches, large lagoons, low-lying wetlands and extensive savannahs. Inland from the coast one finds low mountain ranges, tropical forest, and plains crossed by rivers. This vast area has presented a challenge throughout history to human attempts to develop, settle, and exploit it; it continues to be the most inaccessible part of Honduras. There are no highways or even year-round passable roads in the region. Local transportation is by boat on the numerous rivers and lagoons, where all settlements are located.

Historically, this has been an area of cultural and economic encounter and exchange among groups representing the Mesoamerican cultures to the north and the rainforest cultures from the south. The Mesoamerican cultures introduced a sedentary lifestyle, a stratified, hierarchical social structure, subsistence centered on the cultivation of maize and the development of durable structures and implements made from stone and clay. The rainforest cultures, on the other hand, contributed a hunter-gatherer, nomadic or semi-nomadic lifestyle; a tribal social structure based on clans and chiefs; the consumption of yucca and other root vegetables; and the fabrication of dwellings, weapons, tools, and musical instruments using the more perishable materials of the forests and wetlands such as reeds, bark, and feathers.

Archaeologists have yet to thoroughly explore the rich record waiting to reveal the history, cosmology, and daily life of the region's early inhabitants. Cave paintings such as those found at Cuyamel, legends of mythical cities in the jungle, petroglyphs along the banks of rivers, anthropomorphic idols, and ceramics all point to extensive contact among peoples from the north and the south. Analyzing the nature, extent, and consequences of these contacts will surely help us understand this fascinating piece of prehistory.

During the colonial period, the Spanish presence in the region was minimal. English traders and pirates, however, engaged in lively and lucrative commerce with the indigenous inhabitants. Trees were felled, animals were hunted for their pelts, gold was extracted from the rivers, and rubber was harvested from the *castilla* tree. In exchange for their cooperation with the British, the natives were supplied with firearms, tools, and other objects of foreign manufacture. After Honduras became an independent republic in 1829 it initiated efforts to reduce British influence in its territory. In 1850, the Clayton-Bulwer Treaty between the United States and Great Britain was signed, agreeing that neither country would attempt to exercise exclusive control over any part of Central America. But many of the region's indigenous inhabitants continued to identify with Britain more than with Honduras until well into the twentieth century. Although this area has slowly and gradually developed a relationship with the central government, it continues to be the least accessible and most economically and socially marginal part of the country.

This very inaccessibility has fired the imagination of a series of adventurous travelers who have written about their experiences. Their accounts often have an Indiana Jones flavor to them and their descriptions and opinions may seem outdated to the contemporary reader, but they offer firsthand observations of the people and the natural environment of this fascinating region. Of particular interest are *Waikna: Adventures on the Mosquito Shore*, by Samuel A. Bard, first published in 1855, a facsimile of the original was published in 1965 by the University of Florida Press; *Mosquito Coast: An Account of a Journey through the Jungles of Honduras*, by Peter Keenagh (Boston: Houghton Mifflin Co., 1938); and the more recent *Around the Edge: A Journey among Pirates, Guerrillas, Former Cannibals and Turtle Fishermen along the Miskito Coast*, by Peter Ford (New York: Viking, 1991).

Since the mid-twentieth century, the region's sparse and widely scattered population and its large areas of untitled land have attracted farmers and ranchers from other parts of the republic whose presence and patterns of land use often conflict with those of the native residents. The traditional practice of communal ownership of land and the belief that the earth's bounty is limitless and there for the taking, have inevitably come into question. Competition for land and other natural resources such as game, fish, and timber increased in the 1970s and 1980s when regional turmoil from the Nicaraguan Contra War led to the displacement of thousands of Nicaraguans who were housed in refugee camps in the Honduran Mosquitia. The subsequent disruption in land-use patterns, the increased population in fragile ecosystems, and the upsurge in illegal trafficking of drugs and other black market goods, occasioned rapid change in the region. Around the same time, indigenous political action groups such as MASTA (Moskitia Asla Takanka) and MOPAWI (Moskitia Pawasa) came into being to work toward the sustainable development of La Mosquitia and the recognition of indigenous rights to land and natural resources. The stress put on this natural environment and its inhabitants caused the Honduran government in collaboration with UNESCO to create the Río Plátano Biosphere Reserve in 1980 with the intention of protecting its flora and fauna and introducing models of sustainable development.

The Gulf of Fonseca

The southernmost Honduran departments of Valle and Choluteca open onto the Pacific Ocean in the Gulf of Fonseca. Honduras shares the 419 kilometers of coastline with El Salvador to the west and Nicaragua to the east and claims ownership of three of the islands that dot the gulf: El Tigre, Zacate Grande, and Exposición. The town of Amapala on the island of Zacate Grande was historically the only port of entry to Honduras from the Pacific, but the port of San Lorenzo on the mainland now serves that function. Military maneuvers, drug trafficking, and fishing keep this a busy tri-national body of water. Its beaches, estuaries, lagoons, and mangroves provide refuge for numerous species of birds and all manner of marine life. The development of aquaculture in the waters of the Gulf, beginning in the 1980s, has made Honduras a major exporter of farm-raised shrimp, but it has also put a serious strain on the environment. Recently, the governments of Honduras, El Salvador, and Nicaragua signed an agreement to work cooperatively toward peace, security, and sustainable development in the Gulf. A number of non-governmental organizations (NGOs) are active in the Gulf, researching and promoting ways for the local population to participate in sustainable fishing practices.

The beaches are popular with local tourists and many Hondurans own vacation homes and condos in Coyolito and in and around Cedeño. The weather in the Gulf of Fonseca and adjacent departments is hot and dry. The rainy season, from May to October, brings welcome afternoon downpours.

The Chorotega indigenous people, believed to have been related to the Nahuatl-speaking inhabitants of central Mexico, most likely migrated through this region and had contact with the Lenca as they made their way south to the Pacific coast of Nicaragua.

Western Honduras

This section of the country borders Guatemala to the northwest and El Salvador to the southwest. It is a beautiful area of mountains, forests and small towns and villages. In the northwestern region, the proximity to Guatemala and its indigenous influence can be felt, even though the Chortí, of Maya descent, no longer speak their native language, Chol, or wear traditional dress. The ruins of Copán are among the most beautiful, interesting, and studied of the numerous Maya sites throughout Mesoamerica. The interest generated by archaeological excavations and findings has made Copán one of the most visited tourist sites in Honduras, along with Roatán and the Bay Islands. There are other as yet unexplored archaeological sites in western Honduras as well as several national parks and wildlife refuges. This historic, cultural, and environmental richness may some day result in the development of local infrastructure, which currently is rudimentary except in the town of Copán Ruinas. North and east of Copán is the department of Santa Barbara, known for its skilled craftspeople. To the south and east is Cerquín, an area of historic and legendary significance for the Lenca people. It is said that the Lenca chief, Lempira, was in fact not killed by the Spanish in an infamous battle on Cerquin Mountain in 1537, as some historians claim, but rather escaped into the labyrinth of caves and underground passages beneath the mountain where his spirit lives on.

CULTURAL DIVERSITY: HISTORICAL BACKGROUND

Owing to its geographic position, Central America, which serves as a land bridge separating two oceans and linking two continents, has great natural and cultural diversity.[2] Approximately three million years ago, when the one great sea that separated North and South America became the Atlantic and Pacific oceans, divided by the narrow isthmus we call Central America, the great northern and southern migrations of flora and fauna began. Armadillos, porcupines, and yucca traveled north while corn, bears, and camelids, the ancestors of llamas and alpacas, moved south. This migration pattern occasioned the inevitable intermingling among species of flora, fauna, and later, human groups. It has resulted in the extinction of some species and the creation of others.

Honduras, located in the center of this land bridge, has been the setting throughout history for the contact, collision, and intermingling of diverse cultural groups. It has been home to ethnic groups whose origins have been traced both to North and South America as well as Africa and the Caribbean. Since anthropological and archaeological research is by definition cumulative and evolving, it is likely that current theories regarding the settlement of Honduras by indigenous groups will change as more sites are excavated and current populations are studied, but there is currently some evidence that migrants from the north settled in the area about 5,000 years ago. They were hunter-gatherers and farmers who eventually settled in villages, some of which, such as Copán, later became urban centers that participated in far-reaching trade networks. Their culture, known as Maya Mesoamerican, was dominant in the western and southern part of Honduras. The eastern and central regions of Honduras, referred to as the Intermediate Area, were populated by groups evidencing macro-Chibcha influence from northern South America, and on the Caribbean coast there is evidence of the influence of Amazonian culture. The inhabitants of all of these areas in turn had contact with one another, as can be deduced by the hybrid nature of some cultural artifacts. The Lenca, for example, built ceremonial structures that show Mesoamerican influence but also had macro-Chibcha characteristics, whereas the Tolupán language is thought to be of the Hokan group, whose origins were in the southwest United States, although it shares characteristics with Tlequistlatecan from Oaxaca, Mexico. It is currently widely accepted that the Mesoamerican frontier was not at all an easily traceable boundary but rather that Mesoamerican culture permeated ever southward, blending with, influencing, and being influenced by macro-Chibcha culture. Prehistoric Honduras, consequently, was a region of extensive contact among peoples resulting in great cultural diversity.

According to one estimate, at the time of the arrival of the Spanish to the area the native population of Honduras numbered approximately 800,000, with 75 percent of this number occupying the western and central portions. This population was decimated in a few short decades due to the Spanish wars of conquest. By the first half of the seventeenth century, there were only 25,000 native inhabitants left. Those who survived the wars and were captured were often used as slaves on Caribbean plantations and as porters in Spanish expeditions to Peru. Countless numbers died from epidemics of diseases imported from Europe and Africa. Many of those who survived fled to the mountainous interior where the Spanish cavalry could not capture them and lived in small, isolated groups. Others, such as the inhabitants of La Mosquitia, had scant contact with the Spanish during the first two centuries of Spanish colonization due to the inaccessible nature of their environment.

The drastic reduction of the indigenous population occasioned the importation of African slaves to Honduras, beginning in 1542. Subsequent settlement on the north coast and in the Bay Islands by the Dutch, French, and English, who brought African slaves from various Caribbean islands, added to the African population and resulted in increased diversity among the Miskito and Sumo. This mixed African-indigenous population has been referred to as Zambo or Sambo Miskito. Hondurans of mixed Afro-Caribbean and British descent are commonly called Creoles and are English-speaking. The relatively small number of Spanish women in Honduras during the early colonial period led to a rapid process of miscegenation and the early creation of a *mestizo* or mixed European and indigenous population.

The subsequent arrival in the mid-eighteenth century of shipments of slaves to build forts along the north coast further increased the African population. In 1797, two ships carrying Garifuna or Black Caribs brought their human cargo to Roatán in the Bay Islands.

Throughout the later part of the nineteenth century and well into the twentieth, the population continued to diversify with the arrival of individuals from the Caribbean islands, Arabs of Palestinian origin, and a small number of Chinese. During the twentieth century, the political instability throughout the region occasioned the movement of citizens from other Central American countries to reside temporarily or permanently in Honduras, thus adding ever-new ingredients to the ethnic mix.

LANGUAGE DIVERSITY

Spanish is the official language of the Republic of Honduras.[3] In addition to Spanish, a number of other languages are spoken. In some cases only a reduced number of individuals continue to use their indigenous language. Recent interest in ethnic diversity and language extinction on a global scale has prompted a movement within the academic community and also among NGOs to document language use and preserve in written form the lexicon and syntax of native languages that until recently have survived exclusively through the oral tradition. Nonetheless, numerous contradictions characterize the data on population size and numbers of native speakers. Although it has become a commonplace to assert that indigenous populations throughout the world are on the verge of extinction, a recent study among the Tawahka, for example, shows an increase in the birth rate in the village of Krausirpe.[4]

Tol, spoken only by the approximately 600 Tolupán who live on the Montaña de la Flor, is unique in Honduras. Some linguists have posited that it shares characteristics with the Hokan family whose origins are in the southwest United States, whereas others claim it bears greater resemblance to the macro-Chibcha language family.

Other native languages include Pech, spoken by some 1,500 people living in a remote section of northern Olancho Department and Tawahka, whose speakers in Honduran territory number around 1,000. They live in small villages on the banks of the Patuca River in La Mosquitia. Many Tawahka are trilingual as they speak *twanka*, their name for their language, Miskito, the language of their neighbors, and Spanish. Tawahka men all speak Miskito and/or Spanish. *Twanka* is the language used at home, especially by women and children, and in personal communication among members of their community. The morphology and syntax of the Miskito language suggest that it shares a common ancestry with Pech and Tawahka, although it has incorporated numerous English words as a result of this group's historic relationship with English traders. Most of the approximately 40,000 Miskito are bilingual, speaking Miskito as well as Spanish.

The Chortí, who live in northwestern Honduras, in Copán and Ocotepeque, number approximately 3,000, but very few still speak the native language, Chol or Chortí, of the Mayense family.

The Garífuna language is still spoken or understood by many of the 250,000 Garífuna or Garinagu who originally lived in small fishing villages scattered along the North Coast but today also live in Tegucigalpa, San Pedro Sula, and other Honduran cities as well in various cities in the United States. Their language is unique on the planet, being a mix of African languages, English, Dutch, Portuguese, and Arawak, the ancient and now virtually extinct language of the pre-Hispanic inhabitants of many Caribbean islands. This uniqueness prompted UNESCO to declare the Garífuna language a World Heritage treasure.

An undocumented number of the approximately 32,000 Creoles, sometimes referred to as *Negros ingleses* (English Blacks) of the North Coast and the Bay Islands, descendents of Jamaicans, Cayman Islanders, and Scots, also speak Creole English.

One of the largest present-day ethnic groups, the Lenca, who live throughout central, southern, and western Honduras and number approximately 350,000, is believed to have no more living speakers of their indigenous language. There are, however, people of Lenca ancestry living in Guatemala and El Salvador, so it is possible that some individuals have retained knowledge of this language of the Mayense family.

NOTES

1. Population statistics are from the July 2008 report of the *CIA World Factbook*. A sad footnote to this demographic data is the need to factor in a high mortality rate due to AIDS and inadequate medical services.

2. A classic and still one of the most informative studies of Central American prehistory is Doris Stone, *Pre-Columbian Man Finds Central America: The Archaeological Bridge*, Cambridge, MA: Peabody Museum Press, 1972. A more recent account is David Rains Wallace, *The Monkey's Bridge: Mysteries of Evolution in Central America*, San Francisco: Sierra Club Press, 1997.

3. See Rodolfo Pastor Fasquelle, "History of Cultural Diversity in Honduras," on line and Ramón Rivas, *Pueblos indígenas y garífuna de Honduras*, Tegucigalpa: Guaymuras, 1993.

4. McSweeney, Kendra. "A Demographic Profile of the Tawahka Amerindians of Honduras." *The Geographical Review.* July 1, 2002.

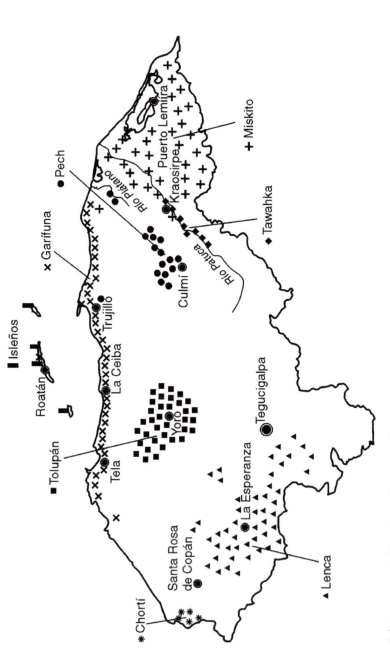

Ethnic groups in Honduras. Courtesy of Bookcomp, Inc.

2

Indigenous Honduras

THE CHORTÍ, LENCA, and Tolupán, who currently reside mostly in the western and central sections of the country, have cultural characteristics in common with groups to the north who share their Mesoamerican roots. The cultures of the Miskito, Tawahka, and Pech, who inhabit the northeastern region of Honduras, bear a closer resemblance to the beliefs and practices of macro-Chibcha groups from northern South America. The Garífuna, who trace their ancestry to Africa and to the Arawak people of the southern Caribbean, are the most recent arrivals of the various groups that contribute to the indigenous cultural diversity of Honduras.[1]

Only one of the seven different indigenous groups, the Tolupán, also known as the Jicaque, resides exclusively in Honduras. The Lenca extend

---

Recent interest in indigenous cultures of the world, occasioned by the realization that many native communities are in danger of extinction, has produced a wealth of material on the Internet that claims to document indigenous practices and beliefs. Although much of this information is reliable, some of it appears to be derived from secondary sources and often is filtered in ways that promote the interests of missionaries, travel companies, and government agencies promoting their own agendas. To avoid misrepresentation, the information in this chapter is based on the published studies of respected scholars, including Ramón D. Rivas, *Pueblos indígenas y garífuna de Honduras*. Tegucigalpa: Guaymuras, 1993; Alessandra Castegnara de Foletti. *Viaje por el universo artesanal de Honduras*. Tegucigalpa: Instituto Hondureño de Antropología e Historia, 2002; Wendy Griffin. *Los garífunas de Honduras: cultura, lucha y derechos bajo el Convenio 169 de la OIT*. Trujillo: CEGAH, 2005; various articles from *Yaxkin*, the journal of the Honduran Institute of Anthropology and History; selected studies by Honduran scholars; and numerous articles in English by Wendy Griffin in *Honduras This Week*.

into El Salvador; there are Chortí in Guatemala and Miskito and Tawahka, also called Sumo, in Nicaragua. There are Garífuna communities in Belize, Guatemala, Nicaragua, and several cities in the United States.

Social scientists have noted that the areas traditionally inhabited by indigenous groups are also the poorest and least serviced areas. In this geography of poverty, those ethnic groups that have retained their native language, customs, and beliefs are also the most isolated from centers of development and consequently receive few services from the state. Many indigenous communities of Honduras lack electricity, running water, clinics, and adequate schools.

MISKITO

According to local legend, on a rock on a hill in Kaunapa on the shores of the Patuca River, a petroglyph depicting a human umbilical cord represents the origin of the Great Mother Itwana and the Great Father Maisahana, parents of the Sumu (also known as Sumo) people. The Sumus were one of the principal indigenous groups living in northeastern Honduras and northwestern Nicaragua in prehistoric times. They are described as a macro-Chibcha tribal rainforest culture with similarities to other indigenous groups that inhabited present-day Colombia, Panama, and Costa Rica. They were semi-nomadic hunter-gatherers and cultivated root vegetables such as manioc. Scholars continue to explore the prehistory of the Sumus and question whether they migrated to the region from the south or were the descendents of earlier Mesoamerican inhabitants who over time assimilated the cultural influences of the south. In any case, their descendents include the contemporary Miskito and Tawahka. The Miskitos (variously spelled Misquito, Mosquito) who live in Honduras currently number approximately 40,000 and live on lands within the Río Plátano Biosphere (Biosfera del Río Plátano), along the banks of the lower Patuca River and the Coco River, on the shores of Caratasca Lagoon and on the North Coast. This region encompasses tropical rainforests, extensive savannahs, lagoons, and the tropical Caribbean coast. They reside in the towns of Puerto Lempira and Brus Laguna and in small, remote settlements including Tukrun, Wampusirpe, Bilalmuk, and Krausirpe.

Miskito origin myths tell of a people's migration from the south, along the Pacific Coast of Nicaragua, around the tenth century A.D. Their chief, Waikna, conquered the coastal region from Costa Rica to Honduras. According to another legend, the warrior chief Miskut descended from the north. Upon arriving at Brus Laguna with his tribe and seeing its natural beauty and its wealth of fish and game, he decided to stay. Some of the Miskito inhabitants of the town of present-day Brus Laguna consider themselves the descendents of this tribe.

Yet another legend claims that the first black African who mixed with the Miskitos came ashore near Brus Laguna after jumping overboard from a slave ship. The town of Brus Laguna is the area's center for commerce and government and has long been important to the Miskito culture. Savannas extend eastward from Brus Laguna, where rural Miskitos graze cattle. Many Miskitos live in areas with no paved roads and rely exclusively on waterways for transportation.

Those Sumus who mixed with Africans, English, and other visitors, invaders, or settlers, became the cultural group today known as Miskitos. By 1700, some 2,000 Miskitos lived along the Caribbean coast of Honduras and Nicaragua. They worked for and with the British in the extraction and sale of natural resources, particularly timber, rubber, gold, and pelts. As a result of this alliance, the Miskitos had access to European weapons, goods, and information, which allowed them to expand, dominate, and assimilate other cultures such as the indigenous Pech and Tawahka and the Honduran mestizo settlers in La Mosquitia. During the eighteenth and nineteenth centuries, when a Miskito king reigned over an extensive territory from Belize to the San Juan River on the Nicaraguan/Costa Rican border, they considered themselves subjects of the British Empire. After years of battles, treaties, and negotiations, Honduras and Britain signed the Wyke-Cruz Treaty in 1859, in which Britain ceded its claims to Honduran territory and the Miskitos officially became Honduran citizens. Toward the end of the nineteenth century, U.S. businesses, primarily companies interested in the cultivation and export of bananas, became an important economic presence in the region. They employed many Miskito men and wage earning subsequently influenced the traditional Miskito lifestyle as money to acquire consumer goods became more available.

The first Moravian missionaries arrived in La Mosquitia in 1849 and have played an important role in the transformation as well as the survival of the Miskito language and culture. Their translation of the Bible into Miskito represented the first effort to write the language; its preservation in written form has undoubtedly contributed to its present survival. In 1930 the Moravian Church established a mission in Cuaquira and in 1935 a congregation was established in Brus Laguna. The church's social and pedagogical mission, which encourages active participation by all in the life of the community, has been influential in preserving Miskito identity, albeit modified from some of its traditional ways and beliefs. According to the official Web site of the Moravian Church, today there are approximately 100 Moravian congregations in La Mosquitia that conduct services in Spanish and Miskito. The Moravian missions have built schools and clinics and currently work with individuals affected by drugs and the drug trade and have been instrumental in reintroducing the production of native crafts, particularly among women, as a means to promote cultural identity and supplement family income.

Despite their history of extensive contact with and assimilation of other cultures, the Miskitos have maintained to a large extent their linguistic and cultural identity, due in part to being a matrilocal society. There are well-defined gender roles: Men are responsible for farming, trade, hunting, fishing, and the production of tools, weapons, and musical instruments; women tend the kitchen garden, care for children and domestic animals, and produce fiber art from the bark of the *tuno* tree. Although tradition demands that Miskito women be looked after by the men in their family, the economic and social reality is that women are often the mainstay of the household and must provide for their families.

Miskito men are known for their fishing skills. They employ harpoons, hooks, and nets in the lakes and rivers. Fishing with a bow and arrow is a skill that is no longer developed and the now illegal methods of poisoning the water of small streams with the *paté* plant or using dynamite are practiced clandestinely if at all. Some fishermen sell their catch fresh. Others are skilled at salting the catch; it is a tradition to buy salted fish from the Miskito camps around Brus Laguna during Holy Week. Young Miskito men, typically fourteen to twenty-five years old, often dive for lobsters on commercial vessels that work the Caribbean coast. As a consequence of not always being properly trained and working long hours, there have been numerous cases of serious illness and even death among these divers. A recent study indicated that nearly half of the 9,000 Miskito divers are living with injuries resulting from unsafe diving practices. They work from twelve to seventeen days at sea and dive to depths of forty-three meters, often with poor equipment. Many of the divers believe that their injuries are caused by Liwa Mairin, the protector of the sea, who looks after marine life and punishes those who overfish. The pay is attractive, however, so young men continue to risk their health. Miskito women are also skilled in fishing, although their fishing is for domestic use and in waters near their homes.

With the exception of lobster diving, occasional work for wages, and illegal drug trafficking, the Miskito economy is primarily one of subsistence. Fish and other marine life such as turtles, otters, and crabs constitute the protein base of their diet along with local game. Overhunting and the destruction of the habitat have occasioned the disappearance or scarcity of many of the small animals that previously added to their diet. Deer, tapirs, iguanas, armadillos, peccaries, agoutis, and wild turkeys were once abundant but are now less numerous.

Small parcels of land along the banks of rivers and lagoons are cultivated with hand tools such as machetes and axes to produce bananas, coconuts, manioc, yams, chili peppers, rice, beans, corn, and cacao. Seasonal flooding puts down new topsoil on these low-lying areas. One of the principal concerns of ecologists analyzing a proposed dam on the Patuca River is that it will block this renewing sediment, which will leave the Miskitos with soils too poor to continue their traditional subsistence agriculture. A family may relocate seasonally to their parcel to care for the crop and return to their community after the harvest, when a portion of the yield may be sold at market. In addition to farming and fishing, Miskitos gather wild fruits and roots to supplement their diet. Traditional Miskito foods that are made using ingredients cultivated and gathered locally include *tapado*, a stew of root crops, plantains and salted meat and *wabul*, mashed plantains or bananas with coconut cream.

The traditional Miskito house, called *utla*, can be found in small settlements called *caseríos* or groupings of between five and forty-five dwellings, always situated near water. The surrounding tropical vegetation is abundant and the land is often wet, with swamps nearby, so the typical dwelling is elevated on four pillars. It has a thatched roof made from the leaves of the palm tree known as *kangku* and walls of wood or bamboo. Nuclear or extended families may live in one dwelling, depending on its size. Some houses consist of a single multi-use room; others have a separate kitchen, which may be enclosed or open-sided. Neighbors and family members typically cooperate in the construction of a new house and it is not uncommon for houses to be abandoned and new ones built as families move or gain members. Natural materials gathered locally are used in house construction. The occasional use of purchased products such as zinc for roofing is an indication that a family member has worked or traveled outside the local area. Miskitos who live in coastal areas or in the larger towns such as Puerto Lempira or Brus Laguna have adopted the mestizo and Garífuna house styles.

Before the arrival of Moravian and Catholic missionaries, the Miskito people possessed a rich and complex cosmogony. *Dawan* or *Wan Aisa*, Our Father, was the supreme being of the universe, the creator of all, who maintained a lordly distance from his creation. A pantheon of deities, incarnate in the sun, *Yu*, moon, *Kati*, stars and planets, and other natural phenomena, traveled through the sky in canoes and were believed to be the forces responsible for individual and collective good or ill fortune. Other supernatural beings were thought to be in charge of the forces of nature and could cause damage if angry. *Prahaku*, for example, the spirit of the wind, could bring storms and hurricanes and *Kumadora*, the spirit of rainbows, was considered a bad omen because it preceded the coming of *Prahaku*. The spirits of the dead interacted with humans and lived in the ceiba tree, *sisin*, which was feared and avoided at night. Numerous hostile or dangerous spirits resided in the natural world in places such as caves, lagoons, and mountains and were the cause of sickness and death. Many traditional rituals and customs, such as the use of amulets and red and black body paint, had their origin in the need to protect oneself from these harmful spirits. Beings called *takaia* or shape-shifters also inhabit the natural world and are the *dueños* or masters of all things in nature such as plants and animals. It is important to ask their permission to use the beings they control and to compensate them for this privilege. It was also believed that specially gifted and trained members of the community, *zukias* or shamans, could intervene to cure one of an illness or bad luck caused by a malicious spirit. They could communicate with the spirit world and were capable of practicing either white or black magic. *Zukias* were consequently very powerful members of the community; they were consulted for all-important decisions and officiated at agricultural and hunting rituals. There are still shamans among the Miskitos, but their assistance is sought primarily to cure illnesses. It is still believed that some maladies are caused by evil shamans and can only be cured by good ones. Community leaders with ties to the departmental or national government have replaced *zukias* in matters that involve political, economic, or legal decisions.

Although the majority of Miskitos today identify themselves as belonging to the Moravian Church, with the Catholic Church claiming an appreciably smaller number of members, they apparently never completely abandoned their traditional beliefs. This may be explained in part due to their vibrant oral tradition. As a people they are known for their love of music, dance, and storytelling. One of their time-honored ritual celebrations was the *Sihkru*, in which the entire community and even several communities gathered to communicate with the ancestors and honor their memory. Music and song played a central role in this ritual. A musical bow held in the mouth, *lungku*, drums, *kungbi*, and a reed flute, *bratara* were played as men sang ceremonial songs called *yul inaia*. Elaborate wooden figures representing the ancestors and wearing long grass skirts were worn by male dancers, giving them the appearance of giants. *Sihkrus* lasted several days and were accompanied by dancing, singing, storytelling, feasting, and the drinking of a fermented beverage made by the women in such large quantities that used canoes to hold the drink. Because of disapproval by the Moravian missionaries, traditional *sihkrus* were not celebrated for many years, although they have been replaced by *tambakus*, popular dances attended primarily by young people from October to January 6. *Tambakus* are purely social gatherings and have not retained the spiritual significance of the *sihkru*. One of the cultural developments resulting from the Nicaraguan Contra War has been renewed interest in preserving and documenting traditional indigenous ways in La Mosquitia. Along with the creation in 1985 of the North Atlantic Autonomous Region (RAAN) and the South Atlantic Autonomous Region (RAAS) in the Nicaraguan Mosquitia, official recognition has been given to the Miskito language and culture in Nicaragua. The influx of Nicaraguan refugees into Honduras has generated a similar political will among the Honduran Miskitos. In honor of International Indigenous Peoples Day, a Honduran–Nicaragua revival of the *sihkru* has been celebrated in recent years in Bilwi, Nicaragua, and Brus Laguna, Honduras. Miskito foods, music, dances, and stories told by elders are enjoyed for three days and nights. It is interesting to note that before the creation of the independent republics of Honduras and Nicaragua, the Miskito people moved freely throughout this now bi-national territory. The rebirth of the *sihkru* represents a new consciousness of tribal rather than national boundaries.

Honduran researchers have documented numerous traditional Miskito dances. There are dances that imitate the movements of animals, such as the Dance of the Vulture (Baile del Zopilote) and the Dance of the Crab (Baile del Cangrejo), and dances that reflect their identity as farmers, such as "Wark Taraka" or "The Man Who Is Working." In this dance the son sings to his father as the father imitates the actions of the song: sharpen your machete, cut the weeds, rest a while. In another work dance, "Tat Sap," the dancers wear work clothes and carry digging sticks. Boys enter pounding their sticks on the ground as girls follow behind bending down to plant seeds. Boys and girls then face each other flirtatiously and the girls warn the boys in song that before they can eat rice and beans they must work.

Another interesting dance is "Miskitu Kuka Nani," the Dance of the Grandmothers, in which elder Miskito, Tawahka, Pech, and mestizo women are invited in song to join in the dance. It has been suggested that this ritualized dance and song demonstrates respect for the elders and also the cultural unity of La Mosquitia. INGWAIA, a Miskito dance troupe, has performed this and other traditional dances at the National Theater in Tegucigalpa.

Miskito men traditionally made a variety of rustic musical instruments, creatively making use of the natural materials at hand. The Miskito flute, *bratara,* is made from reed or bamboo; gourds with seeds inside are used as rattles or maracas, *insuba*; drums, *kungbi,* are made from mahogany and deerskin, turtle shells, and coconut shells. The traditional guitar, *kitar,* is made with catgut strings. Other creative instruments include the jawbone of a horse, the upside-down washtub, an old machete played with a nail, and a kazoo made from a reed and a bat's wing.

The oral tradition among the Miskito has been studied and collected by scholars. Tales and legends have been of particular interest. Wendy Griffin and MISKWAT, the Miskito Cultural Center in Tegucigalpa collaborated to publish, in 1991, *The Ogre Who Carried Away a Boy and Other Stories*, a collection of Miskito tales in Spanish and Miskito. Many Miskito stories are fables with animal characters that illustrate explanations for natural phenomena, such as why vultures are bald and why the dog is man's best friend among the animals.

TAWAHKA

The Tawahkas and Miskitos have much history and culture in common. They most likely both descended from the rainforest people to the south and over time assumed elements of the cultures of their neighbors to the north. Both groups also have been affected by contact with Europeans, Africans, and North Americans. What may be one of their defining differences is the willingness of the Miskito people to mix with and borrow from outside cultures. Historically, the Miskitos have dominated other indigenous groups, either intermarrying, enslaving them, or forcing them to abandon shared territory. Today there are approximately 40,000 Miskito in Honduras and 150,000 in Nicaragua, whereas the Tawahka who live in Honduran territory number barely 1,000, with another 8,000 in Nicaragua.

Although the Miskito population is concentrated in coastal regions, which they share with the Garífuna, the Tawahka have moved more and more inland as hostile neighbors, land invasions, and epidemics have threatened. They now reside principally in seven communities located in or near the Biosphere Tawahka Asagni Preserve (Reserva de la Biosfera Tawahka Asagni) in southwestern Gracias a Dios and eastern Olancho departments. The largest Tawahka communities, Krausirpe and Krautara are on the banks of the Patuca River. The smaller communities consist of one or two extended families. Most of the lands adjacent to their communities are used for hunting, fishing, and the small-scale extraction of timber and other resources for domestic use. Approximately 5 percent of their communal land is under cultivation, for which they employ the time-honored traditions of crop rotation and shift cultivation. They are involved in minimal commerce with the outside world, so one might argue that, although they lack many modern amenities, they have managed to use their land sustainably. They build their dwellings using local wood and plant material; their tools and domestic utensils are typically made from wood and gourds; and they are expert weavers of baskets, mats, and bags using local reeds and fibers. They are very knowledgeable of local plants and their medicinal uses. Like the Miskito, they have revived the tradition of gathering and preparing the bark of the *tunu* tree and with it they make fiber art for sale to tourists using traditional symbols and motifs. They also share with the Miskito the tradition of building shallow-draft canoes called *pipantes* from the trunk of a single large tree, usually mahogany, cedar, or guanacaste. All families have at least one *pipante*, which men, women, and children all use for fishing and transportation.

Most Tawahka families are subsistence farmers who cultivate rice, bananas, plantains, and yucca and keep domestic animals such as cows, pigs, and chickens on a small scale. They supplement their diet with fish and wild game. Some men still use a harpoon to spear fish and a bow and arrow to hunt. They farm with traditional hand tools and typically work communally. A tradition among them known as *mano vuelta* requires that individuals and families assist one another in such tasks as planting, harvesting, and house building. The person whose fields are being planted, for example, will provide his extended family and neighbors with food and drink as they help him, and he is expected to return the favor when they are in need of help.

Individuals of all ages contribute to the livelihood of the family. Women and children participate in the planting, care, and harvesting of crops; they fish, gather wild fruits and roots, and care for domestic animals. The elderly continue to work at whatever tasks they are capable of performing and are considered active and integral members of the community. Elderly women, for example, play an important role in childcare and are often skilled basket weavers. Elderly men occupy positions of authority in the community. It is considered appropriate for an elderly person to let him or herself die when he or she no longer feels capable of contributing to the well-being of the family. It is believed that death is caused by natural forces or may be a punishment from God. Most Tawahkas consider themselves Catholic, although they may subscribe to beliefs about the afterlife, for example, that do not conform to Catholic doctrine. It is likely that their respectful use of their communal land and its resources is related to their traditional belief in the essential equilibrium of the universe and the importance of preserving harmony in one's life through right behavior and reciprocal relationship with the beings who control all aspects of the natural world. The small and isolated nature of their communities does not lend itself to having resident priests, although all communities, no matter how poor, have a house of worship where men, women, and children gather on Sundays to pray and read the Bible. They annually celebrate the Feast of the Immaculate Conception, patroness of their communities.

Tawahka history has been marked by a series of incursions by other groups, to evangelize, conquer, help, or exploit them. The first missionaries to arrive in their lands were the Spanish Franciscan priests Padre Esteban Verdelete and Juan de Monteagudo, in 1604. Despite their attempts to convert the indigenous population peacefully and later with military help, they failed miserably. There are various versions of just how unsuccessful they were, one of the most colorful is that they were eaten by the very souls they were trying to save. Notwithstanding these initial failed attempts, the Catholic Church eventually became the dominant religious institution among the Tawahka. The efforts by the Moravian Church and other Protestant missionaries among the Tawahka have not been successful, unlike their experience with the Miskito. Subsequent incursions into their territory by the

British, the Miskitos, the Honduran government, mestizo farmers and cattle ranchers, refugees from Nicaragua and assorted other groups and individuals have led to some intermarrying and cultural assimilation, but it may be asserted that those Tawahka who have most resisted foreign influence are those who today remain the poorest, most isolated, and closest to their ancient traditions. It is both surprising and heartening, then, that as their ethnic identity is eroded through assimilation with other cultures, a countermovement to preserve their uniqueness is also growing. In 1987 the Tawahka Indigenous Federation of Honduras (Federación Indígena Tawahka de Honduras [FITH]) came into being. An international organization comprised of Tawahkas and sympathetic professionals and intellectuals from Honduras and other countries, FITH had three major goals: to acquire title to ancestral lands; to create and fund bilingual, intercultural education programs for adults and children; and to create a reserve to protect Tawahka ancestral lands from encroachment and development. By employing a variety of political strategies such as public marches and manifestoes to publicize their projects and demands, the formation of networks with other indigenous groups, NGOs, and environmental groups both within Honduras and internationally and negotiations with banks and government officials, they have made significant progress in all three areas. And with the assistance of the Honduran Institute of Anthropology and History (IHAH), and the government-sponsored Program of Rescue and Promotion of the Artisan, Indigenous, and Traditional Production in Honduras (PROPAITH), they have not only revived the traditional practice of making fiber art from the bark of the *tunu* tree, but are creating new designs and motifs to reflect their present cultural reality.

An important milestone for the Tawahka people was reached in 1999 when the Honduran government declared the Tawahka Asangni Biosphere Reserve a protected area. The reserve is located in the departments of Olancho and Gracias a Dios. It is bordered to the north by the Río Platano Biosphere Reserve (a World Heritage Site), to the south by the Patuca National Park, and to the east by the Bosawas National Park in Nicaragua, making it very important to the national park system and the Mesoamerican Biological Corridor. In 1994, Honduras signed the Central American Alliance for Sustainable Development (ALIDES), an international agreement that established an eco-corridor from Guatemala to Panama to preserve biodiversity. This agreement recognizes that above and beyond the political reality that Central America is composed of seven sovereign nations, is the biological reality that ecosystems do not respect national boundaries. The seven nations agreed to create the Mesoamerican Biological Corridor, which they imagine not as one uninterrupted nature preserve but as an ecological network that includes humans and is managed sustainably. The problem with such a broad definition, however, is that sustainability today has as many definitions as people defining it. When the Honduran government, in cooperation with the Tai Power Co. of Taiwan, to justify their plans to dam the Patuca River, insists that it can be done sustainably, one cannot help but question the use of the term. And there is no guarantee that the Tawahka Asangni Biosphere Reserve will be preserved or developed sustainably. The Honduran Forestry Department (CODEFOR) manages the reserve and government agencies do not have a good track record for the enforcement of existing laws. Illegal logging, mining, and burning continue. The most recent threat to the biological and cultural integrity of the reserve is the above-mentioned Patuca-3 hydropower project.

PECH

The Pech live primarily in the departments of Olancho, Colón, and Gracias a Dios in northeastern Honduras. Their towns and villages vary in size from a few families in Waikatara on the banks of the Plátano River to upward of 1,100 individuals in Santa María del Carbón, also known as El Carbón, in the Sierra de Agalta. Waiknatara was settled in 1990 by a small group of Pech who left Vallecito, Olancho as a result of conflicts over land with mestizos. It is remote, reached only by small boat or *pipante*. El Carbón, in contrast, is shared by Miskito, Tawahka, and mestizo residents and is an active Pech community; it has a school and a clinic and has promoted the revival of traditional handcrafts through the organization, KATAHA, which means *artesano* or craftsperson in Pech.

The Pech have migrated frequently throughout their history and have had to adapt to new circumstances in order to survive as a people. It is believed that they are descendents of the Paya, who, before the arrival of the Spanish, occupied the Bay Islands, the north coast of Honduras, and extended south into present-day Olancho. They were one of several different ethnic groups of varying populations who lived in a vast area that the Spanish later named Taguzgalpa and Tologalpa, which encompassed the Atlantic region of Honduras from Trujillo and continuing east and south into Nicaragua.

These groups most probably experienced some level of contact and mutual influence. Indeed, this is considered one of the most diverse cultural regions of prehistoric Central America, where cultural influences from the south and north were both prevalent, to the extent of making it difficult if not impossible to unravel its complex web of cultures and languages. Notwithstanding the melting pot nature of the region, archaeological evidence as well as history in the form of tales, legends, and beliefs passed down through the oral tradition, indicate the persistence of distinct cultures. Numerous archaeological remains can be found in Pech territory, including ceramics, stonework, finely carved ceremonial grinding stones, cave drawings, mounds, and the ruins of entire towns. Carvings on a rock wall on the banks of the Kinikisné River, known as the Rock of Flowers (Piedra Floreada), present botanical and zoological motifs. Of particular interest are carvings of a corn plant and a plumed serpent, two primordial Mesoamerican motifs. The Pech oral tradition tells of a city in the jungle with buildings made from white stone. This mythical city has come to be known as the White City (Ciudad Blanca). Numerous parties have searched for it but to no avail. To the Pech it is the Place of the Ancients (Lugar de los Antiguos) and, if they know its location they do not tell outsiders. Some scholars speculate that these may be the ruins of a distant outpost of the Olmec or Maya; others wonder if ancestors of the Paya were an advanced civilization that, like the Maya, abandoned their city for reasons that remain a mystery.

With the arrival of the Spanish and the English to the north coast of Honduras the balance of power shifted dramatically. The Paya were forcibly removed from the Bay Islands by the Spanish, who suspected them of aiding the British. The were brought to the north coast of Honduras where the Miskito, strengthened and armed as a result of their alliance with the British, exacted tribute from the Paya and captured them and sold them as slaves. Descendents of the Paya who successfully resisted these incursions on their sovereignty moved further inland and eventually came to be known as the Pech. Spanish Catholic missionaries attempted to gather the dispersed and isolated Pech population into settlements, the better to evangelize them, but it was common for the nonconformist Pech to abandon these missions. Today, most Pech identify themselves as Catholic, although Protestant Evangelical missionaries are active among them.

The importance of land cannot be overestimated in the construction and preservation of indigenous cultural identity. When the Spanish missionary Father Manuel de Jesús Subirana helped the Pech acquire title to their lands in 1862, the battle for possession in fact had just begun. The Pech have been able to live peacefully and to survive as a people when they have settled in lands that were either inaccessible or undesirable to outsiders. But gold, timber, and the sarsaparilla plant have attracted locals as well as foreigners who have variously enslaved or employed the Pech in their extraction or simply moved in and taken their land from them. Today, with the exception of the people of Santa María del Carbon, the Pech continue to face the challenges posed by mestizo farmers and ranchers desirous of ever more land, who are more knowledgeable of the legalities involved and more financially able to pursue ownership. Their poverty and high rate of illiteracy have been barriers to gaining equitable treatment by the authorities. Even in the Río Plátano Biosphere, a protected reserve where only indigenous people are allowed to live, lack of enforcement has allowed others to exploit their land and natural resources.

An important part of their culture that is in serious danger of extinction is the Pech language. Most Pech speakers are older adults. Although women and children may speak Pech in the home, most children speak Spanish and/or Miskito in school and at play. As the adult speakers pass away, the motivation to speak Pech will diminish even further. According to a census sponsored by the Honduran Institute of Anthropology and History in 1994, at that time there were 1,518 Pech in Honduras, 993 of whom spoke their native language. Of those aged six to twenty, approximately 50 percent could speak Pech.

The preservation of a language helps to keep alive the oral tradition. Fortunately, scholars have collected many of the Pech myths and legends. One source of these tales is *Gods, Heroes and Men in the Mythical Universe of the Pech (Dioses, héroes y hombres en el universo mítico pech)* by Lázaro Flores and Wendy Griffin (1991). According to legend, the Pech believe they were created from the bark of the *tuno* tree. They perceive the world as a complex of dualities: east–west, good–evil, cold–hot. This world is inhabited by spirits who make themselves felt or known through natural phenomena such as wind and rain and can cause harm if they are not respected and treated with consideration. All animals have female spirit beings who own or control them, an indication of the importance afforded to the mother figure in Pech culture. Patakako is their hero-god who brought them civilization and continues to protect them. His older brother represents the opposite pole and causes death and destruction. Numerous tales recount battles between the two men in which Patakako defeats his brother. Another hero is the hunter Seatuska, who traveled to the Island of the Corn Mother (Isla de la Madre del Maíz), an island inhabited only by women. There the women gave him seeds for three kinds of corn and taught him how to plant them. When he returned to the land of the Pech he gave them this knowledge.

The Pech traditionally practiced an important ritual called *kesh* during which the celebrants, through the mediation of a shaman, came into contact with the spirit world. A *kesh* might be held for various reasons, such as to assist a member of the community on his or her journey after death, to petition for a good harvest or to placate the spirits for a wrong done. Prayers were chanted by the *arñatajá* accompanied by two women singers covered in white sheets and music was played on traditional instruments. *Chicha* made from yucca, *minia,* and yucca tamales, *sasal,* were consumed during the ritual. The *kesh* is no longer commonly practiced but it may well happen that, like the Miskito, who have recently revived their *sihkru,* the Pech revive this unique practice.

Some traditional musical instruments are still fashioned by hand, a craft practiced only by men. When a boy is invited for the first time to play the ritual Pech drum, *tempuká*, it is an indication of his passage into manhood. The drum is covered with the skin of a snake or frog, which it is said must be taken from a live animal. Reed flutes with four openings, *arwá*, are thought to be descended from the first sacred flute, *chawuawuaká*, made from the leg bone of a jaguar and symbolizing the victory of the Twins of the Sky (the planet Venus) over the Black Panther of the Night. Rattles or maracas, *kamachá*, are made from gourds. Instruments no longer commonly used include the horseshoe-shaped *birimbao*, and the *caramba*, a wooden bow as tall as a person. The musical group Piriwa plays traditional Pech songs using the old-style instruments.

A sad footnote to the disappearance of traditional music is that this loss is intimately connected to the loss of the group's natural environment. It is said that it is impossible to play the old flutes properly, for example, because the player should strive to imitate the songs of the *pavón* and the *pahjuil*, local birds that no longer can be found in Pech territory due to timber extraction and clear-cutting. Mahogany, the wood favored for making drums, is also very scarce now. The same is true for some of the traditional dances that are no longer performed such as hunting dances, given that the deer, tapir, and wild pig that lived in Pech forests no longer have a habitat and have retreated from the area.

Traditional handcrafts, on the other hand, have continued to be made; in some instances the necessary skills have been revived owing to an awareness of the potential income-producing value of the products. The Pech today are known as expert woodworkers and fiber artists. Men and women from Las Marías and Santa María del Carbón in particular weave hammocks, bags, hats, baskets, and mats. The men work with wood, making a variety of objects for domestic use; recently they have begun to make furniture for sale as well. Because electricity is rare in Pech communities, craftspeople must employ hand tools for all their wares, a practice particularly impressive among woodworkers.

The old-style weapons for hunting and fishing are still used in the more traditional communities, but have become rare. Hunters use the *cerbatana* and handmade bow and arrow; spears, arrows, and hooks are used for fishing as well as nets made from poles and woven vines.

A typical Pech house is situated on a hillock or raised parcel of land with the front door facing west and a window or a second door facing east. Its walls are *bahareque*, a kind of wattle and daub construction using bamboo poles and a mixture of clay soil, water, and twigs. This style of construction dates back to at least 1300 B.C. among the Lencas of Honduras, although it was only adopted in the last sixty years by the Pech. A *bahareque* house consists of four main posts called *horcones* connected at the top by roof beams called *vigas*. A lattice of woven wood that reaches from floor to roof forms the wall that is then filled with mud. The surface is finished with layers of yellow and white mud called *repello*. Houses have a thatched roof made with locally gathered reeds and grasses, and a packed earth floor. Older dwellings were usually one multiple-use room, but today, if a family can afford it, they build their home with a separate room for sleeping. A nuclear or extended family will live in each dwelling. Sons and their wives may return to the father's home to share the family dwelling.

The kitchen is usually indoors, although a family also may have a simple outdoor fire pit made of stones on the ground. The most common method of cooking is on a structure made by women of wood, stones, and clay and mounted on a table. As a result of eye and lung damage from the smoke produced by this method, especially among women, a government initiative to introduce a chimney to evacuate the smoke has been quite successful. The metal chimney is called a "*lorena*." Wood, clay, and gourd bowls, pots, and domestic utensils are used, along with metal and plastic items. Hand-woven bags and baskets are suspended from the rafters to keep food away from animals. Hammocks are hung for sitting and sleeping. Rustic beds called *tapescos*, simple raised platforms made of wood or bamboo covered with a woven straw mat, are also used.

When Hurricane Mitch pounded Honduras in October 1998, fierce winds and torrential rains destroyed many Pech homes. International relief agencies were at first at a loss because they did not understand this age-old method of construction. Disaster Relief International eventually figured it out and helped rebuild Pech homes in Selin.

Yucca is the staple food of the Pech and is prepared in many ways, including tortillas (*pak-ká*), tamales (*sasal*), and *kuni*, a drink made by boiling the root. Other important staples in their diet are corn, rice, beans, eggs, fish, and chicken. Traditional fermented drinks are made from yucca, corn, and fruits.

Like most indigenous peoples who have a history of living close to nature, the Pech descend from a long line of shamans, herb doctors, and healers. Most Pech today, particularly young people, are accustomed to seeking medical help from more modern sources, even though they might have to take a bus or walk to a distant clinic. This is unfortunate as there are situations when local plant knowledge could be useful. There are several poisonous species of snake in areas where the Pech live, for example, such as the fer-de-lance, the coral snake, and the tree boa. The traditional cure for snakebites is known by only a few living Pech. The Honduran NGO, Madre Tierra Honduras, is one group that is working in partnership with the international NGO community to promote the preservation of biodiversity and habitat and to encourage the use of traditional healing practices in Honduras.

The natural environment where the Pech reside today encompasses mountains, plateaus, valleys, rivers, and savannahs, with their accompanying variations in temperature and rainfall. Some of this area has suffered severely from deforestation and the resulting loss of flora and fauna. Because the Pech do not live on a reserve and their communities are scattered throughout a large area, it has been difficult for them to organize to preserve their land and culture. Nevertheless, a consciousness of their plight exists among them and efforts have been made to join together to work toward solutions. In 1985, *caciques* or tribal leaders from each of the Pech communities joined to organize the Honduran Federation of Pech Tribes (Federación de Tribus Pech [FETRIPH]) to address the situation of land titles and to work toward preserving their traditional culture and customs. At the First Pech Indigenous Congress (Primer Congreso Indígena Pech), held that same year in Pueblo Nuevo Subirana and attended by delegates from the communities of Santa María del Carbón, Agua Zarca, Vallecito, Culuco, Pisijire, and Jocomico, the Declaration of Nuevo Pueblo Subirana was drawn up. This document reflects their concerns and priorities: acquisition of secure title to their lands; primary education in the Pech language, by Pech teachers; access to scholarships for Pech children to allow them to attend high school and university; respect for and preservation of their language and culture; and the right to self-determination for their communities.

An example of their work in this direction was the creation of the environmental group WATA, whose headquarters are in Santa María del Carbón. WATA has built a visitors' center and simple lodging to encourage responsible tourism in their communal forest land and the Pech members of this ecological group have been trained to give guided tours of the area's medicinal plants. WATA is also working for government recognition of the area around Carbón National Forest as a Pech anthropological preserve.

TOLUPÁN AND/OR JICAQUE

The indigenous people referred to here as Jicaque (also spelled Xicaque) are also known as Tolupán (also Torrupan, Tol, Tolpan) Some scholars believe they are the oldest indigenous group in Honduras. It has been asserted that their language is related to Hokan-Sioux and that ancestors of this group migrated from the southwestern United States 5,000 years ago. They inhabited a large area along the Atlantic coast from the Ulúa River eastward to Trujillo and south to the Sulaco River. At the time of the arrival of the Spaniards, their neighbors to the west of the Ulúa River were the Maya and they shared resources in the eastern reaches of their territory with the Pech, Tawahka, and Miskito. Like their neighbors to the east, they were semi-nomadic hunter-gatherers who lived in small groups with an egalitarian rather than a stratified social order. Perhaps because of their intransigence and unwillingness to be subdued, the Spanish called them xicaques, a Nahuatl term that indicated savage or wild.

Like the Tawahka and the Pech, the Jicaque gradually abandoned the flat, accessible lands along the coast and migrated inland to more mountainous land to remain out of reach of the military and evangelizing grasp of the Spanish. They eventually settled in the mountains of the department of Yoro in north central Honduras. One of the most notorious attempts to exploit the Jicaque occurred beginning around 1863 when the sarsaparilla plant was in great demand as the principal ingredient of a popular beverage in Europe and the United States. The plant grew abundantly in the tropical forests of north central Honduras and the Jicaque were forced to collect and transport the roots over the mountains to ports on the Atlantic coast. To escape this enslavement, a small group fled the area and settled in the even more remote Montaña de la Flor (Mountain of the Flower). They founded two neighboring hamlets and lived in isolation for a century. The descendents of this group today are the only remaining speakers of the Tolupán language. They refer to themselves as the Tolupán and among them can be found the last remnants of the traditional culture and lifestyle. Most of the other members of the Jicaque people live in the department of Yoro, in small settlements or in larger mestizo towns and identify themselves as Jicaque. Although Tolupán is most likely the original or authentic name of this indigenous group, today it is used almost exclusively by the inhabitants of the Montaña de la Flor, possibly because their ancestors lived for almost 100 years with little contact with anyone outside their tribe. It is also preferred by scholars who believe Jicaque to have been a name imposed by outsiders.

Various attempts were made by Spanish missionaries to gather the Jicaque into agricultural communities, however, these reductions, as they were called, did not particularly thrive until Padre Manuel de Jesús Subirana realized that helping them acquire legal title to their land would encourage stability as well as allegiance to the Catholic Church. Of the twenty-three known Jicaque tribes identified in 1863, twenty-one were granted title to their land. Due largely to his pioneering efforts in this regard, the Jicaque today can claim ownership of their ancestral lands.

It is significant in the history of the Jicaque-Tolupán people that the missionary work of Padre Subirana and the sarsaparilla exploitation occurred at the time. So when a significant number of Jicaque chose to adopt a sedentary lifestyle and become Catholics, albeit retaining some of their traditional beliefs

and worldview, the small group that separated itself geographically and culturally managed to keep alive their language, customs, and belief system. When
anthropologist Anne Chapman lived among the Tolupán of the Montaña de
la Flor at various times, beginning in 1955, there were still individuals with
knowledge of the rich and complex oral tradition. Her invaluable work, *Masters of Animals: Oral Traditions of the Tolupan Indians, Honduras* (1992), documents a wealth of stories, legends, beliefs, and practices that might otherwise
be irreparably lost.

Among the myths she documented is the story of the creation of human
beings. It claims that the Tolupán are the descendants of a female monkey
and a male mouse, who were of the First Nation. The first children of their
union were Grandmother Moon and Grandfather Sun. During the time of
the First Nation, there was no death, suffering or fighting. The First Nation
humans ate only wild sweet potatoes (*camotes*) and lived peacefully with the
Supreme Being, *Tomam*, and the Grandfathers and Grandmothers: the sun,
moon, stars, thunder; and with the masters of animals and the animals they
watched over. But then *Tomam* sent the Devils, who came to harm the Indians.
They brought fetid vapors that caused sickness and the Indians quarreled so
the Grandparents got angry and left the earth and went to live in the sky. Now
the Indians die, they are mortals: This is what it means to be human.

There are also many stories about Mother Earth and the Masters of Animals.
It is believed that everything is alive and that nothing owns itself, but has a
master or owner (*dueño*) who controls and protects it. *Tomam* created and
protects Mother Earth, who in turn generously nourishes all creatures. But in
keeping with the essential dualism of the Tolupán worldview, Mother Earth
is also vindictive. Living creatures make her suffer when they walk on her, dig
into her, take things from her. So when a mortal dies, she rejoices, because
she will be fed when the mortal is buried. The Tolupán worldview is one of
reciprocity in which ultimately all is returned to balance and everything has
its place and purpose. All beings belong to a Nation and every Nation has its
domicile. *Jo'popjil Jamayón*, for example, is the Master of the Deer and lives
in caves and in the first layer underground. *Tomam* sent the deer to earth so
people could feed their families. If a human kills a deer and does not eat it,
or kills too many deer, *Jo'popjil Jamayón* gets angry and the offending hunter
will suffer a misfortune as punishment.

Certain individuals, called *punakpanes* or shamans, were believed to have
the ability to mediate between humans and supernatural beings. They also
were healers and diviners and very respected members of the community. They
were able to visit the levels below the world and converse with the Masters
of Animals. They healed by sucking, blowing, or shaking the sickness out
of the body. The Tolupán believed that the future was not predetermined

but that it could be known or foretold and with this knowledge one could avoid misfortune or obtain a desired outcome. Although the last traditional *punakpanes* died many years ago, divinatory methods such as the proof of the shinbone (*prueba de la canilla*) and the proof of the cord (*prueba de la cabuya*) may still be practiced in some form. The proof of the shinbone is a way of interpreting a physical accident or involuntary movement in relation to one's activities. Tripping or stumbling with both feet, for instance, is an indication that one's objective or destination should be avoided or postponed. Or if a hunter trips on his right leg, this means he should go left to find his prey. The proof of the cord is a complex manipulation of four knotted cords and its accompanying interpretation to determine such information as whether a loved one will recover from an illness or which of two women will make the better wife.

According to a recent report by Anne Chapman, who has continued to visit the two original Tolupán communities of Montaña de la Flor, there are two very different attitudes among them toward the outside world. Cipriano Martínez, the leader of the east hamlet, wears ladino clothing, has welcomed evangelical missionaries and the Summer School of Linguistics, has allowed a chapel to be built near his house, travels throughout the country to attend conferences on indigenous problems, and agrees to be interviewed by journalists. Julio Soto, the *cacique* of the west hamlet, avoids outsiders and proudly continues to wear the traditional *balandrán* or loose-fitting tunic. He is proud to be self-sufficient, does not want gifts from outsiders, and wants only to be allowed to keep his community's land. Whether or not the young people, as they become bilingual or even Spanish-dominant, will ignore their oral tradition or discover a new interest in it, remains to be seen. Today there are approximately 600 individuals who speak Tol, the vast majority of them residing in the Montaña de la Flor.

The Tolupán-Jicaque who did not isolate themselves in the Montaña de la Flor live primarily in the department of Yoro and number approximately 18,000. They have adopted ladino dress, speak Spanish, and are generally integrated into their mixed communities, although it is common to hear that prejudice and discrimination continue to be a part of their lives. They have by and large abandoned the use of the *cerbatana* and the bow and arrow for hunting and the most common musical instrument among them is the guitar, a Spanish import. They have retained their reputation as skilled basket weavers, a tradition that dates from pre-Columbian times. And although the production of ceramics was not a traditional craft among the Tolupán, many Jicaque women today have learned this skill.

Interestingly, the Jicaque, who have lost so much of their history and traditions, are arguably the most organized of all the indigenous groups of

Honduras and many identify themselves as descendents of the ancient Tolupán. In the 1970s the *caciques* of the various Jicaque-Tolupán communities began organizing to create a federation that would work to recover ancestral lands and to promote the Tolupán language and culture. Their organization, the Federation of Xicaque Tribes of Yoro, FETRIXY (*Federación de Tribus Xicaques de Yoro*) is aligned with the Confederation of Indigenous Peoples of Honduras, CONPAH (*Confederación de Pueblos Autóctonos de Honduras*). Ownership of land and natural resources is unarguably at the center of their concerns. Sadly, numerous Jicaques have been threatened and even murdered by those who desire access to their land, timber, and water.

LENCA

When the Spanish first arrived in Honduran territory, the Lenca were the most populous and powerful native group, occupying most of the mountains and valleys of the central and southern part of the country. Their influence extended to the Pacific coast in the south and included the eastern portion of present-day El Salvador. Most scholars currently accept the theory that the Lenca people originally migrated from the south around 3,000 years ago. Over time they interacted with Mesoamerican groups from the north and gradually their language, of macro-Chibcha origin, acquired Mesoamerican characteristics, particularly nahuatl vocabulary. The Maya were their closest neighbors to the north and east. The Ulúa River, in fact, which marks the westernmost frontier of Lenca territory, has often been designated as the easternmost frontier of the Maya civilization. The Spanish later brought Aztec warriors and farmers to assist in the conquest and colonization of Honduras and this influence contributed further to the transformation of the Lenca language and culture. There are no longer any Lenca speakers, only a scattering of Lenca words in Honduran Spanish, many of which are similar to or the same as Nahuatl vocabulary.

The Lenca at the time of the conquest were at least four different yet related linguistic groups. Anthropologist Anne Chapman has identified the Care, Cerquín, Lenca, and Potón subgroups. The pre-Columbian Lenca were highly organized and stratified societies, composed of priests, warriors, nobles, and commoners. They were organized into *cacicazgos* or groups of settlements under the authority of a civilian-military leader who inherited his position through his father. A *cacique's* center of population may have consisted of as many as 400 families. Wars or military skirmishes were common between villages, particularly those of different linguistic groups. The need for subsequent peace treaties gave rise to the practice of ritual peace accords between villages called *guancascos*, when the inhabitants of one village marched in festive procession to a rival village, whose inhabitants would return the favor at a later date, thereby establishing the opportunity to trade, discuss differences and solve problems. This custom, albeit in modified form and purpose, continues today in a number of locations. Each year, to celebrate a town's patron saint, the saint's statue is carried in procession to the neighboring town, accompanied by musicians who play drums and flutes, wear ritual wooden masks called *gracejos*, and carry flags. The saint "visits" the neighboring church for a number of days before returning to its home. The town so honored returns the favor on the occasion of its neighbor's patron saint's day. The *guancascos* of Ojojona-Lepaterique and Intibucá-Yamaranguila, among others, are well attended and have been studied and documented by scholars.

Some Lenca people who lived in relative isolation, especially in the mountainous regions of Intibucá, Lempira, and La Paz, retained their native language and vestiges of the traditional ways until about the mid-twentieth century. There are now no living speakers of the Lenca language and no one wears the traditional dress, making it difficult to determine Lenca identity. Some observers refer to the Lenca today as people of Lenca background rather than as an indigenous group because of their high level of acculturation. Nevertheless, there is an active movement among the Lenca to reassume their ethnic identity. Numerous local groups have formed to promote the Lenca heritage. The National Indigenous Lenca Organization of Honduras, Organización Nacional Indígena Lenca de Honduras (ONILH) represents this effort on the national level.

The Honduran government, in recognition of the importance of Lenca history to the history and identity of the nation, initiated "Lempira Day" (*Día de Lempira*), which is celebrated annually on July 20. Although Lempira Day is celebrated throughout the country, for the Lencas it is a day of ethnic pride, as Lempira was a Lenca *cacique* who led a rebellion against the Spanish in 1546. His heroic fight has made him a legendary figure in Honduras, a symbol of resistance to foreign invasion and oppression. A portrait of Lempira graces Honduran money, which is also called *lempiras*. Towns celebrate with the election of a queen, whom they call "Pretty Indian" (*India Bonita*). School children dress up as "Indians" and there is a fiesta that includes dancing to the *ranchera* music of Lenca *conjuntos*. These musical groups are typically composed of guitars, a fiddle, and a base fiddle.

Honduran novelist Marta Susana Prieto has written a well researched and beautifully conceived historical novel, *Memory of the Shadows* (*Memoria de las Sombras*) that recreates the story of Lempira and his heroic resistance from the perspective of a young Lenca girl who survives her people's defeat by the Spanish. Its numerous descriptions of Lenca customs and beliefs make it a valuable contribution to both the literature and the historical memory of Honduras.

Individuals of Lenca descent may be large landowners, small business owners, artisans, professionals, and farmers, although those who have remained closest to the traditional Lenca lifestyle and belief system are typically those who live in small towns and villages and are farmers and artisans. They live in an estimated 100 settlements, many of which have a mixed population. In those towns and villages that still celebrate traditional fiestas, the non-Lenca population participates in the festivities, making these events perhaps as much "Honduran" as "Lenca." It is estimated that the Lenca population numbers around 100,000.

For many Lencas, topography and climate are important determining factors in their lives. Most live in one of two ecosystems, either the low coastal region, which is hot and dry or the mountainous interior, which enjoys a wetter and more temperature climate. Their staple foods continue to be the traditional Mesoamerican diet of corn, beans, and squash in addition to chicken and turkey, although the cultivation of such crops as potatoes, apples, and coffee has been introduced and diets of course vary according to a family's resources, including access to arable land. Some Lencas, such as the residents of Guajiquiro, still practice the age-old custom of migrating between the two climate zones to farm and gather the local raw materials for use in their handcrafts.

Many Lencas are skilled artisans. Traditional crafts still practiced include pottery, basketry, weaving with grasses and other natural fibers and the fabrication of candles and soap. They are still respected today for skills their ancestors acquired through contact with the Spanish, such as carpentry, saddlery, and metalwork. They also learned the arts of working with adobe and stucco through their participation in the construction and decoration of churches and public buildings in Colonial times. The practice of weaving on the back-strap loom, so common among indigenous women of neighboring Guatemala, was abandoned around 1950 but was recently reintroduced in the town of Togopala in the department of Intibucá. A group of weavers there formed the Alianza Cooperative (*Cooperativa Alianza*); the women have become known for their brightly colored utilitarian and decorative fabric. Many Lenca women are skilled embroiderers. They decorate textiles for domestic use such as aprons, tablecloths, and napkins. The women of Guajiquiro are known for their imaginative designs that incorporate floral motifs, birds, and animals, religious symbols, and calligraphy. Another craft typically practiced by Lenca women is the weaving of *petates* or floor mats using fibers from the stem of the tule plant (*Iperus canus*). *Petates* have been used since pre-Columbian times as carpets and sleeping mats and even burial shrouds. Men assist with the cutting and gathering of the plant but the task of weaving the mats is reserved for women. The community of El Níspero in the department of Santa Bárbara is known for its high quality *petates*. Weavers there adhere to the tradition of cutting the *tule* plant during the full moon and they believe the most auspicious time for weaving is during the summer.

Perhaps the craft among the Lenca that is most widely practiced is that of pottery. It is a domestic craft, practiced in the home by women and their daughters. Men may assist with the gathering of firewood for the firing of the pieces, but women locate and extract the clay and are the artisans who produce a variety of utilitarian pots, bowls, jugs, and other objects. In domestic production the wheel is seldom used; women fashion the clay using molds, hand fashioning, and the coil method. Pieces are sometimes fired in rustic open-air pits, a method referred to as *quema en tenemaste*, an allusion to the pre-Hispanic custom of using three stones to form a fire pit. Or they may be fired in a mud oven heated with wood. Large-scale production requires more modern and efficient firing techniques, so pottery factories also produce ceramic items for commercial markets.

Numerous cooperatives have been formed throughout the country for the purpose of encouraging indigenous artisans to continue their craft, develop new skills, and learn to market their crafts effectively so they can be a source of income. Examples among the Lenca are the San Cristóbal Association of Pine Tree Handcrafts of Guascotoro in Yamaranguila, a cooperative of some twenty families dedicated to the manufacture and sale of handcrafts made from pine tree needles and *Petateras Lencas*, a regional association of women *petate* weavers. Several potters' cooperatives also exist: one of the largest and most successful is the Lenca Industrial Ceramic Cooperative of Ojojona and Santa Ana, *Cooperativa Industrial de Alfarería Lenca de Ojojona y Santa Ana* (CIALOSA), that has developed a style of decorative ceramics employing colonial and religious motifs.

The spiritual worldview and accompanying practices of the Lenca people are a complex syncretism of Spanish Catholic and pre-Hispanic divinities, cosmogonies, and rituals. According to anthropologist Ramón D. Rivas, the salient features of Lenca spirituality include an animistic conception of reality, a hierarchy of spiritual entities, the persistence of prayers and ritual offerings, *nahualismo* or the belief in animal spirit-beings and a vestigial shamanism. The majority of Lencas are Catholic, although their Catholicism differs in significant ways from mainstream beliefs and practices. Christ and the Virgin Mary, for example, represent for them the original Father and Mother. The agrarian ritual called a *compostura* is an example of this syncretism in practice. *Composturas* are private or domestic agrarian rituals performed as offerings to the earth. They are usually held in the fields, where an altar is constructed following a prescribed design that specifies an exact number of stakes and branches and includes pine boughs, a cross, and *sumos*, an epiphyte that represents the spirits called upon in the ritual. Other essential elements are beeswax candles; *copal*, a resin from a local tree that is burned as incense; *chicha*, a fermented beverage; and a chicken to be sacrificed. *Composturas* range from simple to complex but always include prayers, the ritual drinking of *chicha*, the sacrifice of a chicken or turkey, and a shared meal.

In conjunction with the animistic concept that all things in nature are alive and have spirits is the belief that human beings are constantly relating to and negotiating with spirits, saints, and angels. There are numerous tales, legends, and myths that are part of the Lenca oral tradition and that describe these beings, explain their role in the creation and ongoing functioning of the world, and recount anecdotes that exemplify their relation to humans. Numerous spirit-beings play an important role in the Lenca worldview. *El Cacalote* is a black bird believed to have flown away in search of the first ear of corn, which he found and brought back to the Lenca people. Many angels inhabit the Lenca universe, each with its purpose: They bring rain, wind, good harvests, and diseases. They are capable of causing horrific disasters and must be honored and placated with offerings and ceremonies. *Chalchiguas* are jadeite carvings that predate the Spanish; they brought good luck until people converted to Catholicism, so they were buried deep in the earth and will reappear when people are no longer Catholic. A *nahual* is one's animal spirit or protector. Everyone is born with a *nahual*, who accompanies him or her throughout life. There are various ways of determining one's *nahual*. In some communities it is still the custom to sprinkle ashes at the entrance to the house where a child is born; the first animal to leave its print in the ashes is considered the child's *nahual*. *Los dueños de los cerros* are the owners or spirits of the hills, who will exact revenge if materials are extracted without their permission. Ritual offerings are made to them when clay, for example, is removed for the making of pottery or when animals are hunted. The *Sisimite* is a large creature, half human and half animal, whose feet point backward. He is notorious for abducting women and taking them to his cave, where they produce an offspring who later kills him. The son then tries to return to his human community but realizes he is not understood or accepted, returns to the cave and takes up the life of the *Sisimite*.

In 1985 a group of students from the Honduran National University presented as their thesis for graduation, a manuscript that represented the task of interviewing, recording, and transcribing stories from the oral tradition among the residents of Yamaranguila. They spoke with many elders who are no longer alive and were able to preserve some of the rich oral tradition of this

Lenca community. The thesis was published in 1988 (*Tradición oral indígena de Yamaranguila*) and represents an extremely valuable cultural project. It describes, in the words of their informants, beliefs, rituals, stories, and explanations for natural phenomena.

This type of work that attempts to rescue native beliefs and practices from the slow but sure death of oblivion serves as a countermeasure to the efforts of both the Catholic Church and the numerous Protestant evangelical missions who work among the Lenca. In the 1970s the Catholic Church instituted an initiative to train lay preachers to become Delegates or Celebrants of the Word (*Delegados o Celebradores de la Palabra*), who meet regularly to discuss the Church's teachings and lead their rural congregations in religious celebrations, thereby assisting priests but also usurping the role of the traditional Lenca prayer leaders (*rezadores tradicionales*). Evangelical missionaries often teach that the traditional beliefs come from the devil and that the poverty and ill treatment so many indigenous people suffer is the result not of an unjust social system or an uncaring government, but of worshipping false gods.

CHORTÍ

The Chortí are the southernmost subgroup of the Maya-Quiché people. They live in eastern Guatemala in the department of Chiquimula and there are estimates that those who live in the neighboring Honduran departments of Ocotepque and Copán number between 3,000 and 10,000. Most of the Honduran Chortí live alongside their ladino neighbors, although they are highly concentrated in the mountainous region around Copán Ruinas in small villages and hamlets within twenty kilometers of the Guatemalan border. Although the Chortí of Guatemala have been studied extensively by various scholars, the Honduran branch has received much less attention. Believed to be descendents of the Maya who founded the ancient city of Copán, the Honduran Chortí, like the Lenca, no longer wear the traditional dress and few speak the native language, Chol or Chortí. Many of their traditional crafts are no longer practiced and their beliefs are a complex blend of Catholic and pre-Hispanic influences. However, like the other indigenous communities of Honduras, the Chortí have formed an ethnic federation, the National Council of Chortí Indians of Honduras (CONICH) for the purpose of reclaiming their ethnic identity as well as their ancestral lands. Vestiges of the old ways have served as inspiration for the formation of new generations of artisans who have found a market for their skills and imagination among those Hondurans who have acquired a new appreciation for their indigenous national identity and among the many international travelers who come to visit the exquisite ruins and archaeological museum at Copán. Historically, their closest and most influential neighbors were the Lenca and the Pipil, so their traditions bear a strong resemblance to theirs.

The topography of Chortí territory is mountainous, interspersed with small valleys, numerous rivers, and impressive waterfalls. It has a temperate climate, with seasonal variations ranging from quite cold during the rainy season, *invierno*, May through November, and especially at night, to hot and dry in the months of December through April, *verano*.

Traditional Chortí houses are constructed from *zacate*, a dried straw collected locally and tied to wooden poles, or from *bahareque*, a style found throughout rural Honduras. The exterior walls of homes of *bahareque* construction are typically whitewashed and decorated with floral, animal, or geometric designs using paint made from red clay. Homes are normally one multiple-use room with a packed earth floor. The cooking area occupies the center of this room and may be a simple *tenamaste* or fireplace made with three stones placed in a circle on the floor, or a mud oven. The more prosperous Chortí may build an adobe home with a zinc or ceramic tile roof and add a separate kitchen, either enclosed or an open-sided structure with a roof. A Chortí home is simply furnished with a table and stools or benches made from locally gathered wood. Family members sleep on *tapesco*-style beds, on *petates* on the ground or in hammocks hung from the rafters. The Chortí who live in or around Copán Ruinas produce baskets, *petates*, and other woven articles for domestic use and for the market. They no longer practice traditional weaving like their Guatemalan counterparts, but they have continued to make ceramics and have revived the practice of stone carving and sculpture in order to create items to sell to tourists visiting the Maya city of Copán.

Chortí dietary staples are corn and beans, supplemented by meats, eggs, and vegetables such as squash when the budget allows. Chortí women grind their corn using the traditional stone mortar and pestle, shape their tortillas by hand and cook them on flat, round pans.

The religious life of the present-day Chortí reflects a profound blending of Mayan and Catholic beliefs and practices, although it is important to mention the presence in western Honduras of numerous Protestant missionaries of various tendencies, notably evangelical and fundamentalist, whose attention to civic and communal needs and whose charismatic and even messianic and prophetic orientation have appealed to many Chortí. An interesting example of this contemporary syncretism of Mayan and Protestant influences is the case of Guillermo García, a Chortí shaman or prayer leader (*chucurero*) from the village of Carrizalón who has founded a church called New Century (*Nuevo Siglo*). He preaches a millenarian vision of the return of a messiah and prophesizes the overturning of the system that has oppressed the Maya for centuries. Included in his vision and teachings is the reclaiming of the Chortí language, traditions, and beliefs.

The syncretism of Maya and Catholic in the religious beliefs of the Chortí manifests in many ways, such as their devotion to the Virgin Mary as well as the Earth Goddess of Maya origin, two beings who have been conflated into a caring, nurturing female deity. The Virgin Mary is the Guardian of Corn, for example, and assists the rain god, Chaac, who in turn is under the authority of St. Michael the Archangel. Although some 90 percent of the Chortí profess to be Catholic, their acceptance of the Catholic sacraments is uneven. Many couples live together and/or have families without sanctifying their union through marriage, for example, while the Catholic rite of baptism is considered very important because it is believed to confer personhood on an infant. The cross is a central symbol in Christianity and also was revered among the ancient Maya, for whom it represented the four directions or the four corners of the universe. A large cross is typically located in the central plaza of a Chortí community and important rituals occur there, such as the celebration of May 3, when the cross is decorated with flowers and can help a sick person become well. Crosses are believed to protect against evil spirits, which partially explains their presence on the roofs of buildings, on family altars, and in burial grounds. Each community has its patron saint, whose statue is kept in the local church. The identity of the saint is often a combination of the attributes of a Catholic saint and a Maya deity, although it will be known by its Catholic name. The deity of dreams and sleep is masculine for men and feminine for women and often accompanies the deity of death, who has the form of a skeleton wrapped in white cloth. He carries a tall staff with a knife fashioned from bone on one end and can be seen only by an individual about to die. If he appears near the suffering person's head, there is a chance of recovery, but if he stands at the foot of the bed, there is no hope.

The living have ongoing contact with the spirits of the dead. It is important to speak affectionately of the dead because they can attack the living and cause them harm. The preferred place of the dead is the local church, where they spend a good deal of time and where the living leave them offerings of flowers, candles, and alcohol. The entire month of November is dedicated to the dead. The commemoration is called *tzikin*, which begins on October 31. In homes, altars covered with banana leaves and vines are built and offerings such as tamales, corn, cigars, *copal* incense, and candles are set out as gifts for the dead. There are prayers and ceremonies in memory of the dead throughout the month.

Other rituals that have their origin in pre-Columbian times are agrarian in nature. It is customary to celebrate a ritual to ask for rain in May, the usual beginning of the rainy season. The ritual, called the *padrineo del agua*, takes places at *cenotes*, springs, or other sources of water. It traditionally was celebrated at the Copán ruins in front of Stella 22. The *Padrino* or Godfather who officiates at the ritual places the ceremonial objects on the altar. The altar is constructed in two sections and decorated with green foliage to represent the union of above and below, sky and earth. All ritual objects are in groups of nine or thirteen: flowers, candles, *copal* incense, gourd bowls called boats (*barcos*), and squash cut in half. Sweet *chilate*, a thick drink made from corn and brown sugar, is placed on the upper altar along with yellow and white candles and the gourd bowls filled with water. Bitter *chilate* is placed on the lower altar, where the blood of the sacrificed animal, usually a chicken or turkey, is spilled. Celebrants recite the rosary, pray to the saints and especially to the angels, who bring the rain clouds. The smoke from the burning *copal* symbolizes clouds. Some of the *chilate* and the flesh of the sacrificed animal are buried in the four cardinal directions and are considered offerings to the earth and the saints. The music of guitars, violins, whistles, and rattles accompanies the ceremony. Sexual abstinence by both men and women participants was required in the past.

Rituals in honor of the sun are also still performed. *Cofradías* or brotherhoods are responsible for the ceremony and it is customary for each *cofradía* to have a wooden chest where the sacred objects are carefully kept: five *petates* or woven mats; metal candle holders, preferably gold; copper bells; coins; red, yellow, and white capes; the staff or wand, considered the ultimate symbol of authority; flags; and antique books or manuscripts.

GARÍFUNA

The Garífuna[1] are a unique people who today may number as many as 400,000 living around the world. Population estimates from different sources vary widely; it is likely that the actual number is around 250,000. Their history can be traced to two distinct ethnic groups, the Island Caribs and Africans brought to the Caribbean as slaves. The Island Caribs were a mix of Carib and Arawak peoples who migrated north to the Greater Antilles Islands in the Caribbean from northern South America beginning in the second century A.D. The early sixteenth century saw the importation of African slaves to work on the sugar plantations of the Caribbean islands. Runaway slaves, known as *cimarrones* began to mix with the native Carib population. Other intended slaves, who survived two shipwrecks off the coast of St. Vincent in 1635, also mixed with the indigenous inhabitants. Their offspring were the first generation of the people known today as the Garífuna or Garinagu. It has been argued that, given these beginnings, the Garífuna may be the only African Americans who were never enslaved. They continued to live on

St. Vincent throughout the seventeenth and much of the eighteenth centuries, when the Spanish, French, British, and Dutch were all interested in owning and profiting from the island. In 1796 the British did battle with and defeated the French, thereby gaining control of the island. Because the Garífuna had formed alliances with the French, the British forcibly deported an estimated 2,000 to the island of Roatán in 1797. Some few stayed on the island, founding the community of Punta Gorda, where their descendents live today. Most however migrated to the north coast of Honduras and from there moved east and west and established settlements along the Caribbean coast of Central America from Nicaragua to Belize. Many Garífuna continue to think of the island of St. Vincent as their spiritual home, which they call *Yarumei*. For the Garífuna of Honduras, April 12 is a day of ethnic pride, when they commemorate their arrival in Honduras.

Some of the Garífuna who settled on the Honduran coast moved inland and mixed with the Miskito people. Others stayed on the coast and lived a subsistence lifestyle. Some later worked as loggers for the British and in the first half of the twentieth century many found work with the North American banana companies. Around the time of World War II, many Garífuna men began leaving Honduras to work at a variety of marine-related jobs, particularly with the U.S. and British merchant marines. Today it is common for both men and women to seek opportunities abroad. There are sizeable Garífuna communities in many U.S. cities, including Los Angeles, Miami, Houston, Boston, and the Bronx, New York. Family members living abroad regularly send money and gifts to their relatives in Honduras and many older Garífuna dream of returning to their villages to retire. Although many Garífuna living abroad have adapted to the culture of their new home, it has become increasingly more common for expatriates to reclaim their Garífuna identity with pride. Numerous organizations have been formed to promote cultural awareness and community cohesion.

There are also many Garífuna who live in urban centers in Honduras including Tela, La Ceiba, Trujillo, San Pedro Sula, and Tegucigalpa. Many of those who have moved to the cities are professionals such as teachers, lawyers, doctors, and musicians. Scholars in both Honduras and the United States have been captivated by the history as well as the living culture of the Garífuna, so it is possible to find studies in both languages on a variety of topics ranging from traditional medicine to gender roles to the Garífuna diaspora.[2] Some Garífuna writers, such as Victor Virgilio López García have recently published works on the language, culture, and current political situation of their people.

An interesting example of a foreign artist being inspired by the Garífuna culture is the film "El espíritu de mi mamá" (Spirit of My Mother), written, produced, and directed by actor and independent filmmaker, Alí Allié, in

1999. It tells the story of a young Garífuna woman from Los Angeles whose mother asks her in a dream to perform a traditional *dugú* or ceremony for the ancestors so that the mother may rest in peace. The young woman journeys to Honduras and learns the ceremony from the elders as she is surrounded by the music, dance, food, and family ties of her people. The journey and the ritual serve to reunite her with her past and heal the wounds of the present. It was filmed in Los Angeles and Honduras and all the actors are Garífuna.

There are forty Garífuna villages in the Bay Islands and on the north coast of Honduras. In many of these villages there are still vestiges of the traditional culture. The subsistence lifestyle practiced by many Garífuna who live in these small villages is based on fishing and farming. The men are skilled divers and fishermen while the women cultivate plants that thrive in the hot, dry summers and hot, wet winters of their coastal environment, such as bananas, plantains, *malanga*, *ñame*, yucca, okra, and *camote* or sweet potato. They grow tropical fruits such as coconut, mango, tamarind, papaya, and guava. The coastal villages are typically located close to the shore, behind the line of coconut palms that line the beach and offer protection from storms. The Garífuna do not tend to enclose their homes within fences of any kind, in stark contrast to the ladino custom of security walls often topped with barbed wire or jagged glass. Land is both privately and communally owned. And it is customary for friends and neighbors to enter each other's homes, even in the owner's absence, to borrow an item.

Many of the traditional rituals and ceremonies are no longer widely practiced in the old way, although they have not been completely lost or forgotten. One practice that has become less common due to its incompatibility with the expectations of the contemporary labor market is honoring the *uwani*. An age-old Garífuna belief is that children inherit their spirit or life force from their father. Their health is directly related to the quality of their father's *uwani* and to his ability to provide them with *uwani*-fortifying food, namely fish and meat. The traditional division of labor determines that the men are the hunters and fishermen, but because one's *uwani* is diminished through sweating, the father is required to stop working for a period of time after the birth of his offspring and the mother's brother takes on the responsibility of providing food.

It is still common for the Garífuna to honor their dead and to maintain ongoing relationships with their ancestors. Many Garífuna homes have small altars with candles and photographs of deceased family members. Ritual bathing of the body, wakes, and a ceremony that takes places one year after one's death are important observances. *Punta* is a traditional dance performed at wakes. Women wear long, full skirts and bandanas to cover their hair. They step forward, back, and to each side and move their hips as the men dance around them but without touching them. In the 1980s, traditional *punta* rhythms and instruments were combined with modern musical influences to create what has become known as punta rock, danced and performed in nightclubs and discos throughout Central America and beyond.

The deceased remain active and may communicate with the living through dreams. Their spirits are called *gubida* and they can cause illness and may request attentions to satisfy their needs. When this happens a *buyei* or healer may be called on to remedy the situation. He or she will communicate with the spirit of the deceased to determine its demands by entering into a trance or interpreting signs such as the movements of a candle flame. There are three traditional offerings or appeasements that the *gubida* may request: *lemessi*, *chugu*, or *dugú*. Each ceremony has specific prayers, songs, or dances associated with it. It may be a simple *lemessi*, which involves the guests first attending a Catholic mass, then gathering in the home of the deceased's relatives where a *rezadora* or woman who knows the traditional prayers will lead the singing, after which the guests are served white bread, *guaro* or cane liquor, and a drink made from water, flour, and cacao.

A *dugú*, on the other hand, involves the entire community and can cost thousands of dollars. The main ceremony lasts three days and two nights, but preparations begin well in advance with the construction of a thatched house that has three sections: an area for dancing, a separate space for the altar, and a section where hammocks are hung. The house is blessed and a fire is kept burning in the center for a month. Crosses, candles, and food are placed in the house to attract the ancestors. During the week before the ceremony, women go from house to house with baskets, asking for donations of food. The food is placed in the house. Three days before the *dugú*, fishermen set out to fish for three days and three nights. They salt their catch and arrive with it at daybreak on the first day of the celebration. They decorate their *cayucos* and a child representing an angel rides in each boat. A gala procession with singing and dancing accompanies the fishermen to the *dugú* house, where for the next three days there are songs, dances, food, and rituals. At the end of the ceremony, any leftover food is thrown in the sea, a table is burned and water brought from the sea is sprinkled around the house—rituals to ensure that the ceremony is complete and the ancestor(s) satisfied. The house is left standing for one year, when the ceremony called *lagusiri gayu* is performed, after which the house can be taken down as it is assumed that the ancestors have returned to their home.

It is obvious that any level of ceremony for the ancestors can be costly and time-consuming. It is believed that what one gives to the ancestors will be returned in some measure and that neglecting them is the sign of an ungenerous soul, who will eventually pay the price for his or her stinginess.

Many Garífuna today speak two and even three languages, usually Garífuna, English, and Spanish. The Garífuna language is classified as Arawakan although, given the migration and mixing with other cultures that has characterized Garífuna history, it is not surprising that linguists have also identified the influence of English, French, Yoruba, Bantu, and Portuguese. The language is still widely spoken, although it is taught mostly informally. In 1977, the Garífuna Nation adopted a Language Policy Statement addressed to the governments of Belize, Guatemala, Honduras, and Nicaragua that expressed the desire to develop policies to document and promote the language, but efforts to provide bilingual education to Garífuna children have been poorly financed. In 2001 UNESCO declared the language, dance, and music of the Garífuna an outstanding example of the world's intangible cultural heritage.

Some scholars, both Garífuna and foreign, have begun the task of interviewing elders and recording, transcribing, and publishing some of the rich oral tradition, a wealth of tales, beliefs, songs, history, and practices. One example is *Uraga: La tradición oral del pueblo garífuna,* published in 1992 by the Center for Community Development, Centro de Desarrollo Comunitario (CEDEC) in Tegucigalpa. *Uragas* are tales traditionally told by elders, both women and men (*uragebuna*), at wakes and masses to entertain and teach. The characters of the *úragas* are humans who have greater than normal strengths or powers and are besieged by passions such as envy, love, revenge, sadness, or deceit; or they may be animals who are uncommonly clever or capable and interact with humans as equals. *Uragas* are told with great flair, accompanied by gestures, facial expressions, humor, and imagination and always with a moralizing intent.

Garífuna legends have a clear African influence, as seen in the many stories about Anasi the Spider, hero of Ashanti legends from Ghana. Rabbits and tortoises, popular characters in traditional Yoruba and Bantu tales, also figure prominently.

The importance of preserving and documenting the Garífuna oral tradition cannot be overestimated, for it is not only in many cases the sole source of knowledge of their unique cosmovision and spiritual beliefs and the rituals and practices they inspire, but it has been a precious source of stories, memories, and attitudes that have allowed them to reconstruct their history. Very little historical documentation has been found to help flesh out the broad outlines of the story of the Garífuna people over time: their origins, challenges, migrations, and survival. In 1979 Honduran playwright Rafael Murillo Selva Rendón began working with individuals from villages on the Caribbean coast to create an original musical play that attempts to recreate the history of the Garífuna people. The residents themselves participated in the interviewing of elders which, along with information gleaned from non-Garífuna sources such as chronicles and historical documents and the author's own imagination, formed the basis for the story that unfolds through music, dance, song, and the enactment of actual or symbolic events in Garífuna history. All of the participants in the production were nonprofessional Garífuna actors, dancers, and musicians between the ages of seven and sixty-five. The musical, *Loubavagu*, was presented in Garífuna communities as well as other Honduran venues and abroad. Murilla Selva recalls that when he began the project he observed that the Garífuna with whom he worked had little or no knowledge of the history of their people. If that were indeed the case, it is quite extraordinary that in the less than three decades since that project, the Garífuna story can be easily found on numerous web pages and the deportation of their ancestors from St. Vincent and their subsequent arrival on the Caribbean coast are reenacted annually in Garífuna villages from Belize to Nicaragua. It appears that, with the help of electronic media, the oral tradition lives on.

If events from the far reaches of historical memory had fallen into oblivion, this has not been the case with more recent history. The dramatic massacre of at least a dozen Garífuna leaders in 1937 in the village of San Juan by the government of Tiburcio Carías Andino, for example, has not been forgotten, although it is not a story that commonly appears in Honduran history books. In 1997 U.S.-Honduran writer Guillermo Yuscarán published *When Chona Sang* (*Cuando Chona cantaba*), a fictional account of the massacre that he reconstructed through the stories told to him by Garífuna friends and family.

The recent international popularity of their culture has been greeted by some Garífuna with pride. They see it as recognition of their ethnic identity and as a means of encouraging the younger generations to appreciate their heritage and learn their history and customs, which many young people ignore as they get immersed in the consumer culture offered by globalization. Others are critical of changes that they see as diluting and commercializing their culture. An example that illustrates the inescapable contradictions inherent in attempting to preserve a living culture was the opening of a Garífuna Cultural Center in Tela in 1997. The Center is located in Tela in part because there is an active and numerous Garífuna community in the area, but also because Tela and its beaches have become a popular vacation destination. The Center has an art gallery, a shop that offers handcrafts, a restaurant that prepares Garífuna cuisine, and a museum of Garífuna history, run by the Garífuna Women's Association, *Lanigi Wanichugu*. The museum, which is housed in a traditional Garífuna dwelling made of wild cane and manaca palm leaves, has organized exhibits of musical instruments, dance costumes, traditional tools, and domestic utensils. Although one could argue that such a museum helps to validate and preserve a traditional culture, the nature of museums implies stasis and observation of the surface of a culture. An exhibit that includes a *dugú* house, for example, can only approximate or skim the surface of the living reality of this age-old ritual. Even the restaurant, which offers traditional Garífuna food, finds itself hampered by the complexity of preparation required if the food served is to be truly traditional. The making of coconut oil, for example, is a time-consuming process that requires manually gathering the coconuts from the trees, splitting them open with a machete and grating them with a hand grater. The grated coconut is then pressed to make coconut milk, which in turn is boiled, allowed to ferment, and skimmed. Another classic example is the preparation of *casabe* or *erebe*, a staple food among the Garífuna made from the bitter yucca root (the "sweet" yucca is also eaten), which is poisonous until it is processed to express the bitter juices. The extraction process involves peeling and grating the root and then pressing it through a long sieve called a *rugama* or *culebra* (snake). Flour made from the dried starchy root is the basis of the thin, flat bread known as *casabe*.

Another example of celebrating Garífuna culture and bringing it to the attention of Honduran as well as international audiences is the successful *Ballet Folklórico Garífuna* (Garífuna Folkloric Ballet). Founded in 1976 by Garífuna choreographer Crisanto Meléndez, the company of dancers, actors, and musicians performs a medley of numbers that recreate daily life in a Garífuna village, honor the ancestors, illustrate scenes from their history, and display many of the traditional rhythms and dances such as *punta* and *parranda*.

On a more political note, the international attention directed to the Garífuna culture and the concern by activist groups for the health and well-being of the Garífuna people, has led to the creation of two short documentaries that have been screened around the world. These films expose the precarious situation of Garífuna communities in danger of extinction due to the unwillingness of the Honduran government to enforce its own laws that protect their rights and their environment. The documentaries, *Lucha garífuna/Garífunas Holding Ground* (2002) and *When the River Met the Sea/Cuando el río y el mar se unieron* (2004) were made by the *Comité de Emergencia Garífuna de Honduras* (Garífuna Emergency Committee of Honduras [CEGAH]) in partnership with Witness. The first one tells the story of a road that was illegally built through Garífuna lands and that is causing a negative environmental impact that in turn is affecting their livelihood. *When the River Met the Sea*, which won an award at the Latin American Environmental Film Festival in 2005, describes the devastation caused in Garífuna communities by Hurricane Mitch in 1998 and criticizes the ongoing neglect on the part of the Honduran government.

The Garífuna Emergency Committee is a Honduran NGO created in response to the destruction caused by Hurricane Mitch. From their head-quarters in Barrio Cristales, Trujillo, CEGAH works to resist the taking of Garífuna land by tourism development entrepreneurs and others and supports efforts that promote sustainable development and Garífuna cultural preservation. They worked with Wendy Griffin to publish in 2005, *Los Garífunas de Honduras: cultura, lucha y derechos bajo el Convenio 169 de la OIT.* This text represents an important accomplishment in the ongoing work to gather and document Garífuna beliefs, stories, and practices while there are still individuals alive who carry this knowledge in their memories. Although it is designed for use by teachers interested in passing the traditional Garífuna culture on to children and young adults, anyone can benefit from the wealth of information it contains.

INDIGENOUS ACTIVISM

The seven major indigenous and ethnic groups described above constitute approximately 10 percent of the total population of Honduras. Nevertheless, until the 1970s, very few Hondurans were knowledgeable or even aware of the diversity within their nation. Indeed, the prevailing notion was that Honduras was essentially a mestizo nation: that the fusion of Spanish and indigenous blood had created a new mestizo identity and that there simply were no Indians in Honduras. But the awakening of ethnic consciousness and pride among indigenous groups, their insistence that their history, their cultural heritage, and their rights to land and resources be acknowledged and respected, has made scholars and politicians pay more attention to these previously ignored voices. The indigenous movement that began in Honduras in the 1970s gained momentum in the late 1980s and 1990s and today every indigenous group in the country has organized into coalitions or federations, often with the help and participation of nonindigenous activists in solidarity with their situation. These groups are working on several fronts to retain ownership of ancestral lands; revive traditional handcrafts; promote bilingual education, health care, and sanitation; and preserve or revive traditional celebrations. The Pech (FETRIP), the Miskito (MASTA), the Tawahka (FITH), the Lenca (ONIHL), the Xicaque (FETRIXY), the Chortí (CONICH), and the Garífuna (OFRANEH) also have joined together to form the Confederation of Indigenous Peoples of Honduras (Confederación de Pueblos Autóctonos de Honduras [CONPAH]), created in 1992. This group has become an important presence in Honduran public life.

A dramatic example of the energy and organization of CONPAH was a demonstration carried out in October 1998. On October 11, an estimated

2,500 Lenca protesters arrived in Tegucigalpa; the following day some 3,000 Chortí activists blocked all entrances to the Copán Ruins Archaeological Park 180 kilometers west of the capital as part of their demand for land suitable for farming. That same day, October 12, celebrated as Columbus Day in the United States and the Day of the Race (Día de la Raza) in Honduras but chosen symbolically to demonstrate the protesters' resistance to foreign invasion and domination, 2,000 indigenous activists marched through the streets of Tegucigalpa. They participated in a mock trial of Christopher Columbus during which Columbus was found guilty of ten crimes, including theft of cultural heritage, slave trafficking and genocide. On October 16, four members of CONPAH began a hunger strike, with four additional members pledged to join the strike every four days until their demands were met. Their demands included the fulfillment of unkept promises, primarily for land, made in earlier negotiations between the government and indigenous leaders; an end to the proposed Patuca and Tigre dam projects, which would have a heavy impact on indigenous lands; and justice in the more than forty recent murders of indigenous people due to land conflicts. They asked the government to fulfill their pledge to purchase 1,200 hectares of agricultural land for Chortí indigenous people in the departments of Copán and Ocotepeque and criticized the Honduran Institute of Anthropology and History for allowing the looting of the archaeological sites of Copán and Tagua. Pech, Lenca, and Garífuna protesters camped in the plaza outside the Legislative Assembly building for three weeks and the entrances to Copán remained blocked for several days. This well-orchestrated protest caused the Honduran government to meet with the indigenous leaders and agree to expedite the land purchase.

But the Chortí are not the only people desirous of land in western Honduras. Large landowners, most of them tobacco and coffee farmers, bought thousands of hectares of land on both sides of the Honduras–Guatemala border in the 1950s, thereby displacing thousands of Chortís, who ended up working as laborers on the land they had once farmed. The landowners, represented by the Organization of Farmers and Ranchers (Organización de Agricultores y Ganaderos [AGRACOR]), claim that the Chortí cannot prove their indigenous ethnicity and accordingly are not entitled to the land. The government nevertheless granted land to the Chortí but never paid the current owners for it, so the Chortí were evicted. But now that the Chortí are cognizant of their political power, they are willing to continue the fight. They closed down the Copán Archaeological Park for fourteen hours in 2000, when Honduran police broke up the protest using tear gas and batons and injuring seventeen demonstrators, and again for five days in June 2005 and for six days in September of the same year.

The five different indigenous and ethnic groups that today reside in north-eastern Honduras came to the region at different historical times and migrated from different directions. At various times in their histories they were enemies or formed alliances, intermarried or remained aloof and isolated. Today they collectively face the possible future extinction of their cultures as the forces of the modern world enter this region that once was imagined by outsiders as wild, dangerous, mysterious, and impenetrable. Their undeveloped land and the lure of abundant natural resources are attracting adventure travelers, eco-tourists, *campesinos* in search of land to farm and raise livestock, and most ominously, national and international corporations desirous of exploiting the forests and waterways. So while indigenous groups organize themselves to protect their land and preserve and revive their cultures; while NGOs work in the region to promote bilingual, intercultural education, indigenous women's rights, and the revival of traditional handcrafts; while biological and anthropological reserves are being created by private and government entities, at the same time, massive projects such as the plan to create a dam on the Patuca River to provide hydroelectric power throughout Central America, move forward. This plan, if executed, would have serious environmental consequences for the indigenous Miskitos and Tawakas. In 1998, the first attempt to begin this project generated heated public debate and resulted in the postponement of the plan to build the first in a series of dams on the Patuca River as part of the Puebla-Panamá Plan, which envisions the construction of an unknown number of dams to supply energy through the Central American Electric Interconnection Initiative. Honduran President Manuel Zelaya has entered into an agreement with the Tai Power Company of Taiwan, which has been granted a fifteen-year concession for energy production, although an environmental permit has not been issued. Opposition is once again surfacing, however, and on December 20, 2007, two activists from the Olancho Environmental Movement (MAO) were arrested and then murdered by National Police agents at a police station close to the dam site. In March 2008 an open forum on the Patuca-3 project was held in Brus Laguna, La Mosquitia. Representatives of Miskito, Tawahka, Pech, and Lenca federations, along with members of national and international environmental organizations, drew up a declaration (Declaración de Uhri-Brus) of principles denouncing the project and urging the Honduran government to consider the impact that the proposed dams will have on the communities, given that they live on the shores of the river and it serves as their means of transportation, and major source of food.

There is additional irony in the fact that, although numerous indigenous and grassroots organizations are working with limited budgets to create and sustain micro-projects to promote the care and preservation of nature such as a sea turtle protection campaign, a butterfly farm, and an iguana raising project, the national government enters into agreements to sell its natural treasures.

Marches, protests, hunger strikes, manifestoes, negotiations, and the support of international NGOs have given indigenous movements visibility, voice, and a political presence. The Honduran government has accordingly recognized the importance of linguistic and cultural diversity to the nation's economic and social well-being. The Constitution of 1982, title III, chapter VIII, article 173 asserts that the State will preserve and stimulate native cultures and genuine expressions of national folklore. A series of bilingual education projects that encompassed kindergarten through adult education among the Miskitos, Garífunas, Tawahkas, and Pech, were piloted in the 1990s. Educational materials have been developed with funds from the United States Agency for International Development (USAID), the United States Information Service (USIS), and UNICEF. Sadly, the Honduran government has adopted a practice of meeting and discussing demands with indigenous representatives, promising land and financial support, and then not enforcing laws or carrying through with promises. On a more sinister note, numerous indigenous leaders and activists have been killed in recent decades and their murderers go unpunished. How long these political and judicial tactics can continue remains to be seen.

All of the indigenous cultures described here are facing the reality of their possible extinction. The growing awareness of this fact and the various communities' responses to the loss of their language, the destruction of their natural environment and the loss of cultural memory as elders die and the younger generations abandon the passing on of the rich history embedded in their oral tradition, all indicate that this is a time of growth and renewal for many of Honduras' indigenous people. Complicating the efforts of indigenous groups to preserve their land and their way of life is the realization on the part of the Honduran government and private business that the indigenous peoples of the country—their culture, their handcrafts, the natural environment—are a saleable commodity in a global world concerned with the immanent extinction of species, plant, animal, and human.

This is a precarious time: the future will most certainly bring change to their communities. Can true cultural diversity survive in today's world? Given its rich and varied history of encounter, assimilation, and resistance, Honduras may well be one place where it is possible.

NOTES

1. Although commonly known as the Garífuna, the name Garinagu is also used. Some sources explain that Garinagu is the plural form of Garífuna, others assert that Garinagu is the name for this group in the Garífuna language.

2. The following brief sample of recent scholarship on the Garífuna demonstrates this range of interest: Milton Cohen. "The Ethnomedicine of Garífuna (Black Caribes) of Río Tinto, Honduras." *Anthropological Quarterly*. 57:1 (January 1984) 16–27; Oliver N. Greene, Jr. "Ethnicity, Modernity, and Retention in the Garífuna Punta." *Black Music Research Journal*. 22:2 (Autumn 2002) 189–216; Sarah England. "Negotiating Race and Place in the Garífuna Diaspora: Identity Formation and Transnational Grassroots Politics in New York City and Honduras." *Identities*. 6:1 (1999) 5–53; Eva Thorne. "Land Rights and Garífuna Identity," *NACLA Reports on the Americas*. 38:2 (September/October 2004) 21–25.

3

Religion

RELIGIOUS SYNCRETISM

THE VARIOUS INDIGENOUS groups that before the arrival of the Spanish inhabited the area that is today Honduras, most certainly had beliefs and practices that reflected their understanding of the creation of the world and their relationship to the forces of nature. Contact with soldiers, settlers, traders, and missionaries from various European and African countries, all with their own religions, initiated profound changes in the lives of the indigenous inhabitants, who gradually adapted their ways to those of the newcomers, whereas the newcomers in turn absorbed elements of the religious beliefs and practices of the indigenous groups. The new religions shaped through the various dynamics of force, persuasion, and attraction are syncretic blends that over time became difficult if not impossible to separate into their original components. Just as there are very few if any individuals in Honduras today who can claim a direct and unmixed indigenous heritage, the religions of the majority of Honduras' contemporary population are composites of traditional beliefs and practices with those of Catholicism or one of the Protestant denominations. Observation and study of oral tales, rituals, and ceremonies among the Lenca and Tawahka, for example, reveal vestiges of beliefs and practices that may well date to pre-Columbian times, although individuals will identify themselves as Catholic or Protestant.

THE ROMAN CATHOLIC CHURCH

As was the case in most of Latin America, Roman Catholic clergy played an important role in the conquest and settlement of Honduras. Priests accompanied the first Spanish soldiers and some stayed to evangelize the indigenous people, which generally was accomplished by convincing them through persuasion or force to abandon their traditional lifestyles and live in settlements under the supervision and protection of the Church.[1] These settlements, called *reducciones* or *misiones*, were somewhat more successful in the western and southern regions than in La Mosquitia to the east, given the Lenca propensity to settle in stable, highly organized communities. The mining and ranching opportunities afforded in the west attracted more Spanish settlers and churches were built in the new towns. The Payas and other groups of the eastern region, on the other hand, had a semi-nomadic lifestyle and the hot, wet climate was less attractive to settlers, so even when Catholic priests managed to convince the indigenous people to settle in *reducciones*, they often abandoned them in short order. Priests of the Franciscan Order carried out much of the missionary work among the indigenous peoples. Fathers Esteban Verdelete and Juan de Montegudo have secured a place in Honduran history as the first Catholic priests to penetrate the jungles and mountains of eastern Olancho, c. 1604, to evangelize the indigenous population. The inhospitable reception they received led them to solicit military assistance from the Spanish Crown, occasioning the first slaughter of Spanish soldiers at the hands of the Indians, in 1612. Subsequent incursions by Spanish soldiers, often with the assistance of Spanish settlers, were equally unsuccessful, convincing the Crown that peaceful means of conversion would be a better strategy, although in practice both methods were employed. In 1667 Father Pedro de Ovalle went to Olancho, bringing with him a statue of Nuestra Señora de la Limpia Concepción (Our Lady of the Virgin Conception), which was placed in the church of Santa María to become the patron saint of the town. A few years later Father Ovalle penetrated the difficult terrain further east, this time carrying an image of San Francisco (St. Francis). He reported that he baptized 200 people, built a chapel, and organized a settlement that he named San Francisco. The Indians soon learned, however, that any benefits from living in these settlements had to be weighed against the dangers of contracting diseases for which they had no cures and the possibility of being rounded up and forced to work for the Spanish. This method and its consequences were typical and became the foundation on which the Church constructed its presence in rural Honduras.

Given that the native population was linguistically and culturally diverse and that the various ethnic groups lived in relative isolation as a result of the constraints of geography, the challenges to evangelization were great during colonial times. There were few priests and their territories were extensive. Despite the impediments, the early priests, legitimized and empowered by the Spanish Catholic monarchs, not only converted the indigenous population and built churches and convents, they also owned large amounts of land and livestock and exercised significant political, economic, and moral influence in colonial society. Although rivalries and power struggles among the Spanish conquerors and colonizers created political instability and slowed the progress of urbanization, cities gradually grew and prospered in the mineral-rich interior. Tegucigalpa and Comayagua were the major centers of population during the Colonial period and in both cities major churches were constructed: In Comayagua the Church of La Merced was completed in 1551, the Church and Convent of San Francisco in 1560, and the Cathedral in 1711, and the Cathedral of San Miguel in Tegucigalpa was completed in 1765.

It is important to note that although the Church in Spain was an institution of vast power and privilege, it also was not homogeneous in its outlook, focus, and motivation. Members of the different orders came to the New World with different ideas regarding their role there as well as varying degrees of commitment to the ecclesiastical hierarchy. It was soon the case that the Catholic clergy were native born or *criollos*, in many cases the sons of Spanish fathers and Indian mothers. Their allegiance to family and their native land often preempted their obedience to the official Church and eventually led to conflicts between the Church in Spain and the growing power and influence of the Honduran Church. Priests in Honduras also were more independent than their counterparts in the wealthier and more populated areas of the Spanish Empire, because of their geographic and political isolation.

The story of Father José Simeón de Celaya illustrates these characteristics and helps one to imagine the Catholic presence in colonial Honduras. In 1756, Monsignor Rivas de Velasco, Bishop of Comayagua (then the seat of government of Honduras), visited Real de Minas (later called Tegucigalpa) and gave Father Celaya permission to establish a parish there. The monsignor's observations during his visit prompted him to compose a document in which he outlined not only the customary economic relationship to be established between the new parish and the bishopric of Comayagua, but also what he deemed to be appropriate behavior for the parish priest. Apparently there were Indians, mestizos, and mulattoes in Father Celaya's household as well as in his parish and he was admonished neither to permit excessive dancing and drinking at religious celebrations nor to allow Indians to control the keys to the church.[2]

The Catholic Church, by and large, has been a more benign presence in Honduran society than was the case in neighboring Guatemala, for example.

And although there certainly has been a long and sad history of abuses suffered by the native population at the hands of the Catholic Church, there also have been many priests who are remembered as defenders of the people. Among the latter, one priest stands out in the nineteenth century, Manuel Jesús de Subirana. Father Subirana was born in Manresa, Cataluña, Spain in 1807, became a priest at age twenty-seven, and traveled to Cuba to work as a missionary in 1850. Six years later he traveled to Honduras where he spent the next eight years as an itinerant priest, traveling throughout the country performing baptisms and weddings, saying mass, delivering sermons, and collecting geographical information that he included in his reports to his superiors. He became a familiar and welcome friend in many rural indigenous settlements, particularly those of the Jicaque or Tolupán groups in Yoro, and soon became interested in helping them gain legal title to their ancestral lands. He spent months accompanying government topographers as they traveled over difficult terrain through areas with no roads to measure and map the land. He was instrumental in getting legal title to twenty tracts of land and perhaps of even greater importance, demonstrated to the indigenous inhabitants that there were legal channels through which they could demand justice and land. He died in 1864 and is still revered today as a saintly man who worked tirelessly to help indigenous communities retain ownership of their lands. Because he did not limit his efforts to spiritual ministrations but worked to improve the legal and material conditions of his parishioners, he may be seen as a precursor in Honduras of priests and nuns in the second half of the twentieth century who worked for social change and reform, particularly after the historic meeting of the Latin American Conference of Bishops in Medellín, Colombia in 1968.[3]

The Medellín Conference marked the official recognition of the Theology of Liberation by the hierarchy of the Catholic Church. During the 1960s, priests and nuns throughout Latin America and elsewhere adopted what became known as the "preferential option for the poor." They chose to live and work at the grassroots level to help communities improve the material aspects of their lives. In the case of Honduras, Catholic priests have faced almost insurmountable difficulties in their efforts to minister effectively to their parishioners: Honduras has the lowest ratio of ordained priests to population of any country in Latin America, and the lack of roads and infrastructure in the countryside has perpetuated the isolation and poverty of rural communities. In response to this situation, a movement was founded in 1966 to train men and women to become "Delegates of the Word" in their own parishes. These individuals lead Sunday services and spiritual discussion groups and generally take the place of the parish priest in his absence. Taking advantage of radio as a means of communicating across distances and reaching remote communities, the Church also set up "radio schools," which by 1972 numbered 100, with more than 15,000 students. The vitality and activism that resulted from these and similar programs, in conjunction with the influence of the ideas of Liberation Theology, evolved into an acute political awareness and social consciousness among clergy as well as parishioners. By the late 1960s and 1970s, certain orders of clergy, particularly the Jesuits, Franciscans and various individual priests, were denouncing military repression, U.S. foreign policy in Central America, and the social and legal exploitation of the poor. In 1968, rural laity whose analysis of the political reality of their country was formed at this time started the Honduran Christian Democratic Movement. As Central America gained international visibility in the Cold War in the 1970s and 1980s because of revolutionary movements in Nicaragua and El Salvador, activist priests and nuns, some of them foreign, were accused of being communists. The Church hierarchy was initially somewhat sympathetic but withdrew its support as social activism increased.

In 1975, a dramatic incident occurred that shocked Hondurans and marked the beginning of a fifteen-year period of government repression. In what has come to be known as the Massacre at Los Horcones, large landowners contracted soldiers from the local barracks to murder ten peasants, two students, and two priests on a cattle ranch in rural Olancho. They dumped the mutilated bodies in a well, probably as a warning to activists who at that time were pressuring the government to pass an agrarian reform law. The priests were both Franciscans: Father Casimir Cypher, an American, and Father Ivan Betancúr, a Colombian. This was not the only incident of its kind, but its proportions and brutality were uncommon in Honduras. Expulsions and arrests of foreign priests began at this time and some rural *campesino* centers with ties to the Church were forced to close. A much-publicized example of the strained relationship between Catholic priests and the military government was the case of Father James Carney, a fifty-eight-year-old priest from St. Louis, Missouri, known as Father Guadalupe, who lived and worked in Honduras from 1961 until shortly before his mysterious death in 1982. As a Jesuit and a devoted practitioner of the principles of Liberation Theology, Father Carney dedicated his time in Honduras to working with the rural poor in their efforts to acquire land. Although he had been granted Honduran citizenship in 1973, the government of General Policarpo Paz García later rescinded that privilege and expelled him from the country after accusing him of promoting destabilizing doctrines. He made his way to Nicaragua, where he continued to work with the poor while he wrote his autobiography, *To Be a Revolutionary*. In 1983 he became the chaplain of a group of ninety-six Honduran guerrillas who had joined together near the Nicaraguan–Honduran border to initiate a revolution for social change. They crossed into Honduras and a mere two months later the Honduran military announced that Father Carney had died of starvation in the jungles of Olancho. A subsequent investigation by his family has convinced them that this was not the case. They believe he was captured, interrogated, and tortured by Honduran and U.S. troops as part of a counterinsurgency mission during the Contra War. Father Carney's autobiography is an excellent source of information about the principles and practices of Liberation Theology and the particular realities faced by Catholic priests in Honduras in the 1960s and 1970s.

Father Emil Cook is another example of a Catholic priest who has devoted his life to working with the poor of Honduras. According to Father Cook, in the United States the ratio of priests to parishioners is approximately one priest per 1,300 parishioners. In Honduras there is one priest per 45,000 parishioners. Father Cook first traveled to Honduras as a Franciscan missionary in 1970 to work in a remote area in the department of Olancho, where there are numerous small villages scattered throughout mountainous terrain with few paved roads. He was the only parish priest in an area the size of the entire country of El Salvador, approximately 500 square miles. He ministered to thirty-four villages. At the time there were four high schools in the entire department of Olancho. An adherent of Liberation Theology, Father Cook recognized the need to minister to the whole person and not only the person's spiritual needs. His goal became to address the widespread poverty and high rate of illiteracy by founding schools where students would acquire the knowledge and skills to improve their lives. The headquarters of his mission, which is known as Mission Honduras International, is now in the town of Flores in the Comayagua Valley. Its legal entity, APUFRAM, has a variety of sites, including schools that provide elementary through high school education with a residential option for students who live far from the schools; five houses, three in Tegucigalpa and two in La Ceiba, where graduates of the high schools can live as they attend the university; orphanages; chapels; and a retreat center. A number of students who have been educated at the mission schools have gone on to become teachers and principals of new schools that continue to be built. In the spirit of giving back and sharing, members of APUFRAM now work in missions in the Dominican Republic and Liberia, Africa.[4]

The lives and works of Father Carney and Father Cook represent the challenges, possibilities, dangers, and successes as well as failures that Catholic clergy have experienced in the second half of the twentieth century and into the new millennium. Tensions between the Church's hierarchy and activist priests, that continued until the 1990s, when the region regained a semblance of political stability with the signing of peace accords in Guatemala and El Salvador and the overturn of Sandinista control in Nicaragua, have relaxed. Perhaps the greatest challenge the Catholic Church now faces in Honduras as in the rest of Latin America, is the rapidly growing popularity of evangelical Protestantism.

PROTESTANTISM

Until relatively recent times, the Protestant presence in Honduras was numerically small and concentrated in a few geographic regions. Because of the historic influence of Britain in the Bay Islands and La Mosquitia, Methodist, Moravian, and Baptist congregations are common. Since the 1980s, however, the number of Protestants in Honduras has grown enormously, although they are not members of the traditional Protestant denominations but rather of numerous fundamentalist, evangelical, and Pentecostal sects. Although there are no reliable recent government statistics on the distribution of membership in churches, there is no question that evangelical Protestantism in Honduras is expanding vigorously. Estimates by social scientists, church groups, and informal observers vary widely, in part due to their opposing political agendas, but also because of the difficulties involved in compiling up-to-date and accurate statistics of this nature. The evangelical protestant phenomenon in Honduras as well as in many other Latin American countries is dynamic, varied, and constantly changing. Evangelical Protestantism has been characterized as having three main beliefs: the Bible as the undisputable word of God; salvation through a personal relation with Jesus Christ; and the duty to spread this message of salvation to all peoples of the world. The majority of Hondurans who have become members of one or another evangelical church are of the Pentecostal persuasion, meaning that a direct and personal ecstatic experience with the Holy Spirit is of primary importance to them.

It has been estimated that there are currently well over 200 different sects represented in Honduras with congregations ranging from a handful of believers in isolated rural communities to mega-churches in Tegucigalpa and San Pedro Sula with thousands of members. Many churches in the United States send missions to Honduras. These churches may be large and well-established institutions such as the Assemblies of God and the Abundant Life Ministry, or single-congregation churches such as Bible Holiness in Elkton, Virginia. Regardless of their size and notwithstanding certain doctrinal or methodological emphases, they share a passionate commitment to spreading the word of salvation through Jesus Christ. They share with Catholic adherents of Liberation Theology a holistic approach to serving the whole person and an understanding of the need to make the material welfare of the congregation a central part of their mission. But whereas Liberation Theology led many Catholic priests to work to organize their parishioners to protest social injustices and inequalities and to challenge the political status quo, the focus of the new Christian evangelism is on personal salvation. A direct experience with Jesus, often in the supportive company of the congregation and during a worship service, inspires one to be saved, meaning that one accepts Jesus as his or her savior and makes a commitment not only to change one's personal life but also to work to bring others to salvation. This work in the community is often expressed as planting new churches or planting the seeds of new life by converting others. There is a shared vision of changing the world from the inside out, assuming that one's personal experience of salvation will cause a ripple effect that will bring positive changes to society.

The story of Herb and Joan, taken from the Honduras link of the Abundant Life Church Web site, illustrates the rapid growth of this particular church in Honduras as well as the social service component of their work. Herb and Joan, a married couple with two teenage daughters, moved to Honduras in the 1980s as ministers of the Abundant Life Church. They lived for a year in the coastal city of La Ceiba and for seventeen years in the rural community of El Tomate. In 2001, they relocated to the capital, Tegucigalpa, where Joan directs the Center of Love and Life, an outpatient facility for children with cancer. Herb is working to acquire property and relocate the Alas de Fe Bible Institute to Esperanza. Students from this school in turn "plant" churches throughout the country. The Abundant Life Ministry claims to now have more than 100 churches in rural villages in Honduras.

The story of Orphanage Emmanuel illustrates the spiritual and social service nature of its evangelical founders and is similar to many other projects founded and staffed by evangelical Christians. David Martinez, a Vietnam veteran and his wife, Lydia, became Christians in 1983. David tells of a vision he had a short time later in which God appeared to him and told him that Honduran children needed care and that He wanted someone to plant them as seeds for Christ. Motivated by this calling, the couple sold everything, were ordained for missionary work through *Amor Cristiano Internacional* (Christian Love International) and with their savings as well as donations they raised, went to Honduras, bought land in Guaimaca, a rural area 70 miles northeast of Tegucigalpa, and opened an orphanage in 1989 with five children. They and a staff of ten, with the help of visiting volunteers, now care for more than 400 children. They have a school, a church, and a clinic. Their philosophy is to raise the children in a Christian environment and equip them with practical skills so they can become citizens who give back to their country.

Explanations for the rapid expansion of evangelical Christianity in Honduras include the practical matter of financing.[5] Funding sources that range from individual donations to money raised through congregations in the United States and elsewhere to a lesser extent, to the corporate funding by large international churches, allow missionaries to travel to remote locations and provide the material and technical support so badly needed. They build schools and clinics, provide medical assistance, dig wells, and set up irrigation systems. They identify local leaders and partner with them to establish a trusted presence in their communities. Many people may also convert to an evangelical form of Protestantism because of the focus on salvation through a direct and personal experience with the Holy Spirit. The idea that one's economic situation, social class, or level of education are not hindrances to one's salvation, is surely attractive in a country where the average per capita annual income in 2008, according to a U.S. Department of State report, is $1,600 or $133 per month and according to the 2008 statistics of the CIA World Factbook, 50.7 percent of the population lives below the poverty line and 27.8 percent are unemployed. It also has been observed that women may benefit if they and their families belong to an evangelical Christian congregation because sobriety and paternal responsibility are typically emphasized, both of which are problems that profoundly affect Honduran women's lives. The emotional support a woman can derive from a congregation that condemns domestic violence, for example, cannot be underestimated.

THE STATE AND RELIGIOUS DIVERSITY

At the time of Independence, the Honduran state reduced the social and economic power of the Catholic Church. In 1829, for example, the State confiscated all Church property and title to lands were reissued to supporters of the new Republic. Despite the fact that the predominantly Liberal administrations of the last decades of the nineteenth century reduced the power of the Church even further, it has continued to be the single most significant religious institution in the country.

The Honduran Constitution today provides for freedom of religion and the separation of church and state. However, the armed forces have an official Roman Catholic patron saint, the Virgin of Suyapa, and the government sometimes consults with the Roman Catholic Church and occasionally invites Catholic leaders to participate in initiatives of public concern. Religious groups are not required to register with the government and are eligible for tax-exempt status, but to qualify they must submit an application through the Ministry of Government and Justice. The government requires that foreign missionaries obtain permits to enter and reside in the country and be sponsored by a Honduran individual or institution. The government allows for the deportation of foreign missionaries who practice witchcraft or satanic rituals. In 2007 José Luis Miranda, who claimed to be the Antichrist, was denied entry to the country.

There are church-operated schools of diverse denominations in Honduras, which officially receive no special treatment from the government, nor do they face any restrictions. In September 2000, the Congress adopted a controversial measure requiring that, beginning in 2001, all school classes begin with ten minutes of readings from the Bible; however, the legislation has not been put into effect as a result of protests.[6]

Until the last decades of the twentieth century, it was commonly estimated that approximately 95 percent to 97 percent of the population was Catholic. The remaining 3 percent to 5 percent represented members of traditional Protestant churches, including Methodist and Moravian. Members of indigenous groups such as the Lenca and Chortí, as well as the Garífuna, typically identify as Catholics although their religious beliefs and practices may derive from a syncretic blend of native tradition and Roman Catholicism. This simplified and antiquated picture of religion in Honduras is perpetuated because of a paucity of statistical studies and scholarly attention, but the present situation is unquestionably diverse and dynamic.

In January 2002, the Le Vote Harris Company, a leading market research firm in Honduras, conducted personal interviews on religious issues with individuals age eighteen or older in 1,215 households throughout the country. The company reported that 63 percent of the respondents identified themselves as Catholics, 23 percent as evangelical Christians, and 14 percent as "other" or provided no answer. The principal faiths included Roman Catholicism, Judaism, the Greek Orthodox rite, the Episcopal Church, the Lutheran Church, Jehovah's Witnesses, the Mennonite Church, the Church of Jesus Christ of Latter-day Saints (Mormons), the Union Church, and some 300 evangelical Protestant churches. The most prominent evangelical churches include the Abundant Life, Living Love, and Grand Commission churches. The National Association of Evangelical Pastors represents the evangelical leadership. The Catholic Church reported a membership of just more than 80 percent of the population. Synagogues in Tegucigalpa and San Pedro Sula service the Jewish community and there is a mosque in San Pedro Sula.

Theologian Harvey Cox has estimated that the evangelical Protestant population of Honduras as well as other countries in Latin America will quadruple by the year 2010. The Catholic Church in Honduras is acutely aware of the challenge that this rapid conversion rate presents. It remains to be seen how this contemporary religious dynamic, characterized by a passionately energized spirituality on the individual and congregational level and a desire to harness this spiritual energy to effect change in the economic, social, and political realms takes shape in the future.

HONDURAS' JEWISH COMMUNITY

There has been a Jewish presence in Honduras since colonial times, when Spanish *marranos* or Jews who had converted to Christianity, either voluntarily or to escape persecution, settled in the small towns and villages in the northwestern region of the country. These individuals soon assimilated into the larger population and lost most traces of their Jewish heritage. In the late nineteenth and early twentieth centuries a small number of Jews from central Europe and the Near East settled in Tegucigalpa and San Pedro Sula, forming the nucleus from which grew the two small but thriving Jewish communities in Honduras today. Despite restrictions imposed by the Honduran government in 1939 on the entry of Jews into the country, there have been successive waves of Jewish immigration. Newly arrived Jews tend to be more observant of Jewish religious and cultural practices, whereas second- and third-generation family members often lose touch with the traditional ways, nevertheless there are today approximately fifty families who actively support their synagogues, located in Tegucigalpa (*Comunidad Hebrea de Tegucigalpa*) and San Pedro Sula (*Unidad Judía de San Pedro Sula*). Links have been established among Honduran synagogues and international Jewish organizations, mitigating the potential sense of isolation that a small community can experience. An example of this solidarity occurred after flooding from Hurricane Mitch severely damaged the Torah of the Tegucigalpa Synagogue and the Jewish Community Center on the Hudson in Tarrytown, New York raised funds to restore the sacred text.[7]

ISLAM IN HONDURAS

According to some estimates, there are as many as 200,000 Hondurans today of Palestinian Arab descent, most of whom are Christian. There is, however, a Muslim population of well over 2,000, which supports two Islamic organizations: the *Centro Islámico de Honduras* (Islamic Center of Honduras) in San Pedro Sula, which has a mosque and the *Comunidad Islámica de Honduras* (Islamic Community of Honduras) in Cortés. An Islamic community of twelve members has recently been organized in Tegucigalpa. They meet regularly at members' homes to study the Koran and one of the women has adopted the use of the veil.

NOTES

1. Two excellent studies and analyses of the activities of the Catholic Church in colonial Honduras are Ethel García Buchard, "Evangelizar a los indios de la frontera de Honduras: una ardua tarea (siglos XVII-XIX)," *Intercambio*, I:1 (2002) and Linda

Newson, *The Cost of Conquest: Indian Decline in Honduras Under Spanish Rule*, Boulder, CO: Westview Press, 1986.

2. This anecdote was reconstructed from ecclesiastical documents by Honduran historian Leticia de Oyuela and can be found in her book *Senderos del mestizaje*.

3. William V. Davidson discusses Father Subirana's life and work in "El Padre Subirana y las tierras concedidas a los indios hondureños en el siglo XIX," *América Indígena*. 44, 3 (1984): 447–459.

4. Father Emil Cook's story can be read in Barbara Pawlikowski, *Man on a Mission: On the Road with Father Emil Cook and Mission Honduras International*, Skoki, IL: ACTA Publications, 2007.

5. Harvey Cox's *Fire from Heaven: The Rise of Spirituality and the Re-shaping of Religion in the Twenty-first Century*, Reading, MA: Addison-Wesley Pub. Co., 1995 is an excellent introduction to Pentecostalism. Two scholars who have studied the recent phenomenon of rising Protestantism in traditionally Catholic Latin America are David Stoll, *Is Latin America Turning Protestant? The Politics of Evangelical Growth*, Berkeley and Los Angeles: University of California Press, 1990 and David Martin, *The Explosion of Protestantism in Latin America*, Oxford: Basil and Blackwell, 1990.

6. The "International Religious Freedom Report" is prepared periodically by the Bureau of Democracy, Human Rights and Labor of the U.S. State Department and is based on interviews with government officials and reports of human rights abuses. The information included here is from the report released in 2007.

7. Information on the Jewish community of Honduras can be found at the Web site of the Union of Jewish Congregations of Latin America and the Caribbean.

4

Daily Living and Lifestyles

THE DETERMINANTS OF DIVERSITY

NO DESCRIPTION OF the daily life and pastimes of Honduran people would be complete or accurate without taking into account the many differences that are determined by social class, economic situation, gender, and physical environment. A young man who lives on the island of Roatán, for example, will dress differently than his counterpart who attends a private bilingual academy in San Pedro Sula or a young campesino who lives in an isolated rural community in the department of Santa Bárbara. These three Hondurans will listen to different music, eat different foods, and have more or less familiarity with how other Hondurans live. And their girlfriends and female relatives will have even different experiences and perspectives.

The hypothetical student from San Pedro Sula probably lives in a quiet residential neighborhood in a spacious home surrounded by a high wall or fence topped with glass shards or barbed wire to keep out intruders. An armed security guard from a private agency may have been hired to patrol the neighborhood. The student most likely has a cell phone and possibly a laptop computer. He may have his own car or at least access to a family vehicle. He will wear a uniform to school as do all Honduran students, but when out of school he will dress much like a U.S. middle-class high school student. He may have acquired his modern clothes during a trip to Miami with his family or he may have purchased them in one of the new shopping malls in the city. He eats homemade food prepared by the maid who works for his family or goes out with his friends to McDonald's and Dunkin' Donuts for fast food. When not in school he is probably hanging out with his friends, maybe at a shopping mall or, if he is athletically inclined he may play golf or tennis at a private club. When he graduates from the bilingual academy he will be reasonably proficient in both Spanish and English and will probably apply to universities in the United States. He hopes to work in his uncle's medical equipment import company after college. His older sister went to Tegucigalpa after high school and lived with their grandparents while she attended the National University. She studied marine biology and now works with an international nonprofit environmental agency that is studying the effects of shrimp farming in the Gulf of Fonseca.

The young man from Roatán may have moved to the island from Juticalpa or La Ceiba or El Progreso. Lured by stories of good wages for work in the construction of luxury resorts and condominiums, he and his older brother are staying with their mother's cousin and her family in a two-room house in Sandy Bay. He dropped out of high school to work, but he can read and write reasonably well. Five mornings a week he walks out to the main road where he meets up with several others who are waiting for the supervisor's pick-up truck to pass by and give them a lift to work. He is on the lawn crew for a property maintenance company but if he is lucky he might get a job with the company that will be building the new cruise ship dock in Coxen Hole. He probably has a cup of black coffee and a roll before he leaves for work. At lunchtime he buys *baleadas* (filled tortillas) or *arroz con pollo* (chicken and rice) from the women who prepare food at their makeshift stalls along the road. He listens to the radio on the job, hears Latin music, rock, sports, and news. He calls his friends on his cell phone but he doesn't have a computer or use e-mail. He buys his clothes from the vendors at the market in Coxen Hole, who sell inexpensive imports and seconds from the maquiladoras around San Pedro Sula. He usually wears jeans, a T-shirt, and a baseball cap. On the weekends he plays soccer with a local team and goes to the bars to drink and pick up girls, but his real sweetheart doesn't go to bars, that's why he likes her. She works in the gift shop at one of the dive resorts. Sometimes he borrows his cousin's car and picks her up after work. He doesn't want her riding on the bus where other men can touch her. She swears she never looks at other men but one can never be sure. She told him last week that she was going to have his baby. She's hoping he will want to get married but she knows it isn't likely. That's how men are. Oh, well, her mother will help her out with the baby and maybe he will give her some money now and then to buy food and clothes.

The young campesino from a rural area in Santa Bárbara may have attended the local elementary school for three years. According to Honduran law he should have attended school until age fourteen, but the teacher assigned to his school left and then he had to help his father in the fields and soon he had stopped attending altogether. He can sign his name and knows his numbers but he doesn't have the time or inclination to read, so he has lost some of his literacy skills. He works with his family cultivating their small piece of land. His family owns a five-acre plot, but some day it will be divided among six children and he is most likely thinking that he would like to go to the United States to find work. His family lives in a two-room house of *bahareque* with a dirt floor. He eats the food his mother prepares in their outdoor kitchen, mostly rice and beans and corn tortillas, sometimes eggs and chicken, and spends some of the little money he has on snacks such as chips or peanuts or *chicharrón*. He wears clothes purchased in local markets or stores, probably cotton or polyester pants, a T-shirt or long-sleeved cotton shirt, and a baseball cap or straw hat. He often carries his machete, as do most of the men he knows. On the weekends he plays soccer with his friends, sometimes they buy a bottle of *guaro* and sit around and talk and play music. One of his older sisters is eighteen years old and has two children. Her husband is a good man but there was no work so he left for the United States last year. Twice he has sent her money. She bought medicine for the babies and gave her father the rest of the money to buy fertilizer. She worries about her husband in the United States. She has no phone and doesn't know how to contact him. She is grateful for the money he has sent but she wishes he would come home.

Notwithstanding the different social and economic circumstances that play such an important role in the lives of Honduran men, women, and children from the various regions of the country, it would not be an overgeneralization to say that most Hondurans know and appreciate many of the country's traditional foods, are aware of and perhaps participate in some of the festivals and sports and are exposed to the same radio, television, and press.

TRADITIONAL FOODS

In Guillermo Anderson's popular song "El Encarguito" (The Package from Home), a person back home in Honduras is preparing a package to send to a relative living in the United States who had written a letter saying he is homesick. Because familiar foods are such a basic and ever-present part of our cultural lives, the absence of those foods that we associate with home can cause deep longing. The foods that go into the package are some of the typical, traditional foods of Honduras, among them *nacatamales, chicharrón con yuca, atol, tapado olanchano, flor de izote, pan de yema, totopostes, semitas,* and numerous other dishes whose names have no simple English translation.

There are regional variations of typical foods, in part determined by the crops traditionally cultivated in the different climate zones, although residents of different regions will most likely be familiar with the favorite foods of other parts of the country. The main ingredients of many of the typical foods of the North Coast, for example, are coconut, yucca, and fish. These ingredients are grown, gathered, or caught locally and are used in countless variations. Coconut meat is used in bread, coconut milk in soups and stews, and coconut oil for frying. Many residents of Tegucigalpa travel to the towns and beaches of the North Coast to celebrate Holy Week and sampling the local cuisine is an anticipated part of their holiday.

In much of Honduras, the staples of everyday meals continue to be those same foods eaten since pre-Hispanic times: corn, beans, and rice. Corn is the basic ingredient of Honduran tortillas, which are smaller and thicker than those of Mexico and may be plain or filled with meat, beans, or cheese. Tortillas made from wheat flour are common in urban areas. Ground corn is also used for making *atol* or *pozol*, a thick beverage served hot and *nacatamales*, as Honduran tamales are called. These consist of cornmeal with one of a variety of fillings, either sweet or savory. The filled cornmeal patties are wrapped in banana leaves and steamed and are a favorite treat at holiday times, especially Christmas. An example of a festive *nacatamal* filling might consist of pork, lard, potatoes, carrots, onion, garlic, capers, salt, cilantro, chili, and achiote, which imparts a reddish color to foods.

Many nonalcoholic beverages are made from a variety of locally available fruits such as tamarind, guayaba, papaya, passion fruit, mango, and pineapple; a typical fermented drink is *chicha*, which can be made from corn, pineapple, or cane juice, among other things. *Ronpopo* (also called *ronpope*) or eggnog, which is traditionally enjoyed at Christmas, is drunk hot or cold. It is made with milk, egg yolks, sugar, cinnamon, cloves, and a splash of *guaro* or Honduran rum. Hondurans are coffee drinkers and Honduras produces world-class coffee, although most of the best-quality beans are exported.

Many of the traditional foods of Honduras require labor-intensive preparation. Women spend a great deal of time cooking food for their families and many women also rely on the income they earn from selling food in the streets and markets. In fact, the local markets are one of the best places to find typical foods. Some women operate stalls where they prepare and serve such favorites as *sopa de mondongo* or tripe soup, said to cure a hangover; *tapado*, a meat and vegetable stew with numerous regional variations; and *pinchos* or grilled strips of meat. Other women prepare baked goods at home, such as *rosquillas* (also called *rosquetes*) and *semitas*, and sell them locally. They are biscuit-like cookies that often accompany a coffee break. It is common for women to carry large baskets of these items through the streets or to sit under a tree or on a favorite street corner to sell them to passersby.

The accelerated tempo of the modern world has generated many changes in Honduran lifestyles, but it may be safe to say that one of the things that most Hondurans still hold dear is the pleasure of sharing a cooked meal with family or friends. Stores and offices no longer universally close down from noon to 2 P.M. for the midday meal, as was common as recently as the 1970s, but most people will stop their busy lives and have a substantial meal at this time. Of course fast food chains also thrive in the larger cities. They are frequented by people of means, as a meal cooked at home or purchased in the market is more affordable. Fast food snacks, on the other hand, such as chips made from potatoes or plantains and *chicharrón* or fried pig skin, are available everywhere and are extremely popular.

DRESS

All Honduran students wear uniforms. Public school students normally wear the official Honduran colors: blue skirts and white blouses for the girls, blue pants and white shirts for the boys. Students who attend private schools may wear different colors. The media keeps young Hondurans aware of the changing fads in the United States and the rest of Central America so, when not in school, they like to dress like their counterparts in other countries. In the coastal areas and beach towns, men and boys will wear shorts, and, of course, bathing suits on the beach, but it is not common for men to wear shorts in other regions, except for the prevalent use of uniforms among sports teams, especially soccer. Adults and people from rural areas tend to dress conservatively and with a degree of formality. Some men still wear the *guayabera*, a lightweight shirt well-suited for hot climates, with either short or long sleeves, that buttons in the front and typically has vertical rows of pleats, stitching, or embroidery on the front and back. Pants have become common among urban women but rural women often prefer skirts and dresses. Some women sew their own clothing or enlist the services of a seamstress to confect styles to their specifications. Rural women and vendors in the markets wear aprons, which often are utilitarian as well as colorful and attractive, with pockets, ruffles, and embroidery. With few exceptions, indigenous peoples of Honduras have not retained the use of their traditional dress.[1]

FESTIVALS

A number of festivals[2] are held throughout the year in all regions of the country. Many are annual events held in towns and villages in honor of the Catholic saint believed to be the patron and protector of the community. The most celebrated of all Honduran saints is the Virgin of Suyapa, officially declared the Patron Saint of Honduras in 1925 by Pope Pius XII and in 1982 she became the Patron Saint of all Central America as well. February 3 was chosen as the day when Honduras celebrates its patron saint. It is said that the original statue of the Virgin, which is carved in cedar wood and is a mere 2.3 inches tall, was found in the month of February 1747 by two campesinos from the village of Suyapa, Alejandro Colindres and Jorge Martínez. The men were returning to their village after working in a distant cornfield when nightfall overtook them, so they decided to sleep beside a stream. During the night Colindres was awakened several times by something hard on the ground beneath him. In the morning he discovered it was a tiny carving of the Virgin. Dressed in pale pink with her hands clasped in prayer, her long, straight hair and dark skin gave her an indigenous appearance. Colindres brought the statue to his mother's house; she set up an altar and soon her neighbors began to perceive the statue's powers. A rustic chapel was built in the Virgin's honor in 1780 and the first officially recorded miracle occurred in 1796. The statue resides in the Church of Suyapa in a poor, outlying neighborhood of Tegucigalpa, although on February 3 she is moved to the nearby large basilica that was built in the 1950s, where there is a week-long celebration, the Feria or Fair of Suyapa, when throngs of visitors from around Central America travel to Tegucigalpa. Pilgrims crowd into the basilica to light candles, pray, and get a glimpse of the small statue adorned with a blue robe and a golden crown, enclosed in a protective case. In the plaza outside the basilica there is a festive feeling. Vendors sell food and souvenirs, musicians play, and friends gather.

Another popular event is the Festival of Traditional Foods, which was first held in 1995 in Cantarranas, a picturesque town about an hour from Tegucigalpa. In large part due to the enthusiasm and hard work of Edilberto Borjas, writer and professor at the National University, it began as an attempt to rekindle interest in traditional Honduran dishes, some of which have become less common as people adopt a more modern, processed and fast food diet. It has become a well-attended annual event where people not only prepare, sample and learn about Honduran cuisine, but enjoy music, dance, handcrafts, and performance art.

The Honduran government has designated the month of July as "El Mes de la Hondureñidad" or Honduran National Identity Month. Lempira Day is celebrated on July 20, when Hondurans remember the Lenca chief who heroically resisted the Spanish invasion and was killed in battle in 1537. School children all over the country learn about this national hero, participate in plays, dances and musical performances and elect "La India Bonita" (The Pretty Indian Girl), who marches in the September 15 Independence Day parade. The Garífuna community, noting that not all Hondurans are descended from the Lenca, has begun to choose "La Niña Garífuna" (The Garífuna Girl), who now also marches in the Independence Day parade, wearing traditional Garífuna dress. July is a time when folk music and dances are enjoyed, articles appear in the press debating the nature of being Honduran and academic forums address the issues of national sovereignty.

On April 12, the Garífuna people celebrate their arrival in Honduras in 1797. Many towns on the North Coast host activities, in particular a symbolic reenactment of the arrival of the Garífuna by boat. Dancing, drumming, and the preparation of traditional foods are central to the celebration. Community leaders give speeches, school children march and perform songs and dances, and a Catholic mass is celebrated.

Many towns have begun to hold festivals to celebrate and promote a local product. In February, the village of Suyatal in the department of Francisco Morazán holds a Festival del Café (Coffee Festival) and Guinope in the department of El Paraíso has a Festival de la Naranja (Orange Festival). Siguatepeque celebrates the pine tree in April, and in May Yuscarán honors the mango and Santa Lucía has a Festival de las Flores (Festival of Flowers). Danli's Festival del Maíz (Corn Festival) is held in August and Amapala holds a Festival del Pescado (Fish Festival) in October. Indeed, every month of the year has numerous festivals scheduled, from music to art to foods to traditional dance.

Two time-honored traditions that are still practiced in December are the making of *nacimientos* or nativity scenes and the Christmas *posada*. *Nacimientos* may be small and simple, consisting of statues of Mary, Joseph and the infant Jesus, a rustic cradle and assorted barnyard animals, or they may be as large and elaborate as their maker's skill, imagination, and resources allow. Families typically set up a *nacimiento* in their home and some towns display a large one in a park or other public place. Although the *posada* is no longer so common in the cities, in rural areas, during the nine evenings before Christmas, groups will gather and go from house to house carrying a *nacimiento*. In this ritual reenactment of the Biblical story of the nativity, each group will visit three homes, singing the traditional *posada* song and asking for lodging. The first two will say there is no room but the third will invite them in and serve them *ronpope* and other holiday treats. The nativity scene stays there until the next evening, when the ritual is repeated.

SPORTS

Many different sports are played throughout Honduras, both informally in streets, parks, and open fields as well as professionally. Honduras has professional men's and women's tennis teams. The men's team has competed in the Davis Cup since 1998 in the Americas Zone, Group IV. The women's team began competing for the Fed Cup in 2002 in the Americas Zone, Group II.

Men's and women's basketball teams compete in the Central America Championship for Clubs. Honduran athletes and teams have participated in the Olympics in such events as soccer, swimming, and table tennis.

But soccer is unquestionably the most popular sport in Honduras. Hondurans began to take an interest in the sport in the 1930s and the Francisco Morazán Major League in Soccer was founded in 1948, with the goal of professionalizing the sport in Honduras. The first teams were Olimpia, Federal, Motagua, Argentina, and España. The first championship games were held in 1948 in the new Tiburcio Carías Andino Stadium in Tegucigalpa. In 1962, the first National Soccer League was organized with nine teams, who played their first championship matches in 1965. Today, there are ten teams and eight major stadiums in the country. The Estadio Olímpico in San Pedro Sula is the largest stadium in Central America. The national team, Los Catrachos, qualified once for the World Cup, in 1982. They have twice won the Unión Centroamericana de Fútbol/Central American Soccer Union Cup, in 1993 and 1995.

In July 1969, after a qualifying game between the Honduran and Salvadoran teams for the 1970 World Cup, rioting that broke out eventually led to a six-day war between the two countries. Non-Hondurans refer to the conflict as The Soccer War, although analysts have established that the causes were more serious economic and political differences. Nonetheless, it demonstrates the passion and intensity that many Hondurans feel toward their national sport. Children begin playing soccer informally at an early age and many adult males belong to teams that play on the weekends. Players carrying gym bags are a common sight all over Honduras on Sundays. In 2001, the *Revista de la Universidad Pedagógica Nacional Francisco Morazán (Journal of the Francisco Morazán National Pedagogical University)* devoted an entire issue to exploring the many facets of this sport from sociological, economic, and literary perspectives.

THE MEDIA

Although television has long been popular and recently the Internet has become used more often, radio still may be the most common and widespread form of media communication in Honduras.[3] The principal broadcasting networks are Radio América, Radio Nacional de Honduras, and Emisoras Unidas and according to the *CIA World Factbook* there are 241 AM and 53 FM radio stations in the country. Music, news, and talk shows can be heard 24 hours a day. The government as well as Catholic and evangelical Protestant churches have used the radio as an effective means of propaganda, news dissemination, proselytizing, and education. Viewers, on the other hand, can watch

Honduran news, weather, sports, and culture as well as several telenovelas or soap operas from Mexico, Colombia, and elsewhere on thirteen different channels. Religious programming is very popular and films, dramas and sitcoms from the United States are also broadcast, either dubbed or with Spanish subtitles.

Honduras' own film industry is in its fledgling stages. Although Honduran filmmakers have produced only a few low-budget feature-length films, movie viewers have access to foreign films through the cultural programs sponsored by foreign embassies and organizations such as the *Alliance Francaise*. Tegucigalpa and San Pedro Sula both have multiplex cinemas where one can see films primarily from Mexico, Spain, and the United States.

There are several wide-circulation newspapers in Honduras. The largest and most popular dailies are *El Heraldo, La Tribuna, La Prensa,* and *Diario Tiempo.* Their focus is national news but they all cover international news, particularly from the other Central American countries and the United States. *Honduras This Week* is an English-language weekly that reports on national news, culture, and the environment.

The landline telephone system has been notoriously unreliable, with long waits for installation and service. The introduction of cell phones has made telecommunication much easier for many Hondurans. An estimated one-third of the population now has cell phones. Internet users, however, are far fewer. A 2006 estimate indicated that less than 5 percent of the population has access to the Internet. There are Internet cafés throughout the country but local technical assistance is not always available or reliable and the cost of using the computers puts this media outside the reach of many Hondurans.

NOTES

1. See Chapter 2, Indigenous Honduras, for more information on traditional clothing.

2. Traditional celebrations are also described in the sections devoted to the various indigenous groups; a discussion of the *guancasco* as well as other traditional ritual performances can be found in the chapter on the performing arts.

3. Information on the media in Honduras can be found on line in the *CIA World Factbook* and the Honduran *Sistema Nacional de Cultura.*

5

Literature and the Oral Tradition[1]

THE ORAL TRADITION AND LITERACY

AN UNDERSTANDING OF the literary culture of Honduras must take into account the oral culture in order to recognize the powerful presence both in Honduran literature as well as in Honduran culture in general of popular beliefs, legends, storytelling, songs, and spoken rather than written forms of Honduran Spanish; and to appreciate the effort and dedication required for writers to practice their craft and publish and distribute their work in a country with a high rate of illiteracy. The evolution of the oral tradition and the development of a literary tradition in Honduras are intimately related and inseparable from education and literacy.

Although six years of elementary school are compulsory in Honduras today, many children, particularly from rural poor and indigenous families, attend school irregularly if at all. The official literacy rate of 76 percent, therefore, measures a basic knowledge of reading and writing that may deteriorate over time with disuse. Only an estimated 31 percent of those who complete elementary studies attend junior high school and an even smaller percentage go on to complete high school. The National University is free, although students must purchase their own textbooks and even this expense, in addition to transportation, can prove prohibitive. Also, the time spent attending and preparing for classes is time not available for gainful employment, further limiting the number of prospective students. Notwithstanding these economic impediments, the student body has multiplied to the point where an admissions exam must be passed to limit enrollment; regional branches of the National University have expanded, particularly in San Pedro Sula and La Ceiba; and a number of private universities and technical colleges also have opened in recent decades.

To be a professional writer in Honduras assumes that one will engage in other forms of employment as well. Many poets and novelists also are full- or part-time journalists or teachers and may work for a nonprofit organization or at any one of a number of other jobs. There is only one private publisher of long-standing and solid reputation in Honduras, Editorial Guaymuras (Guaymuras Publishing Co.), although at any given time a number of small, independent publishers may have a more or less limited inventory. A few of these are Editorial Guardabarranco, Ixbalam, and Editorial Pez Dulce. These publishers tend to be dedicated and idealistic but without the financial backing to survive the vicissitudes of the market. It is not uncommon for authors to self-publish small editions of 500 to 1,000 copies and distribute their books through informal channels. The old custom of gifting one's friends and family with an autographed copy of one's book is still practiced, although there is a growing consciousness among writers that their work is valuable and deserves to compensated, making it very desirable to have one's book accepted by a solvent publisher. Some of Honduras' best-known writers have been published internationally by Letra Negra (Guatemala), EDUCA (Costa Rica), and Alfaguara (Spain and Miami), among others. The National University, the National Pedagogical University, and the Honduran Institute of Anthropology and History are three of the major public institutions that also support publishing operations; their publications tend to be academic and pedagogical in nature, although their inventories do include fiction as well as anthologies of poetry. Poetry and short stories are sometimes published in local newspapers and there is a long history in Honduras of individuals and collectives publishing magazines devoted to literature and culture, although these efforts are typically short-lived. Some of the most successful literary journals of recent decades include *Presente, Tragaluz,* and *LiterArte.* Given the constraints faced by writers, it is remarkable that Honduras has produced authors of such numbers and talent: Poets, authors of short fiction and novels, playwrights, and essayists have all enriched the cultural milieu.

THE BEGINNINGS OF A LITERATE SOCIETY

Colonial Honduras

With the exception of the Maya culture that flourished at and around Copán in the western region until some time around 950 C.E., it is believed that none of the indigenous peoples of Honduras had developed a form of writing, so the passing on of family and communal history, the transmission of beliefs, and the preservation of knowledge naturally took the form of the spoken word, which we now refer to as the oral tradition. Many of the European soldiers, traders, and colonizers who arrived in the sixteenth and seventeenth centuries were themselves illiterate. The Spanish Catholic clergy who accompanied them, on the other hand, could read and write Spanish and usually Latin and introduced the concept of literacy to the population they evangelized. Among the first records of the oral tradition in Honduras are written accounts by sixteenth-century Spanish missionaries. These letters and reports on their attempts to convert the indigenous populations offer brief descriptions of a subjective nature but Honduras unfortunately had no ecclesiastic scholar of the likes of Fray Toribio de Benavente, known as "Motolinía" (?–1565) or Fray Bernardino de Sahagún (1499–1590), who documented and preserved the history, beliefs, and practices of the indigenous peoples of Mexico.

As a result of the decimation of the indigenous population caused by the Spanish conquest and the relative lack of interest on the part of the Spanish Crown in exploiting Honduran territory, Honduras during the colonial period became a sparsely populated and predominantly rural country, with small clusters of people living in relative isolation, so education took the form of family members passing on to the younger generations the knowledge and practical skills necessary for survival. The Catholic clergy, who were central figures in the formation and administration of *reducciones* (reductions), *encomiendas* (units of control over land and Indians), and *cofradías* (brotherhoods or associations of mutual assistance), were active in many forms of education, including literacy. In need of a workforce to plant crops, exploit mineral wealth, build, decorate, and maintain churches, and serve as domestic help, they educated the native population to carry out these tasks. During the colonial period, the Church was perhaps the most significant patron of the arts as well; its coffers often financed the training of artists and the execution of paintings to decorate churches.

The Period of Independence: An Age of Ideas

For several decades, at the end of the eighteenth and the beginning of the nineteenth centuries, the region was in a state of turmoil. Independence movements challenged the status quo in countless ways and created an atmosphere of instability. As the Central American provinces came closer to declaring their independence from Spanish colonial rule, Hondurans expressed their thoughts regarding such concepts as freedom, patriotism, independence, and nationhood. They debated and discussed in informal gatherings known as *tertulias,* gave speeches at public rallies and demonstrations, and wrote essays that circulated as broadsides and rudimentary newspapers. Guatemala was still the seat of colonial government of the region, and two early newspapers were published there, *El Editor Constitucional* (*The Constitutional Editor*), a weekly founded in 1820 by the fiery and polemical Pedro Molina and *El Amigo de la Patria* (*The Friend of the Fatherland*), founded by the more measured José Cecilio del Valle, who was a native Honduran living in Guatemala. These weekly periodicals circulated in Honduras and were passionately discussed, along with the imported works of French and Spanish thinkers such as Rousseau, Voltaire, and Feijoo.

In 1829, Honduras became a nation and ratified its first constitution. This was a time of chaos, idealism, and regional rivalries. It was also a time of change and innovation: In 1822 the first public elementary school was opened in Tegucigalpa; in 1829 the first printing press was brought to Honduras by Francisco Morazán, and it was used to print the first newspaper, *La gaceta del gobierno* (*The Government Gazette*) the following year. Poetry printed on single sheets or leaflets also became popular, with themes ranging from religious devotions to tributes to statesmen to commentary on local events to celebrations of births. These poems were most often anonymous or signed with unidentifiable names or titles such as "a friend" or "an observer." Poems published in this fashion between 1840 and 1881 were collected and published by Carlos Maldonado and Mario Argueta in 1996 as *Poesía nacional desconocida del siglo XIX* (*Unknown National Poetry from the 19th Century*) and constitute a valuable source of historical cultural information.

As Hondurans became citizens of a nation in formation, the issues debated included the presence of diverse ethnic groups in Honduran territory and the extent and nature of their rights and responsibilities, the role of the Catholic Church, and land ownership. These, as well as civic themes of importance to the emerging nation such as health, education, agriculture, laws, and good government, inspired numerous poems, essays, tracts, and speeches. Examples of the historical-literary texts of this period include the last testament of Tegucigalpa native Francisco Morazán (1792–1842), who served as president of Central America from 1830 to 1838, in which he urges the youth of Central America to have faith in the eventual union of Central America and to carry on the fight for liberty and the speech delivered by Dionisio de Herrera (1780–1850) at the opening of Honduras' first legislative assembly in Comayagua in 1822.

It is indeed impressive that these ideas were so eloquently expressed, given that Hondurans had not yet developed their own centers of higher learning. Literary inclinations had to be nurtured privately and were not compensated. The University of San Carlos in Guatemala City was the preeminent institution of higher learning in Central America and Hondurans continued to travel to Guatemala and to institutions such as the university in León, Nicaragua even after the Honduran National University was founded in 1847; it took many years for it to grow to a size and prestige that satisfied young intellectuals' desire for knowledge.

José Cecilio del Valle (1777–1834), editor of the aforementioned *El Amigo de la Patria*, is remembered not only for his role in Central American politics, having contributed to the writing of the first Central American constitution in 1824, but also for his writings on topics of practical and philosophical importance to the new nation. He was known as *El Sabio* (The Sage) for his knowledge of such diverse areas as laws and government, agriculture, geography, education, and astronomy. He kept in touch with the world of ideas through his correspondence with intellectuals from England and America and wrote thoughtful essays that can still be read and appreciated today.

Another leading cultural figure at this time was Father José Trinidad Reyes (1797–1855), who was born into a humble mestizo family in Tegucigalpa. As a young man he moved to León, Nicaragua, where, because of his musical talent, he obtained the position of assistant to the choirmaster at the cathedral. At this time, only the sons of the Spanish elite were allowed access to higher education, but a humanistic education was available to members of the clergy, so Father Reyes was ordained as a Catholic priest in León in 1822. In 1824, when many Catholic clergy were expelled from Nicaragua because of the prominence of post-independence anticlericalism, he entered his order's monastery in Guatemala, where he continued his studies. During the suppression of religious orders throughout Central America in 1829, Father Reyes returned to Tegucigalpa, where churches had been closed or abandoned and priests were not officially allowed to say mass. Choosing to ignore these restrictions, Father Reyes performed liturgical services, opened a series of primary schools, and became a much loved and respected figure about town. He spent the remainder of his life in Honduras, where he continues to be remembered as a nonpartisan humanist who helped restore a sense of cultural purpose and continuity to a population in search of its identity. He was a scholar, poet, playwright, and composer, remembered for having brought the first piano to Honduras and for being the founder of the Honduran National University and the University Library. Considered Honduras' first playwright, Father Reyes wrote the scripts as well as the musical scores for his *pastorelas* or plays in the medieval European tradition performed to celebrate the Nativity. He staged these plays as entertainments but also as a way to teach or communicate moral and political points of view. It is interesting to note that the style and intent embodied in his *pastorelas* can be seen today in the many popular theater groups that often perform outdoors and in public places and see their art form as being uniquely suited to audience participation and as a vehicle for education and activism as well as entertainment.

Romanticism, Positivism, and the Period of Liberal Reform

The period known in Honduras as the liberal reform began during the presidency (1876–1883) of Marco Aurelio Soto (1846–1908). Soto's government was responsible for the creation of the National Library and Archives and the national postal and telegraph systems. Prominent intellectuals, including Ramón Rosa (1848–1893), who was minister from Honduras to the United States in 1883 and Adolfo Zúniga (1836–1900), were his trusted advisers. They were instrumental in the opening of public schools throughout the country and worked to introduce science and technology into the curriculum and to create Honduras' first teachers' colleges. Soto surrounded himself with writers as well; his private secretary, José Joaquín Palma, a Cuban national who was granted Honduran citizenship, is credited with the publication of Honduras' first book of poetry, in 1882. Palma was the friend and teacher of many young poets. His influence was such that an entire generation of poets has been called "La Generación de José Joaquín Palma" (the José Joaquín Palma Generation). In 1881, the Academia Literaria de Tegucigalpa, founded by Father Reyes in 1845, became the Universidad Central de la República (Central University of the Republic). Ramón Rosa, an eloquent orator and essayist, delivered the inaugural address at the opening of the newly organized institution, in which he outlined his vision of a practical, positivist higher education oriented toward preparing professionals who would be productive citizens capable of ushering Honduras into the twentieth century. His concern that future Hondurans have models of integrity and public service inspired him to write numerous biographies. His biographical subjects include José Trinidad Reyes, José Cecilio del Valle, and Francisco Morazán.

Soto's willingness to devote public revenues to education and culture contributed to the relative stability and openness of Honduras society at this time. Government sponsorship of study abroad allowed for more international cultural exchange, which in turn influenced the styles and themes adopted by the new generation of writers. Poetry was the most common form of literary expression in the late nineteenth century, although few if any poets devoted themselves exclusively to a literary occupation. Among the numerous late nineteenth-century poets are Adán Cuevas (1852–1895), Lucila Estrada de Pérez (1856–?), and Manuel Molina Vigil (1853–1883). Their preferred subjects were nature, romantic love, patriotism and meditations on such concepts as beauty and the fleeting passage of time. The combination of describing natural wonders with a love of Honduras inspired poems such as "Adiós al Lago de Yojoa" (Farewell, Lake Yojoa) by Josefa Carrasco (1855–1945). José Antonio Domínguez (1869–1903), who is known primarily for his poem "Himno a la materia" (Hymn to Matter), is considered the most accomplished poet of this group.

HONDURAN *MODERNISMO*

Honduran writers at the turn of the century were enthusiastic practitioners of the movement popular throughout Latin America known as *modernismo*. The literary term *modernismo* (modernism) should not be confused with the movement known as modernism in English, the general term applied retrospectively to the wide range of experimental and *avant-garde* trends in the art and literature of early twentieth-century Europe and the United States. In the Latin American context it refers to a conjunction of style, theme, and authorial attitude inaugurated by Nicaraguan poet Rubén Darío with the publication of a slim volume of poetry, *Azul* (Blue), in 1888 in Buenos Aires. The salient characteristics of *modernismo* include preference for exotic and sensual themes; frequent reference to ancient and medieval mythologies; a stylistic devotion to rhyme, rhythm, and musicality; and a kinship with the symbolist and Parnassian aesthetic movements of Europe. Central American modernist writers felt a strong attraction to Paris, which they saw as a cultural mecca. They typically defined themselves as alienated artists in search of aesthetic perfection and many of them eschewed material gain and lived bohemian lifestyles. Not a few of them took their own lives and/or died young, the result of poverty, alcohol, and drugs.

Juan Ramón Molina (1875–1908) was the quintessential modernist poet. He was born in Comayagua and went to study in Guatemala at the age of eighteen, where he pursued a career in law and journalism and began to build a reputation as an accomplished poet. He returned to Honduras in 1897 and grew increasingly dissatisfied with and openly critical of what he considered to be the lack of culture and the provincial narrow-mindedness of his homeland. In 1906 he traveled to Rio de Janeiro, New York, Spain, and Paris. When civil strife in Honduras escalated in 1907 he fled to neighboring El Salvador, where he died of an overdose of morphine in 1908. During his brief life he founded several literary reviews, including *Espíritu* (*Spirit*) and *Ritos* (*Rites*) and published numerous poems, prefaces, articles, and essays. He achieved international acclaim and is considered one of Central America's finest modernist poets. His collected lyrics were published posthumously by his friend and fellow poet Froylán Turcios in 1911 as *Tierras, mares y cielos* (*Lands, Seas and Skies*).

The career of Froylán Turcios (1875–1943) spanned the final decade of the nineteenth century and the first three decades of the twentieth, a period that coincides with the rise and decline of the modernist style in Central America.[2]

Turcios founded and/or directed numerous newspapers and literary journals such as *Esfinge* (*Sphinx*) and *Ariel*. In keeping with the international and classical aesthetic of modernism, he published the work of Honduran writers as well as contemporary European writers and selections from the classics of world literature. He was an advisor to Honduran presidents and a friend and supporter of Nicaraguan patriot Augusto Sandino. In the journal *Hispano-América*, he forcefully and eloquently expressed his nationalist and anti-imperialist sentiments and worked to further the cause of Central American union. His *Boletín de la defensa nacional* (*Bulletin of National Defense*) was an important political publication that denounced the occupation of Tegucigalpa by U.S. Marines in 1924. In addition to journalism, he wrote novellas, short stories, poetry, and memoirs. His fiction displays elements typical of romanticism as well as modernism. Both *Almas trágicas* (*Tragic Souls*), published in 1900 in serial form in the newspaper *Diario de Honduras* (*Honduran Daily*), and his 1910 novel *El vampiro* (*The Vampire*) are stories of ill-fated love, peopled with idealized characters burdened with somber thoughts and prone to bouts of melancholy. Crimes of passion, suicide seen as the only noble alternative to a tragic destiny, and adjective-rich descriptions identify the texts as romantic while discussions among the characters about poetry introduce the aesthetics of modernism. *El vampiro* is the first example in Honduras of horror fiction. In 1929, while serving as general consul for Honduras in Paris, he published a collection of sixty-nine short stories entitled *Cuentos del amor y de la muerte* (*Stories of Love and Death*), in which the reader can find examples of his romantic, modernist, and fantastic themes and styles. *Memorias* (*Memoirs*), published posthumously in 1980, is a richly detailed narrative of his life and times in which the reader learns about his privileged childhood in Juticalpa, the provincial capital of Olancho, his numerous publishing ventures, his acquaintance and correspondence with countless intellectuals throughout Europe and Latin America, his international travels, his political involvements, and his tireless efforts on behalf of Honduran political autonomy. In 1995, Honduran novelist Alfredo León Gómez (1928–) published a historical novel based on the life of Turcios, *Ariel La vida luminosa de Froylán Turcios* (*Ariel, the Brilliant Life of Froylán Turcios*).

THE TWENTIETH CENTURY

Narrative Fiction

Amalia Montiel, the first Honduran novel, by Lucila Gamero de Medina (1873–1964) of Danlí, was published in serial form in the magazine *La Juventud Hondureña* (*Honduran Youth*) in 1892. A practicing physician, essayist, feminist, and businesswoman, Doña Lucila published *Adriana y Margarita*

(*Adriana and Margarita*) in 1893 and in 1897 *Páginas del corazón* (*Pages from the Heart*). All three of these early novels are typically romantic in theme and style. Gamero's best-known work is *Blanca Olmedo* (1908), a romantic novel that was controversial because of its open attack on the Catholic clergy. Among her later novels, *Aída* (1948) is noteworthy for its strong female characters and the explicit message that a woman who is educated and capable of working outside the home can maintain her dignity even in the face of financial problems. The fact that *Aída* was written in 1918 although it was not published for thirty years, testifies to the progressive and independent character of the author. Although several of her novels are set in locales such as Mexico, New York, and Los Angeles, in *El dolor de amar* (*Love's Pain*, 1955), her last novel, she returns her gaze to Honduras and explores some of the cultural and linguistic richness of her country's rural population. Much like the work of her counterparts in other Latin American countries, such as Clorinda Matto de Turner of Peru and Juana Manuela Gorriti of Argentina, her novels are framed by a romantic sensibility but her social and political concerns are also evident. In *Adriana y Margarita*, she forefronts the relationship between the two female characters; the villain of *Blanca Olmedo* is a Catholic priest who, seeking revenge because she refuses his sexual advances, ruins the heroine's hopes of marrying her true love; and one of the central themes of *Aída* is a denunciation of the corruption and militarization of Honduras' political parties. In addition to her impressive list of novels, Doña Lucila also wrote articles for the national press. In keeping with the ideology of liberal positivism common among many of her contemporaries, she favored the separation of church and state, promoted public education for both sexes, extolled the benefits of opening the country to foreign economic investment and cultural influence, and was openly critical of infringements on the rule of law by both of the dominant political parties. An interesting biographical note is that Doña Lucila's father, Manuel Gamero, was a prominent medical doctor in Danlí. The young Lucila expressed interest in studying medicine but it was not considered an appropriate occupation for a young woman nor were women allowed to take anatomy classes along with their male peers, so she had to content herself with learning medicine by studying her father's textbooks and assisting him in his practice. When he became ill she took over the care of his patients and operated a *botica* or pharmacy that provided the residents of Danlí with tinctures made from local medicinal plants.

Costumbrismo

Costumbrismo, also known as *criollismo*, was one of the most beloved and popular prose styles practiced by Honduran writers in the first half of the twentieth century. This genre, imbued with patriotism and nostalgia, focuses its attention on the people and landscapes of Honduras, describing traditional lifestyles and beliefs. Examples of the variety found in this category might include the short stories of Víctor Cáceres Lara (1915–), collected in *Tierra ardiente* (*Burning Earth*, 1970), stories that expose the difficult life of rural campesinos. In another vein, Arturo Oquelí's (1885–1953) *El gringo lenca* (*The Lenca Gringo*, 1947) is an entertaining compendium of the geography, flora, fauna, mineralogy, and customs of different regions of Honduras, narrated by a mestizo whose father was North American and whose mother was indigenous. Having returned to Honduras after living in the United States, he recounts his travels through the country, describing the natural environment with the affectionate distance of one who is both an observer and a participant. Marco Antonio Rosa's (1899–1983) novels, *Tegucigalpa, ciudad de remembranzas* (*Tegucigalpa, City of Memories*, 1968) and *Mis tías las zanatas* (*My Gossipy Old Aunts*, c. 1963), are chronicles of life in the Honduran capital when it was a sleepy provincial town, told with a dose of romantic nostalgia. Another work that evokes an earlier and slower time is *Peregrinaje* (*Pilgrimage*) by Argentina Díaz Lozano (1917–1999), published in English as *Enriquetta and I* (1944). In this charming blend of *costumbrismo* and autobiography, a young girl narrates her adventures and observations as she travels around Honduras with her widowed mother. A unique variation of the *costumbrismo* genre is the work of Daniel Laínez (1914–1959), whose *Estampas locales* (*Local Sketches*, 1948) and *Manicomio* (*Insane Asylum*, published posthumously, 1980) portray a gallery of local characters from the streets of Tegucigalpa.

SOCIAL REALISM AND THE COMMITMENT TO SOCIAL JUSTICE

It is not surprising that, given Honduras' long history of invasion, conquest, foreign exploitation, and government corruption that allows and at times even promotes social injustice, many Honduran writers have taken on the task of dramatizing these realities in their narrative fiction. Writers from the North Coast were particularly active in describing and denouncing the practices of the Standard and Cuyamel Fruit Companies. The careers of an interesting literary couple from La Ceiba illustrate the activities and concerns of North Coast intellectuals in the first half of the twentieth century. Adolfo Miralda was a lawyer, journalist, and businessman who founded Imprenta Renacimiento (Renaissance Press) in La Ceiba in 1931 and a few years later the newspaper *El Espectador* (*The Spectator*), through which he denounced political corruption and abuses of human rights. Because of his incendiary journalism he and his wife, Paca Navas de Miralda, (1900–1976), who had distinguished herself as a folklorist with the publication of *Ritmos criollos* (*Creole Rhythms*) in 1947, were forced into exile in Guatemala. There Paca published

Barro (*Clay*, 1951), a novel that combines the descriptive and folk-oriented characteristics of *costumbrismo* with a denunciation of the loss of national sovereignty, inhumane working and living conditions, poverty, and illiteracy. The protagonists of this novel of social regionalism, set in a town newly established for workers of an international fruit company, have left their home in rural Olancho, attracted by the promise of jobs and wealth on the North Coast. The novel weaves together scenes of traditional domesticity and daily life with descriptions of the hard work and suffering of the transplanted families, whose lives become immersed in the violence and alcoholism of this new social order based on wage-earning and consumerism. The many conversations in bars, boarding houses, shops, and gatherings in people's homes showcase the author's skill at transcribing the semantic variations and pronunciation idiosyncrasies of the population. The inclusion of songs, legends, sayings, and customs add to the oral quality of the narrative. Numerous descriptions of the land and the weather contribute to making this an important effort to portray the complexity of the characters' lives and the role played by human nature as well as the natural environment in determining their destinies.

Ramón Amaya Amador (1916–1966), a self-taught writer and journalist from a working-class family, was himself a worker on the North Coast banana plantations for many years. A member of the Communist Party, in 1943 he founded *Alerta* (*On Guard*), a weekly newspaper dedicated to defending the interests of the workers. Two years later he began publishing installments in *Alerta* of his novel *Prisión verde*, which has enjoyed several re-editions and has become a classic example of anti-imperialist writing in Honduras. It presents a detailed and multilayered picture of the social, cultural, and political life in the camps and fields of the banana companies that monopolized the North Coast economy. By dramatizing the contrasting situations of local landowners who are convinced by the lawyers employed by the banana company to sell their land and one stubborn landowner who refuses to sell at any cost, the author creates sympathy for the independent-minded character only to then reveal that government troops in league with the foreign company force him off his land regardless and for a paltry compensation. The unhygienic living conditions in the camps, the dangers of working with pesticide-laden fruit, the absence of educational facilities for workers' children, the government's corruption and complicity in the exploitation of Honduran citizens are just a few of the injustices that are denounced in the novel. A leader emerges from within this human misery to lead a strike effort. The strike is put down and the leader is killed, but his memory lives on to inspire a glimmer of hope among the workers. The novel was uncannily prophetic, for on May 2, 1954, some 25,000 United Fruit Co. and 15,000 Standard Fruit Co. workers began a strike that lasted sixty-nine days. Workers from other sectors joined the strike, which finally resulted in official recognition of the right of workers to unionize, the creation of an eight-hour workday, overtime compensation, and paid vacations.

Amaya Amador's other works similarly describe and denounce social injustices and inequalities among various populations, critique imperialism, and offer the ideals of democratic socialism as solutions for a better future. *Amanecer* (*Daybreak*, 1947), for example, is a novel in the Latin American tradition of denouncing dictatorships, inspired by the 1944 revolution in Guatemala that overthrew General Jorge Ubico and inaugurated the democratic presidency of Juan José Arévalo, whereas *Constructores* (*Construction Workers*, 1958) focuses on the conditions of workers in the building trades and *Cipotes* (*Kids*, published posthumously 1981) portrays the lives of street children in Tegucigalpa.

His political activism coupled with his critical writings, led to persecution by the government of Tiburcio Carías Andino, forcing him into exile in Guatemala, Argentina, and Czechoslovakia, where he died in a plane crash in 1966. Consequently, a number of his many novels were published posthumously.

SOCIETY AND VIOLENCE

Honduras has gone through protracted periods of civil conflict, military governments inclined to use force to suppress opposition and the presence of foreign troops in its territory. This climate of violence has exerted a powerful influence over Honduran writers of all genres. During the presidency or dictatorship of Tiburcio Carías Andino (1876–1969) from 1932 to 1954, drastic measures were often taken to assure that the president ruled unopposed. It is said that outspoken and critical intellectuals, writers and artists were silenced through *encierro, destierro, entierro* or imprisonment, exile, or execution. Military governments in the 1960s, 1970s, and 1980s and the war between Honduras and El Salvador in 1969 created a feeling of unending militarism. The situation that caused the most recent concern was the presence of the U.S. military on Honduran soil during the Contra War in Nicaragua (c. 1980–1990). Many Hondurans saw this as yet another example of the United States using their country as its backyard. The influx of dollars and the close relationship promoted between the armed forces of the two countries led to a period of repression against Honduran citizens that included surveillance, threats, killings, and disappearances. The oppressive atmosphere that has permeated the country for so much of the twentieth century has marked the creative output of many fiction writers, journalists, and poets. For some it has manifest itself as outrage or explicit denunciation; but for others it has taken the forms of irony and cynicism; still others have expressed their social concerns obliquely, through the use of allegory, symbolism, and the techniques of magical realism. The major theme of Eduardo Bähr's (1940–) *El cuento de la guerra* (*The War Story*, 1973), and Julio Escoto's (1944–) *Días de ventisca, noches de huracán* (*Days of Blizzard, Nights of Hurricane*, 1980), for example, is the Honduran–Salvadoran War, but language and narrative technique play an equally important role alongside political urgency, which was usually not the case with the committed writers of the past such as Ramón Amaya Amador.

PORTRAYING THE NATION'S CHARACTER

Honduran fiction writers have long been attracted to the challenge of defining what is uniquely Honduran and have written ambitious novels that attempt to describe, analyze, and disentangle the complexities of Honduran history, politics, and culture in the hope of offering an interpretation of the Honduran national character. Perhaps the most comprehensive of these attempts is the two-volume work of Carlos Izaguirre (1895–1956), *Bajo el chubasco* (*Under the Storm*, 1945). Izaguirre was a unique and controversial literary and political figure. He was a close personal friend and advisor to Tiburcio Carías Andino (1876–1969) during Carías' long and dictatorial presidency; he was also a journalist, a poet, a novelist, a pilot, and a diplomat. He studied in the United States, spoke English, worked for the Cuyamel Fruit Company from 1919 to 1921, and founded at least six different newspapers between 1917 and 1932. Like so many of his peers, he was critical of the state of his country; unlike them, he supported the Carías dictatorship. He believed in the value of peace and order and admired even fascist leaders if they were able to create stability in their countries. He was an astute observer of virtually all aspects of Honduran reality and managed to incorporate them in his novel of well over 1,000 pages. The plot of *Bajo el chubasco* is simple: A young man grows up on the family hacienda in harmony not only with nature but with the human beings of all social classes who make up his idyllic world. He goes to Tegucigalpa to study and on a subsequent visit to the hacienda, witnesses the murder of his parents by soldiers in the army of a political strong-man who is leading an insurrection to take over the government. He flees to the mountains and several years later is inspired by a sermon to go to the North Coast to fight for human rights and justice. He is befriended by Mr. Smith, an administrator of a banana company, who helps him establish his utopian dream of a model farm that provides decent and humane conditions and benefits for its workers. His farm is a success, until he is senselessly killed and the experiment collapses. Fleshing out this uncomplicated story are numerous asides, digressions, and analyses of most aspects of Honduran life and culture in the first four decades of the twentieth century, among them are descriptions of the music, dances, and legends of rural communities; the corruption of politicians who are bought off by foreign companies; the complicity of the press with politicians; state censorship; the lack of professionalism in the military; the dearth of state support for the arts; the extreme poverty; and the high rate of illiteracy.

In contrast to Carlos Izaguirre, for whom structural elements and aesthetic experimentation were of lesser import than the communication of ethical positions, Marcos Carías Zapata's (1938–) novels are works of linguistic and metafictional experimentation. *La memoria y sus consecuencias* (*Memory and Its Consequences*, 1977) approaches the riddle of national identity through the lens of history. Oscillating between the colonial period and the twentieth century, an amateur historian presents a series of found documents that ostensibly give alternative versions of Honduran history. The reader is challenged to question official histories and ultimately to reread and reflect on the very practice of writing or interpreting the past. *Una función con móbiles y tentetiesos* (*Function with Mobiles and Roly-Poly Toys*, 1980), on the other hand, plays with sound and meaning; it introduces onomatopoeia, synesthesia, disembodied voices, and neologisms in a playful attempt to reflect the complex reality of Tegucigalpa in the final decades of the twentieth century. This multilayered collage of overheard dialogue and interrupted conversations presents every imaginable character from actors in *telenovelas* (soap operas) to evangelical preachers to street vendors to university professors to beauty queens.

Julio Escoto (1944–) is without question one of contemporary Honduras' most distinguished writers and intellectuals. His work encompasses fiction, both novels and short stories, essays, and literary criticism. He has studied at the Honduran National University, the universities of Florida and Iowa and the University of Costa Rica in San José, where he was the director of *Editorial Universitaria Centroamericana*, Central America's premier university press. He has founded and directed a number of literary journals and chaired the literature department of the National University. Since 1986 he has lived in San Pedro Sula where he continues to play an active role in the cultural life of his country. All of his novels contribute to an understanding of the Honduran experience and identity, but one in particular stands out for its range of vision. *Madrugada Rey del albor* (*Madrugada, King of Dawn*, 1993) is at once a spy novel, an interpretation of the Honduran national character and an imaginative synthesis of Honduran history. Employing the technique of inserting historical vignettes in retrospective chronological order into a contemporary plot of mystery and international intrigue, Escoto juxtaposes past and present to create a mosaic of multiple signifiers that open Honduran history to new interpretations. The spy story centers on an African-American U.S. university professor who has been contracted by the president of Honduras to write a history of the country that diminishes Spain's role and foregrounds the importance of the United States and who inadvertently discovers a plot by the United States to gain control of Central America. Juxtaposed with his efforts to decode the relevant computer files are recreations of significant historical moments such as the 1963 presidential coup, the 1924 occupation of Tegucigalpa by U.S. Marines, and the 1621 story of an African slave. Escoto's most recent novel, *El génesis en Santa Cariba* (*Genesis in Santa Cariba*, 2006) takes place on a Caribbean island colonized by the British. It reflects his interest in the history and culture of the Atlantic coast of Honduras with its obvious Caribbean influence.

Roberto Castillo's (1950–2008) untimely death in January 2008 put premature closure on an illustrious career. Formerly a philosophy professor at the National University, Castillo began publishing fiction in 1980 with *Subida al cielo y otros cuentos* (*Lifted into Heaven and Other Stories*), a collection of short fiction that combines quizzical humor with a taste for the bizarre yet revealing detail. This characteristic may have been what inspired the young filmmaker Hispano Durón to produce Honduras' first feature-length nondocumentary film, *Anita, la cazadora de insectos* (*Anita, the Insect Hunter*), based on the homonymous story from this collection. Castillo's novella *El corneta* (1981) was translated into English as *The Bugler* by Edward Waters Hood and published in a bilingual edition by the University Press of America. Narrated with an unflinching gaze that follows the misfortunes of a young man from a poor family who gets drafted into the army and takes on the job of playing the bugle, *El corneta* portrays a cast of characters from the underprivileged classes with realism and compassion. *Traficante de ángeles* (*The Angel Dealer*, 1996) may be Castillo's most original work. A collection of fictional biographies, it showcases the author's broad, humanistic knowledge and creative imagination. In a tone reminiscent of Borges in its understated ironies and with a generous dose of intertextuality, Castillo creates portraits of authors, inventors, philosophers, and even a mayor of the twenty-third century, guardian of his city's history, in the act of writing his memoirs. An indefatigable reader and scholar, Castillo collected his essays in *Del siglo que se fue* (*The Century That Has Gone*, 2005). The selection reveals his major interests: literature and language; biography; philosophical speculation, particularly regarding the nature of time; the social and cultural realities of the modern world; and his country—its suffering, its beauty, its idiosyncrasies. All of these interests come together in his masterpiece, *La guerra mortal de los sentidos* (*The Fatal War of the Senses*, 2002), which can be counted among the handful of ambitious Honduran novels that attempt to penetrate the national character by offering a panoramic mural of voices, customs, beliefs, and geographies.

The central conceit of Castillo's novel, which begins in the year 2099, is the search for the last speaker of the Lenca language. The narrator reconstructs the quest of his great-grandfather, a Spanish linguist who had set out to record this language that, at the time of the actual writing of the novel, was believed to be extinct in Honduras. This last Lenca speaker takes on mythical proportions as the narrator, now on his own journey of discovery, meets and converses with a variety of characters and witnesses all manner of curious occurrences, which lend the story an air of magical realism. Language itself becomes the protagonist of the narrative as the oral tradition is both honored and recorded in the form of dialectical speech, myths, legends, and popular history. It is hoped that some of Castillo's numerous unpublished manuscripts will become available to the reading public.

POETRY

Like the narrative, Honduran poetry has grown and changed during the twentieth century. Poets have responded to their political situation with works that reflect their social awareness and have transcended politics to create lyric poems of lasting beauty. One poet who has successfully combine these trends is Roberto Sosa, who may very well be remembered as Honduras' most accomplished poet of the twentieth century. Considered an outstanding representative of the Generation of 1950, he was born in 1930 in Yoro, a small town in the northwestern highlands in an area with a strong indigenous presence. His family was poor and from an early age he worked at various jobs, although he acquired a love of reading while still in elementary school and amassing a library has been one of his joys throughout his life. After publishing three books of poetry that reflect his early romantic inclinations and concern for questions of form, the climate of military repression in Honduras in the 1960s inspired him to publish *Los pobres* (*The Poor*, 1969), awarded the Adonais Prize in Spain and *Un mundo para todos dividido* (*A World Divided for All*, 1971), which won the prestigious Casa de las Américas prize in Cuba. These poems are acerbic attacks on militarism and social injustices expressed in startling images and a rich yet accessible vocabulary. His denunciation of corruption and the use of violence by the government and the military has occasioned death threats and the loss of a teaching position at the National University. Notwithstanding these reprisals, his social critique reached its most intense expression in *Secreto militar* (*Military Secret*, 1985), which includes parodic portraits of infamous Latin American dictators such as Carías (Honduras), Duvalier (Haiti), Somoza (Nicaragua), and Pinochet (Chile). Subsequent works foreground eroticism, death, the passage of time, and other universal themes, but Honduras is never distant—its poverty, corruption, beauty, and the powerful hold it has on the poet. In 1990 his *Obra completa* (*Complete Works*) was published, perhaps prematurely, for he has since then continued to write, as evidenced by *El llanto de las cosas* (*The Weeping of Things*, 1995) and *Digo mujer* (*I Say Woman*, 2004). In addition to writing poetry, he has been consistently active in the cultural life of Honduras. He founded the journal *Presente* (*Present*) in 1964 and has published essays on cultural topics (*Prosa armada*, *Armed Prose*, 1981) and interviews with Honduran writers (*Diálogo de sombras*, *Shadows in Dialogue*, 1993). His most ambitious cultural project to date has been a three-volume compilation of essays, statistics, speeches, and scholarly articles intended to illuminate the history and culture of Honduras, *Documentos para la historia de Honduras* (*Documents for Honduran History*, vol. I, 1999, vol. II, 2002, and vol. III, 2004). It contains a wealth of information from firsthand sources and is an invaluable tool for scholars. Sosa is one of the few Honduran writers whose work has been translated into other languages, including French, German, and Russian. Four collections of his poetry are available in English: *Poems*, tr. Edward V. McLaughlin, Spanish Literature Publications, 1984; *The Difficult Days*, tr. Jim Lindsay, Princeton, 1985; *The Common Grief*, tr. Jo Anne Engelbert, Curbstone, 1994; and *The Return of the River*, tr. Jo Anne Engelbert, Curbstone, 2002.

As the first woman to publish a volume of her poetry in Honduras, Clementina Suárez holds an honored place in the pantheon of Honduran poets. Born in 1902 in Juticalpa, capital of the Department of Olancho, Clementina left home and her privileged childhood to move to Tegucigalpa and become a poet. She lived with a man without marrying him, had two children out of wedlock, and supported herself by waitressing in a downtown café where the local literati gathered, giving poetry recitals and publishing, in 1934, six issues of a literary/cultural magazine she called *Mujer* (*Woman*), walking the streets of Tegucigalpa in a bellhop's uniform to publicize and sell copies of her editorial venture. Her first poems, collected in *Corazón sangrante* (*Bleeding Heart*, 1930) and *Los templos de fuego* (*Temples of Fire*, 1931) were the romantic, passionate verses of a fiercely independent and strong-willed young woman struggling against the rigid social norms of a provincial, patriarchal society. During a period of time spent in Cuba from 1936 to 1937, when she was inspired by the political activism of many Cuban writers and intellectuals as well as by reports of the popular struggle against fascism during the Spanish Civil War, her poetic expression underwent a profound transformation. *Veleros* (*Sails*, 1937) and *De la desilusión a la esperanza* (*From Disillusion to Hope*, 1944) reflect a consciousness awakening to the suffering and injustice of a world much larger than the self. Like numerous other Latin American writers and artists, Clementina Suárez entered the compelling and ongoing debate concerning the role and responsibility of the intellectual in the fight for peace and justice. She lived in Mexico in the 1940s, where she founded the *Galería de arte centroamericana* (Gallery of Central American Art) and in El Salvador from 1949 to 1959, presiding over her *Rancho del Artista* (Artist's Ranch), a unique space that functioned as an art gallery, gathering place for writers and artists and lodging for visiting artists. In 1957 the Ministry of Culture of El Salvador published her award-winning *Creciendo con la hierba* (*Growing with the Grass*), a single long poem divided into eight sections that is a plea to the poet's lover to become her comrade as well. In 1958, having returned to Honduras, she published *Canto a la encontrada Patria y su Héroe* (*Song of the Found Fatherland and Its Hero*), another long poem, this one divided into thirteen sections, a truly revolutionary composition in which she redefines fatherland and patriotism and positions herself within this newly conceived homeland as a woman, a poet and a Honduran. In 1969, the National University published an anthology of her poetry, *El poeta y sus señales* (*The Poet and Her Signs*), and *Clementina Suárez*, a compilation of biographical sketches, literary essays, reviews, interviews, and poems composed in her honor, as well as reproductions of the many portraits painted of her over the years. The following year she was awarded the Ramón Rosa National Award for Literature, Honduras' highest literary honor. In 1975, she purchased a house in Barrio La Hoya, an old, centrally located neighborhood of Tegucigalpa near the Choluteca River and created the "Galería Clementina Suárez." She continued to live there, writing poetry and promoting the arts, until, in 1991, an unknown assailant killed her. When Hurricane Mitch devastated Tegucigalpa in 1998, the waters of the Choluteca River flooded Barrio La Hoya and filled the gallery with mud. It remains closed.

Clementina Suárez struggled throughout her life to create a place for herself as a woman and a poet in Honduran and Central American literary history. During her colorful life she was severely criticized by some and lauded by others; she is recognized now as Honduras' foremost woman poet. She continues to be an inspiration to new generations of women writers who admire her lifelong dedication to her art as well as her strength and independence.

Contemporary Poets

Late twentieth century poets such as Rigoberto Paredes (1948–), José Luis Quesada (1948–), and José Adán Castelar (1940–) lived through the traumatic times of militarization and censorship in the 1970s and 1980s, so it is not surprising that their work reflects this in theme and attitude. Social themes of more recent relevance include women's rights and sexual abuse; AIDS; poverty, globalization, and migration; urban violence; and the stresses and angst of a rapidly changing world. All of these concerns are addressed in the works of a prolific, eloquent, and engaged generation of poets. Many poets are active today in Honduras and make use of the Internet, the conventional printed word and recitals and performances to share their work. The following are just a few of the numerous examples that might be chosen to demonstrate the range and variety of Honduras' contemporary poetic expression. María Eugenia Ramos' (1959–) *Porque ningún sol es el último* (*Because No Sun Is the Last*, 1989) expresses an acute awareness of the complexities of modern life and the cultural impoverishment of clichéd approaches to comprehending or changing it, whereas in *Ataduras sueltas* (*Broken Chains*, 1998), Blanca Guifarro (1946–) calls out to women to take control of their lives. Edgardo Florián (1975–) experiments with syntax and typography in *Yazz* (*Jazz*, 2003) in short compositions that reflect pop culture. Fabricio Estrada (1974–) shares his poems, photographs, and iconoclastic aesthetic on his blog *Bitácora del párvulo* (*The Infant's Log*). Armida García's (1971–) *La soledad justificada* (*Justified Silence*, 1997) showcases her rich visual imagination. Amanda Castro's (1962–) powerful, woman-centered voice creates lyrical portraits, angry denunciations of social injustices, and erotic love poems. Gabriel Vallecillo Márques (1976–) is a cultural theorist as well as a poet. His illuminating analyses of contemporary culture have been published in journals and on line. His own creative work includes three books of poetry and experimental video-poems.

Women and Poetry

It is noteworthy that, although just a few decades ago women writers were less prolific and were often ignored or excluded from critical studies, literary histories, and anthologies, this has changed significantly and some of the country's finest poets are now women. Women's active and accepted participation in the literary life of Honduras today stems in large part from the initiative of Adaluz Pineda de Gálvez and others in 1988 to form the Grupo Cultural Femenino Clementina Suárez (Clementina Suárez Women's Culture Group). With the encouragement and moral support of Suárez and the members of the group, including Claudia Torres, Raquel Lobo, Mery Santos, Aída Sabonge, María Eugenia Ramos, and Sara de Medina, Pineda de Gálvez embarked on a landmark project that both reflected and inspired this development: the publication in 1998 of *Honduras: Mujer y Poesía, Antologia de Poesía Escrita por Mujeres 1865–1998* (*Honduras: Woman and Poetry, Anthology of Poetry Written by Women 1865–1998*). A linguist and literary historian, Pineda de Gálvez's research brought to the public's attention the sometimes lost or forgotten works of the foremothers of Honduran women's poetry and honored a number of talented young poets with inclusion in this important publication. All of them have continued to write and publish and encourage a new generation of women to be full participants in their country's literary life.

In 1996 Pineda de Gálvez was instrumental in formalizing the creation of the National Association of Women Writers of Honduras (Asociación Nacional de Escritoras de Honduras [ANDEH]). Many of the original members were participants of the workshop "Casa Tomada." The association's objectives included paying tribute to women writers of the past, encouraging contemporary writers and establishing connections among women writers from different parts of the country. They held a series of poetry recitals in various cities and in 1997 they organized the first national assembly of Honduran women writers. The pioneering board of directors was composed of Adaluz Pineda, María Eugenia Ramos, Waldina Mejía, Indira Flamenco, Lisbeth Valle, and Lety Elvir.

Lety Elvir (1966–) is an outstanding example of a talented poet who, in addition to refining and expanding her own poetic repertoire, has been a courageous voice for change and in defense of women. The quality of her work was recognized internationally even before the publication of her first book of poetry, *Luna que no cesa* (*Moon That Does Not Cease*, 1998). Since then she has become an important presence in the literary culture not only of her own country but also of Central America. She received an advanced degree from the University of Costa Rica and has been a visiting Fulbright professor in the United States. She teaches at the National University, is active in ANDEH as well as regional writers' groups and speaks and publishes on literary, social, and gender-related topics. Her poetry communicates strength, compassion, and sensuality. Other accomplished women poets of this time are Yadira Eguiguren (1971–), Elisa Logan (pseudonym of Elizeth García, 1964–), Deborah Ramos (1962–), Diana Espinal (1964–), Alejandra Flores (1957–), Claudia Torres (1951–), and Rebeca Becerra (1969–).

PERSISTENCE OF THE ORAL TRADITION

The oral tradition of storytelling in its many forms is by definition ephemeral and, although it is the oldest form of using language to create and share the stories and beliefs that become the cultural identity of a community, it is also the most malleable. It may include the wisdom passed down by indigenous elders through the retelling of legends of the ancestors and tales of animals and spirits; songs and dances sung and danced year after year and generation after generation, their meanings modified over time; beliefs about the spirits who inhabit the natural world and their interactions with human beings; and the history of a community or a people, most often the stories that do not form part of the larger official history of a nation. Because the performance of the living word cannot be separated from the stories, they are recounted with gestures, expressions, and emotion. When these narratives are finally written down, either retold by creative writers who endow the telling with their own voice and style or recorded and transcribed in the words of their informants by linguists, anthropologists, and folklorists, they become part of the literary culture of a wider community. They also become static, losing the quality of performance inherent in the oral tradition and taking as their final form, the version that has made its way into print.

During the nineteenth and early twentieth centuries there was a great deal of interest in Central America on the part of Britain, Germany, and the United States. Representatives of these countries saw the potential for economic development in the isthmus and actively traveled through, mapped, and documented the land and the people. Although their interests were not necessarily ethnographic, many of their accounts include references to the oral traditions of the people they described. Eduard Conzemius, probably the first ethnologist to study and document some of the culturally isolated indigenous groups of the country, produced exhaustive studies of the Jicaques or Tolupanes in 1921, the Payas or Pech in 1927, the Garífunas in 1928, and the Misquitos and Sumus in 1932. He documented virtually every aspect of the material as well as spiritual culture of these groups with such thoroughness that his texts are still consulted today. Other pioneers in collecting the oral tradition of indigenous groups include Brazilian anthropologist Ruy Galvao de Andrade Coelho, who documented many of the beliefs and stories of the Garífuna people in the 1940s; Anne Chapman, who, beginning in the 1950s, recorded the creation myths, animal, and spirit tales and many other stories and myths of the Tolupán and Lenca; and Nancie S. Gonzalez, who studied the Garífuna culture in the 1980s.

In 1981, the Department of Language and Literature (*Carrera de Letras*) of the National University initiated a long-term research project to record and study the literature of the oral tradition in Honduras. Teams of students and faculty have since then done extensive fieldwork to interview individuals, usually elders, and to record, transcribe, and publish their authentic and unique versions of traditional stories. This marks a new direction in literary studies at the National University and a new appreciation for the actual speech of indigenous, rural, and often illiterate individuals and communities. Recent publications that reflect this tendency include Claudia Marcela Carías et al. *Tradición oral indígena de Yamaranguila* (*The Indigenous Oral Tradition of Yamaranguila*, 1988) and Mario Gallardo, *La danza que hizo Dugú: la literatura oral en la comunidad garífuna de Masca* (*The Dance of Dugú: Oral Literature of the Garífuna Community of Masca*, 2008).

Long before the academic community began to focus its attention on the oral tradition of indigenous groups, numerous Honduran writers and enthusiasts of folklore were publishing compilations of folktales, legends, sayings, jokes, and other elements of the oral tradition. These commonly were artistic renderings of often-told tales that teach a lesson, reflect a trait associated with the "typical" Honduran personality, or simply entertain the reader. Some well-known examples are Jesús Aguilar Paz (1895–1974), *Tradiciones y leyendas de Honduras* (*Traditions and Legends of Honduras*, 1930) and Pompilio Ortega (1890–1959), *Patrios lares* (*Patriotic Homeland*, 1949). These stories are some-times narrated with an obvious nostalgia for the supposedly simpler life and times when the oral tradition implied communal gatherings, but Medardo Mejía (1907–1981), in *Comizahual, leyendas, tradiciones y relatos de Honduras* (*Comizahual, Legends, Traditions and Stories of Honduras*, 1981), employed irony, sarcasm, and humor in his telling, to deconstruct the social patterns of Honduran society.

Contemporary writers continue to collect and/or recreate Honduran myths, legends, and folklore. *Cuentos y leyendas de Honduras* (*Stories and Leg-ends from Honduras*, 6th ed., 2006), by Jorge Montenegro (1940–), is an art-ful retelling of popular tales familiar to most Hondurans through the oral tradition. Montenegro has had a very popular radio program that broad-casts throughout the country, during which he dramatizes Honduran folk tales. The desire to capture vanishing folk stories in a rapidly changing world has inspired young writers such as Noël Borjas, who published *Despertando el duende: Leyendas de Santa Lucía* (*Awakening the Magical Spirit: Legends of Santa Lucia*, 2007).

One author/raconteur who has achieved extraordinary popularity is Teófilo Trejo. Born in 1941 in La Lima, Cortés, he left school and began working on banana plantations on the North Coast when he was nine years old. He has been active in workers' organizations for many years and is a well-known sto-ryteller who excels at the performance of *perras* or tall tales. These are stories of encounters with *La Sihuanaba* or *El Sisimite*, or scary or comically heroic acts, told with great theatricality and using slang, popular expressions, and colorful language. In 1998 a national farm workers union sponsored the publication of a collection of Teófilo's tall tales, *Las perras de Teofilito* (*Teófilito's Tall Tales*) for use in adult basic education programs in rural areas. The book has sold more than 20,000 copies and he has since then written six more books, including his autobiography.

CHILDREN'S LITERATURE

A perhaps natural outgrowth of this interest in the oral tradition is that increasing numbers of writers are turning their attention to Honduran children. Anthropologist Mario Ardón's (1956–) *Folklore lúdico infantil de Honduras* (*Traditional Children's Games of Honduras*, 1986), for example, is a compilation and transcription of children's songs, rhymes, and games, intended to provide Honduran teachers with authentic material they can use to teach children their own culture and as a corrective or antidote to the computer games, action figures, war games, and extraterrestrials that the global media has introduced to Honduran children who largely cannot afford to purchase these toys and games and may develop a distaste for homegrown games and a sense of dissatisfaction and even cultural inferiority.

Rubén Berriós (?–2007) was a pioneer in the field who devoted his long and distinguished professional career to the promotion, creation, and publication of literature for children. His works range from rhymes and melodic poems that celebrate the simple pleasures of childhood to short anecdotal prose compositions that are often based on traditional tales. His most accomplished work is *Espiga ceremonial* (*Ceremonial Cornstalk*, 2001) a collection of stories that are original recreations of legends and creation myths of the various indigenous peoples of Honduras. Edilberto Borjas (1950–), who also writes adult fiction, published *El Tolupán de la Flor* (*The Tolupán of Flower Mountain*) in 1993, a lyrical story of a young boy of the Tolupán people who live in Montaña de la Flor, very few of whom today speak their native language or have preserved their traditional culture. The story takes the boy on a quest to find the lost members of his tribe and reconnect with his people's history. A number of other recent publications aim to teach Honduran children about the indigenous groups that form an important part of their heritage. One excellent example is *Así es como vivimos aquí* (*This Is How We Live Here*, 2003), with stories by Manuel de Jesús Pineda that illustrate traditional ways of life, accompanied by color photographs of indigenous children by Edmundo Lobo. A number of government-sponsored activities aimed at increasing literacy are aided by NGOs such as the Neruda Foundation, which has been especially active in organizing literary workshops for children and teens. Eduardo Bähr, a much-loved writer, actor, and professor at the National Pedagogical University, directs the Honduran branch of this organization.

TESTIMONIAL NARRATIVES

The genre of testimonial narratives that became popular in Central America in the 1980s took on a unique form in Honduras. Unlike neighboring El Salvador, Guatemala, and Nicaragua, Honduran society did not experience a prolonged revolutionary movement or civil war in the final quarter of the twentieth century. These conflicts inspired the publication of numerous testimonies to the horrors of genocide and military violence as well as first-hand accounts of participation in guerrilla movements and other forms of political activism in their respective countries. Despite not having had a civil war, Honduran writers and intellectuals also experienced the need to record for posterity the unofficial history of their country in the words of those who participated in it. To this end, Rina Villars published in 1991 *Porque quiero seguir viviendo...habla Graciela García* (Because I Want to Keep on Living...Graciela García Speaks). Villars conducted extensive interviews with the now-deceased Graciela García (1895–1995?), which she transcribed and glossed. García was a well-known political activist in the 1920s and 1930s in Honduras and El Salvador, author of *Páginas de la lucha revolucionaria en Centroamérica* (*Pages on the Revolutionary Struggle in Central America,* 1971) and *En las trincheras de la lucha por el socialismo* (*In the Trenches in the Fight for Socialism,* 1975).

In 1990, the Guaymuras Publishing Co. sponsored a contest in testimonial narratives. Numerous manuscripts were submitted and the three award winners were honored with the publication of their testimonies. Public response was very positive so the contest was held again in 1993 and three additional testimonies were published. None of the authors were professional writers, but they were participants in significant events in Honduran history who would otherwise most likely never have left a written record of their experiences to enrich the historical and cultural record. Among the testimonies published were *Soy Andreo Neda, un hombre que no quiso ser cucaracha* (*I Am Andreo Nedo, a Man Who Didn't Want to Be a Cockroach,* 1991) by Andrés Pineda, upon whom the character Andreo Nedo in Ramón Amaya Amador's novel *Constructores* is based; *La promesa* (*The Promise,* 1991) by Doris Hernández, which recounts the experiences of a woman who promised herself as a young girl that she would work to eradicate illiteracy in Honduras; and *Presidiario* (Inmate, 1993), Vidal Antonio Martínez's first-hand account of life in a Honduran penitentiary.

The testimony of Elvia Alvarado, *Don't Be Afraid, Gringo* (1987), unlike its counterparts, has been published only in English. It is the story of a rural working-class woman who became a leader in the agrarian rights movement. Medea Benjamin of The Institute for Food and Development Policy interviewed Alvarado and then was responsible for the transcription, translation into English and publication of her testimony for an international audience. Benjamin and Alvarado subsequently toured the United States to promote the book. Alvarado's testimony unfortunately has not been published in Spanish, nevertheless it is a valuable contribution to Honduran and Central American testimonial literature because of the perspective it offers on the life of a woman from rural Honduras and the light it sheds on popular activism.

All of these testimonies are texts that inhabit that borderland between the oral tradition and written literature. In addition to being cultural and historical documents whose worth will increase with time, they are also precious examples of the spoken Spanish of their time.

THE COLLECTIVE SPIRIT

Although it is certainly true that writing can be a solitary occupation and Honduran writers will often complain that the government does little to support their creative efforts, there is undeniably a collective spirit that is manifest among them. Indeed, it may be because the government offers so little in the way of financial incentives or assistance that a tradition of forming groups that meet to discuss each other's work and sometimes pool resources and join forces to publish literary magazines and anthologies is alive and well. In the early decades of the twentieth century, one of the significant characteristics of literary life in Tegucigalpa was the *tertulia* or informal gathering in favorite cafés, bars, or restaurants to discuss politics, poetry and local gossip. Some locales came to be associated with specific groups. These public gathering places allow individual as well as collective literary identities to form and evolve. In the 1920s and 1930s, the well-respected and established poets and journalists liked to gather at the Café de Paris and the Jardín de Italia, whereas the younger bohemian writers preferred the more rustic and less expensive hangouts. In the 1950s, the Duncan Maya just off the main plaza was popular, while artists and writers enjoyed meeting in the Café Nuevo Continente in the 1960s and the Cafetería San Francisco in the 1980s. The Café Paradiso was opened in the 1980s by Rigoberto Paredes and Anarella Vélez. Rigoberto Paredes is a poet whose work is known throughout Central America and Anarella Vélez is a historian and professor at the National University. Located on a narrow side street in the historic district of Tegucigalpa, it has remained one of most popular meeting places for artists, writers and a wide range of intellectuals and cultural activists. The Café Paradiso, which is also a book store and art gallery, hosts poetry readings, concerts, lectures, films and book presentations; its open and welcoming atmosphere encourages the gathering of groups such as El Cine Club Luis Buñuel (The Luis Buñuel Film Club) and Paíspoesible. An example of a cultural event held at Paradiso was the screening of the documentary film *Oquedad* by Honduran filmmaker Carlos Ordóñez.

Another important dynamic in the literary culture of Honduras is the working group or collective that defines itself either through a manifesto that sets forth its aesthetic principles and goals or through the reputation of a writer around whom the group forms. Four recent examples are *Tahuanka, Casa Tomada, Paíspoesible,* and *Ixbalam.*

Tahuanka was formed in the 1970s by a group of writers with a desire to create a national literature in step with the revolutionary ideals and practices of writers from throughout Latin America. Members included Rigoberto Paredes, José Luis Quesada, Eduardo Bähr, and José Adán Castelar. They published their work in the magazine *Tahuanka*, organized free poetry readings and collaborated with other artists and intellectuals of a similar persuasion in various events of cultural activism with a political agenda.

In 1993 José Luis Quesada (1948–), a well-known and much-loved and admired poet who had taught at the National University and worked at the Ministry of Culture, organized a group of young poets who met regularly to share and critique each other's work. They called their group *Casa Tomada* (House Taken) because a friend, Leda Suárez, had invited them to hold their first gathering at her home, but the meetings continued for months and also in honor of the homonymous short story by Argentine writer Julio Cortázar. Members included Rebeca Becerra, Fabricio Estrada, Rubén Izaguirre, Víctor Saborio, Roberto Becerra, Oscar Flores, Diana Vallejo, Lety Elvir, Edgardo Florián, and Luis Méndez. The municipality of Tegucigalpa published an anthology of their poems in 1996. The group met for several years and finally disbanded, but all the members have continued to be active participants in the cultural life of their country.

A decade later a few of the members of Casa Tomada went on to help form the collective *Paíspoesible* (a play on words that communicates the idea of a country made possible by poetry or the country of possible poetry). Paíspoesible is a group of artists in the broad sense that includes the written, visual, and performing arts, because what defines them is not an interest in a particular genre or form but rather a vision and a commitment to social transformation through art. Their manifesto declares that poetry has died, leaving them free and penniless at ground zero, starting over in a world that embraces cyberspace along with the urban landscape. This iconoclastic and vibrantly original group began as a writers' collective started by Marvin Valladares Drago (1969–), Fabrico Estrada (1974–), Salvador Madrid, and others and has grown and remained active. They receive financial support from a variety of international NGOs as well as the Ministry of Culture. They have organized poetry festivals (*Festival de Poesía Paíspoesible*) and have published a number of local authors such as Dennis Avila (1981–), Mayra Oyuela (1982–), Samuel Trigueros (1967–), Herber Sorto (1973–), and Armida García (1971–) in their series of chapbooks *Papel de oficio* (Official Paper, 2006). Other members include Rolando Kattán (1979–) and Waldina Mejía Medina (1963–).

The collective *Ixbalam* was formed in 2003 through the efforts of poet, linguist and cultural activist Amanda Castro (1962–). While the composition of the group has changed over time, the original guiding principles remain operative: to create and promote a consciousness of the value of autochthonous Honduran culture and its diverse expressions. To this end the collective has been admirably active, given its limited resources and the extreme difficulty of acquiring financing for independent cultural projects in Honduras. They founded a journal of cultural studies, *Ixbalam*, in 2004, edited by Rebeca Becerra. The journal publishes creative writing, book reviews, and articles on such topics as the oral tradition in Honduras and women writers. Editorial Ixbalam (Ixbalam Publishers) has also published a number of books of poetry, including *Exacta*, poems by Juana Pavón (1945–), a well-known *poeta de la calle* (street poet), known for her courageous and uncensored recitals of her independent-minded and honest poems in bars, theaters and on street corners of Tegucigalpa. The collective hopes to publish in the future the poems of some of Tegucigalpa's other street poets, who contribute a dose of color and authenticity to the capital's urban culture but who rarely have the opportunity to see their work in print. Some of their other projects have been poetry workshops for women with AIDS, cultural activities involving vendors in the large public markets of Tegucigalpa and most recently, performances of original woman-centered theater.

Mimalapalabra is not a typical collective and has not published a manifesto of aesthetic principles, but its group identity and unique presence in Honduras' literary life make it noteworthy. The writers and critics who identify with *mimalapalabra* have been contributors to the literary page of the Sunday supplement of *La Prensa* (*The Press*) a daily newspaper from San Pedro Sula. They started a blog in 2006 where they air their often acerbic opinions regarding Honduran literature. Members Mario Gallardo, Gustavo Campos, Ricardo Tomé, Carlos Rodríguez, and Giovanni Rodríguez provide an antidote to what some observers have called the laudatory, noncritical style of many Honduran cultural critics. They are refreshingly iconoclastic.

LITERARY HISTORY AND CRITICISM

Many scholars have contributed to the ongoing compilation, publishing, and evaluation of Honduran literature. In the first half of the twentieth century, the efforts of Rafael Heliodoro Valle (1891–1959), poet, journalist, historian, anthologist, and bibliophile, were significant in the appreciation and professionalization of Honduran letters. A writer and scholar of international stature, he compiled numerous important bibliographies and wrote serious analyses that have served scholars in their study of Honduran culture, among them, *Historia de la cultura hondureña* (*History of Honduran Culture*, published posthumously, 1981). A penchant for inclusive anthologies and wide-ranging histories has long characterized the work of Honduran literary scholars. Rómulo E. Durón (1865–1942), for example, collected the literature of Honduras of the nineteenth century in *Honduras literaria*

(*Literary Honduras*, 1896 and 1899); Manuel Luna Mejía's *Indice general de poesía hondureña* (*General Index of Honduran Poetry*, 1961) contains well over 1,000 pages of poetry; and *Literatura hondureña y su proceso generacional* (*Honduran Literature and Its Generational Process*, 1987) by José Francisco Martínez begins its survey of national literature with the Maya of Copan.

Contemporary Honduras' most prolific and distinguished literary critic and historian, Helen Umaña (1942–) has contributed significantly to the understanding and appreciation of Honduran literature through her excellent critical studies, including *Literatura hondureña contemporánea* (*Contemporary Honduran Literature*, 1986) and *Narradoras hondureñas* (*Honduran Women Novelists*, 1990) and subsequently embarked on the astonishing project of documenting, summarizing and commenting on the Honduran novel, short story and poetry. Her three monumental volumes: *Panorama crítico del cuento hondureño, 1881–1999* (*Critical Survey of the Honduran Short Story*, 1888– 1999, 1999); *La palabra iluminada, el discurso poético en Honduras* (*The Illuminated Word, the Poetic Discourse of Honduras*, 1999); and *La novela hondureña* (*The Honduran Novel*, 2003) are encyclopedic surveys of the three major literary genres.

NOTES

1. There is little scholarship in English that illuminates Honduran literature. Honduran scholars, on the other hand, have produced numerous anthologies, histories, and analyses of their national literature. Many of these scholars and their works are cited in this chapter but special mention must be accorded the extraordinary contribution of contemporary critic and literary historian Helen Umaña, whose work has been a primary and most useful reference. The Internet now provides information, albeit brief, on many individual writers.

2. José Antonio Funes' *Froylán Turcios y el modernismo en Honduras* offers an excellent survey of Turcios' work and a description and analysis of the cultural context of modernism in Honduras.

Museum of National Identity, Tegucialpa. Courtesy of the author.

Street in San Juancito. Courtesy of the author.

View of Santa Lucía. Courtesy of the author.

Street scene in Pespire. Courtesy of *Honduras This Week*.

Reenactment of Garífuna landing on island of Roatan in 1797. AP Photo/Thomas Tomczyk.

Statue of Virgin of Suyapa, Honduras' patron saint. AP Photo/Esteban Felix.

Garífuna houses in Tornabé. Courtesy of *Honduras This Week*.

Gay rights march, San Pedro Sula. Courtesy of *Honduras This Week*.

The Honduran National University. Courtesy of *Honduras This Week*.

Lenca women preparing tortillas. Courtesy of *Honduras This Week*.

Honduras versus Costa Rica in a soccer game. Courtesy of *Honduras This Week*.

Aftermath of Hurricane Mitch, Comayaguela, 1998. Courtesy of *Honduras This Week*.

Students in traditional attire in Independence Day celebration, Tegucigalpa. AP Photo/Antonio Romero.

Lenca protest construction of El Tigre reservoir on Lempa River. AP Photo/Edgard Garrido.

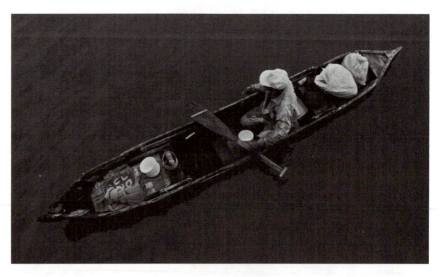

Fisherman in traditional boat, La Ceiba. AP Photo/Esteban Felix.

Author Roberto Castillo. Courtesy of the author.

The National Library, Tegucigalpa. Courtesy of *Honduras This Week*.

An affordable edition of Honduran authors. Courtesy of *Honduras This Week*.

Poet Roberto Sosa at poetry reading in New York. AP Photo/Joe Kohen.

Author Lety Elvir. Courtesy of *Honduras This Week*.

Regina Zelaya in her metalworking studio, San Juancito. Courtesy of the author.

Interior patio of the National Gallery of Art, Tegucigalpa. Courtesy of the author.

Black ceramic Lenca goddess statue. Courtesy of the author.

Wood-fired ceramic vessel. Courtesy of the author.

Melvin Bodden, artist from Roatán. Courtesy of the author.

Artist and author Guillermo Yuscarán at his home in Santa Lucía. Courtesy of *Honduras This Week*.

Mirian Sevilla Rojas, writer, director, and producer of children's theater, Danlí. Courtesy of the author.

6

Traditional Artisanry

HISTORY OF ARTISANRY IN HONDURAS

THE PRE-COLUMBIAN indigenous cultures of the area that is today Honduras were mainly of two types: chiefdoms and nomadic tribes. Chiefdoms, such as the Maya and the Lenca, existed mainly in southern and western sections of the country; their economy was based on agriculture, with maize being their primary crop; and priests, temples, and ceremonial artifacts were a central part of their religion. Artisanry was highly developed in these societies, particularly cotton textiles, ceramics, basketry, and stone work. The numerous and very beautiful stellae of Copán are among the most sophisticated examples of their work. The cultures of the eastern section of the country, on the other hand, among them the Paya, Pech, and Tolupán, were nomadic or semi-nomadic; they relied on hunting, fishing, and gathering; their agriculture was minimal and consisted mainly of tropical root vegetables such as manioc. Their artisanry was more limited and less elaborate. They used cotton to make fabric and, although the warm, wet climate required less clothing, they were adept at fiber art for the fabrication of hammocks, baskets, and bags and fashioned tools and culinary implements from wood, clay, and stone.

Much of the information in this chapter has been synthesized from the following two sources: Rápalo Flores, Oscar. "Diagnóstico de la artesanía de Honduras. Tegucigalpa: UNESCO and IHAH, 2004; and Castegnaro de Foletti, Alessandra. *Viaje por el universo artesanal de Honduras.* Tegucigalpa: PROPAITH, 2002.

As European and African influence resulted in the eventual predominance of a mestizo or mixed racial and ethnic identity, many indigenous communities experienced the gradual loss or transformation of their traditional beliefs and practices. The mestizo or ladino population adopted and adapted many aspects of the local indigenous ways while retaining some European and African traditions, practices, and beliefs. The materials and techniques for the weaving of *petates* or sleeping mats, for example, remains essentially unchanged today. The fabrication of ceramic vessels, on the other hand, has changed significantly in some areas, where the potter's wheel and kiln were introduced and men began to practice this craft traditionally practiced by women. Another important change has been the loss or transformation of the spiritual or magical context in which indigenous artisans worked. The infusion of new materials, techniques, and lifestyles opened the door to new popular art forms as well, such as metalwork, woodwork, hatmaking, silversmithing, and saddlery. During the colonial period, the construction and decoration of Catholic churches created the demand for skilled craftspeople such as masons, woodworkers, sculptors, and embroiderers. In time, certain towns or regions came to be known as centers that specialized in one or another traditional craft. Santa Barbara in western Honduras became known for its fine straw hats; various towns in the south produced high-quality saddles and equestrian supplies; the department of Yoro was famous for its basketry; and Comayagua, in central Honduras, was famous for its tiles and ceramics.

Isolation, geographic as well as economic, is clearly one of the strongest determining factors in the preservation of traditional cultures and their corresponding artisanry. In those still relatively isolated areas of Honduras such as the mountainous western region, northern Olancho, and La Mosquitia, handcrafts continue to be primarily utilitarian and the unit of production is the individual and the family. Ceramic vessels and cookware, wooden and metal tools, fiber hats, hammocks, mats and baskets, wooden and fiber furniture, and musical instruments are made for domestic use and for local market distribution.

These areas also boast small-scale workshops whose employees usually have learned their craft through apprenticeship to older, skilled artisans. These workshops produce decorative articles for sale in souvenir and craft shops to a national and international clientele. Furniture, wood carvings on doors, chests, and boxes, and painted ceramics are among the most popular products of these workshops. Other items include the so-called souvenir or commemorative ceramics, which are a wide variety of objects exchanged among friends and relatives to mark special occasions such as weddings, anniversaries, graduations, and baptisms; dolls, flowers, and other decorative objects made from dried corn husks; and stone sculptures, especially replicas of archaeological objects from Mayan ruins.

Modern methods of communication and transportation, the unrelenting push to develop rural areas and to extract natural resources, the shifting demographics of rural to urban national migration as well as international migration, an evolving gender awareness, and an expanding tourist presence have all contributed to a lessening of the isolation of indigenous and rural communities and in many cases the transformation of the role of handcrafts as well as the materials and techniques employed.

In recognition of the importance of traditional arts and crafts to Honduran national identity, Articles 172 and 173 of the Constitution explicitly refer to these cultural manifestations as part of Honduras' cultural heritage and place them under the protection of the State. In response to the impending loss of traditional knowledge and crafts in indigenous and rural communities, the Honduran government created in the late 1970s the Center for Industrial Development (Centro de Desarrollo Industrial [CDI]), which made loans available to artisans, opened schools to teach traditional crafts in rural areas outside Tegucigalpa, and set up a permanent exhibition space in the town of Valle de Angeles, 22 kilometers from the capital. Oversight of these programs was transferred to the National Association of Artisans of Honduras (Asociación Nacional de Artesanos de Honduras [ANAH]) in the late 1980s, which, according to a 2003 census, has more than 900 members. In 1996 the Ministry of Culture, Arts and Sports, in conjunction with the Honduran Institute of Anthropology and History, created the Program to Rescue and Promote Indigenous and Traditional Crafts (Programa de Rescate y Promoción de la Artesanía Indígena y Tradicional de Honduras [PROPAITH]), charged with researching and reviving the traditional techniques, designs, and worldviews of indigenous and mestizo communities. PROPAITH has been instrumental in organizing and supporting seven cooperatives, among them an association of potters with more than 150 ceramicists located in diverse regions of the country and cooperatives of Miskito and Tawahka women who produce articles made from the bark of the tuno tree. PROPAITH also operates stores where Honduran crafts are sold, at Copán Ruins, the Fort of San Fernando in Omoa, and the archaeological site at Los Naranjos near Lake Yojoa.

Although many craftspeople still learn their skills from family members or local masters, there is also currently one educational institution in Honduras, the National Institute for Professional Formation (Instituto Nacional de Formación Profesional [INFOP]), founded in 1970, where students can study the techniques of woodworking, basketry, ceramics and leatherwork. In addition to practical, hands-on classes, the institute offers instruction in small business management to provide artisans with the financial and legal skills necessary to set up and run their own shops. The institute is comprised of five schools, all of which are located in small cities in areas known for their traditional crafts: Valle de Angeles, La Paz, Sabanagrande, Gracias, and Trujillo. The majority of the students are men and women between the ages of fifteen and eighteen, from various regions of the country.

The support and intervention of official government agencies from France, Spain, and Sweden and the activities of national and international NGOs such as Aid to Artisans, which appreciate the potential economic role that traditional handcrafts can play in alleviating poverty and unemployment, has led to the increased production of decorative rather than utilitarian crafts and the relearning of traditional techniques or in some cases the introduction of new techniques and the use of locally available natural materials. Dependence on market tastes and demands can lead to mass production and an accompanying degeneration of quality; it can also encourage increased care and artistry as artisans compete.

Two crafts that continue to use some of the traditional natural materials, procedures for gathering and preparing the materials, and methods of fabrication from the colonial and even pre-colonial past are ceramics and basketry. Hand-fashioned clay objects fired in open pits are made by the Lenca of southwestern and central Honduras, whereas the Tolupan, Pech, Tawahka, and Mosquito of the northeastern region employ traditional fibers and techniques to make rope, hammocks, and other items for domestic as well as commercial use. The Garífuna of the North Coast still make traditional items for the preparation of yucca (manioc) and drums and masks for ritual religious use.

Experimentation with sustainable practices, such as the fabrication of handmade paper using materials such as byproducts of the processing of coffee and tobacco and the use of recycled fabrics in various forms, has become increasingly popular.

A growing number of women have become involved in making marketable crafts, which allows for flexible and part-time employment.

The following section describes the most common handcrafts today in Honduras.

CONTEMPORARY ARTISANRY

Textiles

Handmade weaving is done only in a very limited area of western Honduras, possibly the result of proximity to the rich textile traditions of neighboring Guatemala, where cotton and woolen items are woven by women on backstrap looms. Embroidery is a common handcraft among women in rural areas. They decorate pillow covers, aprons, napkins, and other articles for domestic use with floral and avian motifs and sentimental phrases. Some women now embroider on T-shirts, men's *guayaberas,* and children's clothing for the tourist market.

Ceramics

Ceramic production is possibly the most common handcraft today in Honduras. Traditional methods of extraction and preparation of the clay as well as the shaping, firing, and decorating of the objects are still used among some indigenous groups, particularly the Lenca. Depending on the nature of the local clay, black or red (terra cotta) objects are made entirely by hand, without the aid of a potter's wheel, either by starting with a circular or cylindrical mass of clay in which the potter forms a concave opening that is then enlarged to the desired size and shape; or using a coiling technique whereby successive rows of clay are joined. The surfaces of the object are worked first with a rough tool such as a corncob or an *ocote* pine branch and then smoothed with a finer utensil such as a *zapote* (sapodilla) seed or a river stone. Some potters fire their ware by placing the objects on the ground and covering them with wood that is then burned. The pieces are hardened and scorched and retain a characteristic blackened exterior, particularly on the upper edges. Some potters use outdoor stucco ovens with large openings and chimneys to fire their ware. The style of these ovens varies from region to region.

Many contemporary ceramic artisans use a variety of other techniques to shape, fire, and finish their ware. Potters' wheels and plaster molds are now widely used among mestizo artisans although the traditional hand-shaping and coiling methods are also still employed. Commercial propane-fired kilns have replaced traditional ovens in some cases. Because much of this pottery is destined for urban markets and souvenir shops, artisans now employ a variety of glazes, incisions, overlay, and painting techniques to produce the desired decorative effects. Among the most commonly produced ceramic objects are vases, flowerpots, dinnerware, objects for nativity scenes displayed during the Christmas season, and religious statues. An interesting example of ceramics inspired by traditional materials and designs is the black pottery from the southwestern region. Contemporary artisans use local clay to create a wide variety of both utilitarian objects such as candleholders, trivets, and dinnerware, as well as decorative pieces such as animal sculptures. Whereas the traditional pottery was all black, artisans now also use white paint on the black surfaces to create simple, bold geometric designs suggestive of pre-Hispanic glyphs.

Woodwork

Working with wood is a time-honored and respected craft in Honduras. Although deforestation and the exporting of prized hardwoods has created obvious problems for them, woodworkers, carpenters, cabinetmakers, furniture makers, and wood sculptors continue to exercise their craft. Items range from rustic spoons, bowls, and children's toys to elaborately carved doors, chests, and room dividers. Common designs for these carvings are flora, fauna, rural landscapes, and motifs evocative of the Mayan culture of Copán. The local woods most prized for their durability and ease of use are oak, chestnut, mahogany, walnut, teak, lime, sycamore, applewood, and pine. Some of the country's finest woodwork comes from Valle de Angeles, where skilled artisans carve complex designs from mahogany and cedar.

Fiber Arts and Basketry

This handcraft is practiced primarily in rural areas where there is an abundance and variety of palms, grasses, and reeds. Items made from palm (*Sabal mexicana martius*) include baskets, hats, cradles, bags, and fans. Palm trees are planted near the home and the fronds or branches gathered as needed.

Reeds (*Cardulovica palmata*) may be gathered in the wild but it is common for commercial growers of this plant to cut and bundle it for sale to craftspeople. The fibers are used naturally or colored with aniline dyes or with dyes from Brazilwood, dyewood (*sacatinta*), or holly (*ilex*) trees. Weavers fashion reed baskets of all sizes, shapes and uses as well as floor mats, placemats, and hats.

The fibers of the henequen plant (*Furcracea cabuya*) are another popular natural material used for making such useful articles as rope, twine, hammocks, and fishing nets. Some artisans have turned to synthetic materials to weave these items, perhaps for their brilliant colors and durability.

The department of Santa Barbara is known for its well-made *petates* or floor mats. They customarily use fibers of tule (*Iperus canus*), although in some areas henequen is used. A Lenca artisans' cooperative from Santa Barbara has diversified its inventory to include a variety of items such as handbags, wallets, cushions, placemats, and wall hangings.

Two indigenous groups from northeastern Honduras, the Tawahka and the Miskito, traditionally used the bark of the tuno tree (*Amata*) to make fabric for clothing. Although they no longer wear such rustic attire, they continue to work with this natural material to make decorative and artistic articles for the international market. In the 1970s, Moravian missionaries taught the women collage techniques so they could make cards and wall hangings from tuno bark. In the 1990s the Honduran government program charged with conserving and promoting indigenous and traditional crafts (PROPAITH) worked with Tawahka and Miskito women, encouraging them to create new designs for their craft that incorporate scenes from indigenous daily life, local flora and fauna and spiritual and mythical symbols and beings from their unique religious tradition. The old-time methods of gathering and processing the bark are employed. The bark is stripped from the tuno tree, then scraped and cleaned. Women beat it with mallets to achieve the desired thickness. The pieces are dyed using local plants, such as manioc root for yellow, *kerosín* bark, which produces brown and guava tree (*guayabillo*) bark for black.

In the villages of Tule and Infiernitos in the municipality of Sabanagrande as well as in the municipalities of Nueva Celilac and La Venta in the department of Santa Barbara, women work with corn husks and seeds to confect Christmas decorations, flowers, dolls, articles for nativity scenes, and many other items. After husking the cobs, they boil the leaves and sometimes color them using aniline dyes. Their work has a rustic quality as a result of the nature of the materials, that belies the high level of detail and care that goes into the articles. Their dolls and figurines are particularly engaging. Children gather the seeds that are used in the confections, particularly cashew (*marañón*), St. Peter's tears (*lagrimas de San Pedro*), and deer eye (*ojo de venado*).

The Garífuna of the North Coast and the Bay islands use vines, palm, bamboo, coconut shells, sea shells and turtle shells in the fabrication of baskets, hats, bags, musical instruments, and, of particular interest, articles used in the traditional preparation of manioc.

Leather Craft

The use of leather to make equestrian articles, known as *talabartería*, has been common since colonial times, particularly in southern Honduras. Practical items such as saddles, chaps, saddlebags, and reins are usually made from cowhide, although the skin of pigs and goats is used as well. In small-scale, traditional operations the hides are cured using lime and dyed with bark containing tannic acids from trees such as *nance, nacascolo,* and mangrove. As market opportunities expand, leather crafters have diversified and one can find finely made wallets, handbags, shoes, portfolios, and numerous other goods in local shops and also for export.

Stone Carving

In western Honduras, particularly near Copán Ruins, artisans sculpt the same kind of soft, white, locally mined stone used by the ancient Maya in their beautiful stellae. Tourists who visit Copán purchase stone replicas of Mayan altars, masks, stellae, and carved animals. Market demand has injected new life into this ancient art and local artisans create an increasingly diverse and appealing variety of articles, including jewelry, for which they also use jade and marble. A harder, green stone is used for large sculptures for hotels, banks, and public buildings.

Artisans in the municipality of Langue in southern Honduras are known for their carvings made from a soft stone known as *toba* or travertine (tufa) and from green jadeite. They also make traditional grinding stones from a local volcanic tufa.

Coral and Tortoise Shell

The use of sea shells, coral, and tortoise shell or *carey* is common among residents of coastal communities, particularly the Garífuna of the North Coast and the Bay Islands, who make a variety of jewelry and hair ornaments for personal use as well as for the tourist market.

Metalwork

Some very interesting and ingenious uses of zinc, tin, and a variety of recycled metals can be seen in markets throughout Honduras. Everything from birdcages to coffee pots, with all the quirks and imperfections one can expect from one-off production, are fashioned by hand for domestic use. Larger scale production of such items as picture frames, crucifixes, and Christmas tree ornaments can now be found in souvenir and gift shops.

7

The Visual Arts

THE VISUAL OR pictorial arts, whether in the caves of Yaguacire, on ceramic vases from Copán, in Catholic Churches, or on canvas, are art forms that have flourished in Honduras. Honduran art historians have discerned four distinct stages in the ongoing evolution of this art form, the various stages and styles corresponding to significant historical eras: the centuries preceding the arrival of the Spanish in the early sixteenth century; the almost 300 years that Honduras was part of the Spanish empire in the new world (c.1550–1829); the early years as an independent nation (1829–1875); and the period following the initiation of liberal reforms (1876–the present).[1]

ARCHAEOLOGY AND PRE-HISPANIC ART

Archaeology in Honduras is a field of study with many discoveries yet to be made. At the present time, Honduran universities do not train students to work as professional anthropologists or archaeologists, although some related courses are offered. Because of the lack of trained professionals, coupled with the scarcity of public funds for archaeological research and excavation, much of the work done in the country has been carried out by foreign archaeologists and funded by foreign universities and international organizations. Foreign interest in Honduran archaeology began with the discovery of the Mayan ruins at Copán by John Lloyd Stephens and Frederick Catherwood in 1839 and the ensuing publication of *Incidents of Travel in Central America, Chiapas and Yucatan* (1841). Stephens' account of their adventures, enhanced by

Catherwood's meticulously rendered illustrations was wildly successful in the United States and England, introducing what has become the most studied of the ancient Maya cities.

Although a vast amount of research and on-site study has been carried out at the Maya ruins of Copán and the sculptures and the paintings on ceramics found there have been described and analyzed, very little field work was done in other parts of Honduras until recently.[2] Although it may be that much of the pictorial art from the cultures that once lived in the area that was to become Honduras has not survived the effects of migrations, wars, cultural invasions, and climate, some examples do exist and point to the possibilities for fresh interpretations of the indigenous past as more evidence becomes available and more pre-Hispanic artwork is unearthed with each new archaeological project. One of the most ambitious and exciting of the recent excavations began in 1978 in the Sula Valley, directed initially by John Henderson, Eugenia Robinson, and Rosemary Joyce. Subsequent stages of the project, which continues to be carried out with the collaboration of the Honduran Institute of Anthropology and History (IHAH), have unearthed the oldest ceramic collection found to date in Honduras, believed to be from approximately 1,500 B.C. Excavations at Yarumela in the Comayagua Valley were previously believed to be the oldest site of ceramic production, dating from 1,400 to 1,000 B.C. The Los Naranjos Archeological Park in the vicinity of Lake Yojoa in central Honduras comprises a number of sites that indicate settlements from 800 B.C. to 1,200 A.D. In the 1930s various archaeological explorations sponsored by the Smithsonian Institution, the Museum of the American Indian, and the American Museum of Natural History explored the Bay Islands and La Mosquitia. Unfortunately, these efforts did not continue to be funded, but they did establish a basis for further research. In 1995 James Brady and George Hasemann discovered the Talgua Caves in eastern Honduras. Additional explorations in the 1990s were the discovery of Cueva del Gigante (Giant's Cave) in southwestern Honduras by Hasemann and Lara Pinto and an extensive inventory and description of rock art by art historian Alison McKittrick.

The IHAH, founded in 1952, has official jurisdiction over archaeological research, funding and legislation. During its first years of operation it dedicated its efforts almost exclusively to the Mayan site at Copán, which, along with the entire Copán Valley was declared a World Heritage Site by UNESCO in 1980 and a Honduran National Monument in 1982. Over the years countless valuable pieces from Copán as well as other sites have ended up in private collections both in Honduras and abroad, and in museums outside the country. As of 1982 the Honduran Constitution establishes national ownership of all anthropological, archaeological, historic, and artistic treasures, thus legally ensuring that these artifacts stay in the country. Illegal art trafficking may well continue, but this legislation reflects the government's recognition of the worth of its cultural heritage. Hondurans have long complained that their art treasures deserve to be displayed and cared for and it seems that this is finally coming about.

Art Museums

In 2006 the beautiful and stately Villa Roy mansion in Barrio Abajo, one of Tegucigalpa's oldest historic neighborhoods, was converted into the Museo de la Identidad Nacional (Museum of National Identity). Its exhibits are organized in three thematic units: geography, history, and ethnic or cultural identity. The Galería Nacional de Arte (National Art Gallery), located in the historic center of Tegucigalpa in the Plaza La Merced, opened to the public in 1996. It is owned and operated by the nonprofit Foundation in Support of Art and Culture (Fundación Pro Arte y Cultura [FUNDARTE]). Housed in the beautiful old building dating from 1654 that was originally the Convento de Nuestra Señora La Merced (Our Lady of Mercy Convent) and later was home to Honduras's first university, FUNDARTE has the most complete collection of Honduran art in the country. A tour of the gallery includes pre-Hispanic rock art and ceramics, religious art from the colonial period, and an excellent collection of representative works by many of Honduras' best-known artists of the nineteenth and twentieth centuries. Other museums that display pre-Hispanic art and pieces of archaeological interest are the Museo de Antropología (Museum of Anthropology) of San Pedro Sula, the Museo de Arqueología (Museum of Archaeology) in Comayagua, the Museo de Arqueología e Historia de las Islas de la Bahía (The Bay Islands Museum of Archaeology and History), and two museums in Copán Ruinas, one at the archaeological site and the other in town.

Rock Art

Painting, etching, and engraving on rock surfaces is one of the oldest forms of art and one of the most likely to survive the ravages of time. Honduran rock art consists of decorated lithic formations such as caves, rock shelters in hillsides and cliffs, and rock walls, particularly beside riverbanks. They may be petroglyphs, engravings carved into the rock surface with stone tools or pictographs or paintings executed on the rock with mineral paints or charcoal. Motifs are typically anthropomorphic, zoomorphic, geometric, and stylized designs resembling elements of nature such as plants, the sun, and the moon.

Between 1993 and 1995, the IHAH carried out the first systematic rock art documentation in the history of Honduras, coordinated by art historian Alison McKittrick. The project was reactivated in 2004. Of the more than fifty rock art sites that have been documented, thirty-seven have petroglyphs and twelve have pictographs. Most of the sites have not been thoroughly studied, in part because they are located in places difficult to access. In mountainous regions, they are typically carved or painted on rocks that form the walls, floor, or ceiling of a shelter such as a cave or a ledge against a cliff. Archaeologists and art historians speculate that indigenous peoples perceived caves as entrances to the underworld and may have been destinations of pilgrimages and venues for sacred rituals and ceremonial offerings. In the wet lowlands of La Mosquitia, on the other hand, there are petroglyphs on rocks along the banks of navigable rivers. Intriguing examples of pictographs are the human, animal, and geometric figures executed with white, red, and orange mineral paints in the caves at Yaguacire just outside of Tegucigalpa. There are as yet undeciphered petroglyphs at Ayasta in four rock shelters in the dry highlands south of the capital and numerous human and animal pictographs including red handprints in the Cueva del Gigante outside the town of Azacualpa near the Salvadoran border. The Talgua Cave near the Talgua River in Olancho has black and red line drawings and two frontal faces. The numerous and diverse petroglyphs in La Mosquitia, such as the animal and plant figures at Walpa Ulban Sirpe in the Río Plátano Biosphere Reserve, offer symbolic clues to the life and beliefs of this region's early inhabitants. The Cueva Pintada (Painted Cave) in the department of La Paz is the most complex rock art site yet found in Honduras. According to Dr. McKittrick, its pictographs and engravings are organized in seven different panels. White, ochre, red, blue, and black mineral colors were used to paint both realistic and stylized anthropomorphic and zoomorphic figures and geometric images. One of the petroglyphs of Santa Rosa de Tenampua in the department of Comayagua is a plumed serpent that resembles a relief in Copán.

Ceramic Art

The most elaborate paintings on ceramic have been found at the Mayan site of Copán. The designs and motifs include quetzals, serpents, lizards, frogs, and other animals found in the high, wet natural environment of Copán as well as the sophisticated, highly stylized human profiles believed to represent their political and religious leaders. Many of the impressive ceramic pieces probably had religious or ceremonial uses. It is likely that this same level of artistry produced mural paintings and codices similar to those found in other parts of the Mayan empire, but no examples have been found to date in Honduras.

ART FROM THE COLONIAL PERIOD

The influence of the European tradition began to appear in the second half of the sixteenth century with the arrival of Catholic priests. As churches, convents, and monasteries were constructed, the structures themselves as well as the sculptures, ceramics, textiles, metalwork, and paintings that adorned them were often imported from Spain. The first paintings identified as being by local artists, some of which can be found in churches, museums, and private collections, date from the late seventeenth and early eighteenth centuries. Groups of artists would travel from parish to parish to decorate churches, convents, monasteries, and cathedrals, which explains the similarities of style and motif one can observe in numerous churches in the Comayagua Valley and the central department of Francisco Morazán. Arguably the most interesting and original religious paintings were those done by anonymous artists. Unsigned works included decorative paintings on plaster and stucco church walls and ceilings that incorporated designs inspired by the natural world such as suns, moons, stars, and flowers. A beautiful example of decorative work can be observed on the arch of the Capilla del Santísimo Sacramento (Chapel of the Most Holy Sacrament) in the seventeenth-century church of Comayagua, where an anthropomorphic sun with sixteen rays extending from its face forms the center of a design that incorporates a floral motif reminiscent of eight giant sunflowers alternating with eight geometric column-like rays.

One artist who distinguished himself from the ranks of anonymous artists in the late colonial period was José Miguel Gómez. He is considered by Honduran art historians to be the first professional native-born Honduran artist. Gómez was born around 1720 in Tegucigalpa. After studying with master artists in Comayagua and Guatemala, he returned to Comayagua, which was then the capital of Honduras, where he accepted a commission by the wealthy Araque family to execute a painting of San José Calasanz. The bishop of Comayagua was impressed with his work and asked him to paint a series of canvasses for the cathedral of Comayagua, including "La Sagrada Familia" and "La Santísima Trinidad." His fame spread and soon the archbishop of Tegucigalpa contracted him to direct the decoration of the new cathedral under construction there. One can still view his frescoes of the four evangelists, Matthew, Mark, Luke, and John, which adorn the cupola. He went on to decorate the chapel that houses the statue of Honduras' patron saint, the Virgin of Suyapa. He died in 1805, poor and forgotten.[3]

ART OF AN INDEPENDENT NATION

During the period of transition from Spanish colonial rule to the formation of the independent nation of Honduras, there was little demand for religious art. Influenced by the ideas and ideals that inspired the French and the American revolutions, the newly formed government closed convents and churches and expelled religious orders. With their powerful religious patrons gone, artists began to rely on wealthy secular patrons to commission paintings and purchase their work. The *criollo* upper classes, however, were inclined to look to Europe for the romantic landscapes in vogue at the time.

A popular art form of the nineteenth century was portraiture. Well-to-do social and political figures often commissioned reputable artists from outside Honduras such as Nicaraguan Toribio Xerez and Francisco Cabrera of Guatemala to paint their portraits. In the second half of the nineteenth century the Honduran artist Toribio Torres painted portraits of various bishops of Comayagua. Responding to the demand for portraits in rural areas, itinerant Honduran artists traveled from hacienda to hacienda, painting family portraits. The works by these artists have a fresh authenticity often lacking in the likenesses executed by more technically sophisticated portraitists.

As Spain's monopoly on trade with its New World colonies was no longer an impediment, travelers from Europe and North America found numerous reasons to explore South and Central America. They were artists in search of exotic landscapes to paint, archeologists interested in exploring ancient ruins, representatives of transportation and mining companies charged with surveying unmapped territories, and representatives of foreign governments hoping to replace Spain's interests with their own. Some of these travelers wrote entertaining and informative accounts of their experiences accompanied by invaluable drawings, maps, and descriptions of people and customs.

Two examples are the aforementioned John Lloyd Stephens, whose illustrator Frederick Catherwood produced masterful drawings of the landscape, structures, and sculptures of Copán and William Wells, an American who spent a year traveling by horse and mule throughout Honduras and published, in 1854, *Explorations and Adventures in Honduras,* comprising sketches of travel in the gold regions of Olancho and a review of the history and general resources of Central America with original maps and numerous illustrations. Wells himself drew the maps and Honduran artist Sotero Lazo provided fifty-seven pen-and-ink sketches of landscapes, villages, and scenes from daily life.

During the last decades of the nineteenth century, known as the Period of Liberal Reform, under the guidance of President Marco Aurelio Soto and his secretary of state, Ramón Rosa, the country confirmed its commitment to representative democracy, encouraged immigration, and opened the door to foreign investment. Peruvians, Cubans, and Nicaraguans came to live in Tegucigalpa, French settled in Comayagua, British in the northeastern section of the country, and Lebanese on the north coast. This atmosphere of openness and international exchange inspired wealthy Hondurans to travel abroad, especially to the cultural centers of Havana and Paris, where they purchased the art-deco lithographs then fashionable and had their portraits painted by foreign artists.

THE TWENTIETH CENTURY

Arts Education

The first instance of formal arts education was the Academy of Fine Arts, opened by the Spanish educator of Rumanian extraction, Thomas Mur in Tegucigalpa in 1890. This private academy offered classes is watercolor, drawing, embroidery, and declamation for women as well as painting, sculpture, architecture, anatomy, and art history and theory for men. As can be seen from these class offerings, women's participation in the fine arts at this time was limited to adornment or decoration. Watercolors were thought to be more appropriate than oils for the fair sex and women were encouraged to excel at those art forms that would add color and comfort to the home, such as embroidery, landscapes, and copies of portraits. Modesty required that men and women not take anatomy classes together and history, theory, and art criticism were considered masculine fields, so women's access to art as a profession was severely limited.

Perhaps because it did not receive government funding and had to rely exclusively on tuition, the Academy closed its doors after a few years. One of the Academy's graduates, Antonio Obando, introduced graphic design to Honduran advertising. The relevance of painting receded at this time as photography and reproducible graphic arts captured the public's attention. Among Honduras' first photographers were Juan T. Aguirre and Manuel Ugarte. Newspapers and magazines from the first decades of the twentieth century offer excellent examples of the skills and inclinations of Honduras' illustrators and graphic artists.

The National School of Fine Arts

The Honduran government historically has been slow to recognize the importance of financial support for the fine arts. The founding of the National School of Fine Arts (Escuela Nacional de Bellas Artes) in 1940 was therefore a national commitment of great importance for the arts. Previous to its founding, with the exception of the brief life of Mur's Academy, there was no professional-level academy in the country, so individual artists either were self-taught or some received funding to study abroad. This was the case with four talented young men who became the most prominent and influential Honduran artists of the first half of the twentieth century. Pablo Zelaya Sierra (1896–1933) studied in Costa Rica and Spain; Confucio Montes de Oca (1896–1925) lived and traveled in France and Italy for six years; and Carlos Zúniga Figueroa (1884–1964) and Max Euceda (1891–1987) both studied in Spain. Although it was stimulating to travel abroad to Guatemala, Costa Rica, Cuba, Mexico, or Europe to study, this opportunity was of course not available to everyone and much potential talent certainly went undeveloped. Even those who went abroad sometimes found that the financial assistance promised to them did not materialize. Such was the case with Montes de Oca, for example, who stopped receiving his promised aid shortly after arriving in Paris. But he was determined to remain in Europe to study art and returned to Honduras only after extended economic deprivation caused his health to deteriorate. Pablo Zelaya Sierra suffered a similar fate. It is noteworthy that all four returned to Honduras enthusiastic about their exposure to European art and eager not only to exercise their profession but also to teach what they had learned abroad to young artists. This desire went unrealized for Confucio Montes de Oca, who died just two months after returning from Italy, as well as for Pablo Zelaya Sierra, who died five months after his return from a twelve-year sojourn in Spain. Carlos Zúniga Figueroa, on the other hand, after studying in Madrid, opened an art academy in Tegucigalpa in 1934 where a number of young artists studied and Max Euceda, after studying in Spain thanks to a scholarship sponsored by the Spanish Embassy, went on to become a well-loved and influential teacher for many years at the National School of Fine Arts.

While the works of these four painters show the influence of the aesthetic movements popular in Europe at the time, including impressionism, realism, and cubism, one can also observe the predominance of Honduran themes in all but Montes de Oca. This syncretism is notable for example in Euceda's romantic and impressionistic Tegucigalpa street scenes and in the subtle geometry reminiscent of the early cubism of Cezanne in Zelaya Sierra's "Las monjas" (The Nuns) and "Mujer con huacal" (Woman with Gourd Bowl). Both Zúniga Figueroa and Euceda excelled in portraiture. Zúniga Figueroa painted individuals from all social classes and walks of life, including portraits of famous leaders of Honduran independence, such as one of Francisco Morazán, which for many years hung in the National Palace in Tegucigalpa, as well as of anonymous beggars and street people.

The importance of the founding of the National School of Fine Arts in 1940 cannot be underestimated, as young Honduran artists would now be able to study with excellent teachers right in Tegucigalpa. It is also significant that women were allowed to study at the National School and there were women on the faculty, thus opening the door for women to participate more fully and professionally as artists. The school was founded largely as a result of the efforts of Arturo López Rodezno, who had studied painting and drawing in Havana and mural painting in Paris. Its beginnings were modest: two small rooms, a few easels, some brushes, and tubes of paint. In its initial conception its goal was to provide students with a minimal theoretical and historical background and to prepare them technically to work in various art forms such as drawing, painting, ceramics, woodworking, and sculpture, including religious sculpture. In 1975 the school's mission was expanded to include teacher preparation and in 1983 it began to offer a complete three-year course of study leading to an undergraduate degree in graphic arts. Under the leadership of Juan Domingo Torres, an active extension program was initiated in 1978 whereby art classes are offered to primary school teachers and also to children. The children's art classes have been very successful; over the years Honduran children have won numerous distinctions in international art shows. The greatest difficulty the school has consistently faced is a meager operating budget. In September 2006, students and faculty joined to demonstrate on the steps of the National Congress. They complained that the government's subsidy is inadequate and cannot provide even the basic materials. Given the lack of art supplies, the poorly maintained physical plant and the low faculty salaries, the number of excellent artists who have studied at Honduras' National School of Fine Arts is truly impressive.

López Rodezno, the school's founder, was himself an excellent muralist. He was inspired by the mural movement popular in Mexico in the 1930s and 1940s and by the paintings and sculptures at Bonampak and Copán as well as by Honduran popular culture. His murals have graced the walls of the National School of Fine Arts, the Banco Atlántida (Atlantida Bank), the Duncan Maya Restaurant, and numerous other large, public spaces. His monumental 1948 "Mural de la producción económica en Honduras" (Mural of Economic Production in Honduras) is currently part of the collection of the Museum of Honduran National Identity.

It has been typical since the 1940s for Honduran artists to begin their formation at the National School of Fine Arts and then go on for further study elsewhere, most commonly Spain and Italy. A few have chosen to pursue their careers outside of Honduras. Notable among this group are Moisés Becerra (1926–), Julio Visquerra (1945–), and Gregorio Sabillón (1945–). After teaching at the National School of Fine Arts for several years, Becerra returned to Italy in 1961and established an art gallery in Milan. It is interesting that being far from his native country has inspired him to focus his work on the land and people he left; in works such as "El gallo muerto" (The Dead Cock) and "El Xique" (xique is a traditional folk dance) he recreates scenes from popular culture with a tender nostalgia tempered by the flattening effect of cubist-inspired geometric lines and shapes. He returned to Honduras in 1995. In 1968, Gregorio Sabillón moved to Barcelona, where, until his recent return to Tegucigalpa, he was an active and prolific participant in the art scene, with numerous solo and collective shows to his credit. His symbolic and surrealistic portraits are suffused with a graceful and ethereal light that lends a charmed atmosphere to his figures, who are often accompanied by unexpected objects,

surroundings or attire, creating a complex mood at once contemplative, eso-
teric, and ironic. Examples of his unique vision are "La Madona del huevo"
(Madonna with Egg) and "Múltiple Femenino" (Woman Multiplied). Julio
Visquerra also lived and worked in Barcelona for many years. Like Sabillón,
he creates figures of haunting mystery, although his subjects are more mythical. His characteristic use of fruits and vegetables as structural elements as well
as adornment lends a sensual and unsettling quality to his work. He currently
lives in Honduras, where he has opened the Galería Sixtina (Sixtina Gallery)
in the picturesque town of Valle de Angeles. The gallery hosts exhibits of the
works of young Honduran artists as well as other cultural events such as concerts and book presentations.

Primitive and Naïf Art

No description of Honduran art of the twentieth century would be complete without the story of the man who for some observers is the quintessential Honduran artist. José Antonio Velásquez was born in the town of Caridad
in southern Honduras, near the Salvadoran border, in 1906.[4] At the age of
eighteen he went to Tela on the North Coast in search of work and there he
learned to be a barber. Three years later he moved to Tegucigalpa, where he
studied to be a telegraph operator. The telegraph company sent him to San
Antonio de Oriente, a quiet village not far from his birthplace. Between running the telegraph office and cutting people's hair he managed to find time
to paint landscapes and scenes of village life in San Antonio. In 1943, he
met William Popenoe, the director of the nearby El Zamorano Agricultural
School, who hired him to be the school's barber. When Mr. and Mrs. Popenoe
saw his paintings they were convinced that they were the work of a true primitivist. They began to supply him with materials and organized an exhibit of his
work at the school. With this initial appreciation of his work as inspiration,
Velásquez devoted himself to his painting and moved with his family to Tegucigalpa where he sold the occasional painting, although his ingenuous scenes
that always included a church, whitewashed stucco houses with tiled roofs,
a black-robed village priest, a dog, and a tidy background with meticulously
rendered trees and an always blue sky, did not sell well in Honduras. It was not
until 1954, when the Popenoes organized an exhibit of his work at the Pan-
American Union in Washington, DC and he became internationally known,
that Hondurans begin to take notice of this quiet and unassuming artist who
never took an art lesson. In 1971, Shirley Temple Black made a documentary
film about the artist and his village. He died in Tegucigalpa in 1983. It is ironic
that the unique and absolutely recognizable style of Velásquez's painting has
spawned countless imitators. Tegucigalpa's markets and the sidewalks around
some of its luxury hotels are lined with canvases that depict scenes of peaceful

villages nestled in perfect hills under a tranquil blue sky. Some of them even include a small black dog and a black-robed priest. But in fact this is the image of Honduras that sells: a rural, preindustrial Honduras, picturesque and Catholic.

Among the numerous practitioners of the primitivist style today Roque Zelaya (1958–) stands out for his exquisitely detailed landscapes and scenes of everyday Honduran life. Zelaya grew up in southern Honduras and worked as a rural schoolteacher before devoting himself full time to his painting. He moved to Tegucigalpa in 1976 where he was assisted and encouraged by a number of artists associated with the Galería Leo. The following year the gallery organized an exhibit of his work, which is now widely recognized and appreciated both within Honduras and internationally. His paintings are luminous, colorful depictions of festivals, weddings, outings, markets, and lively street scenes. In 2007, the Museum of Honduran National Identity exhibited a retrospective of his work in their main gallery.

Two self-taught artists from the North Coast are currently adding their unique visions to the repertoire of Honduran primitivist painting. Virginia Castillo, who signs her work "Virgie," was born in La Ceiba and has spent her life in the Caribbean cultural environment of the North Coast and the Bay Islands, where, as she says, "I just simply look out the window and paint what I see." She is self-taught and uses whatever materials are available, such as oils, watercolors, fibers, and ink. Her work is colorful, strong, nostalgic, and full of affection for her world and her people. Her subjects include portraits of Garífuna people and culture, tropical nature, and appealing semi-abstract compositions that combine bold representations of flora and fauna with an artistic vision rooted in an obvious sensual delight in color and form. Some of her most appealing works depict the many shapes and faces of Caribbean women and situate them in a mythic tropical environment. In her work "Dos Mujeres" (Two Women), for example, two brown-skinned female bathers assume dream-like dancer poses as they appear to emerge from lush vegetation reminiscent of both Cezanne and Cuban artist Wilfredo Lam. Her work is shown at Waves of Art Gallery in West End on the island of Roatán in the Bay Islands.

Roatán is also home to Melvin Bodden. He was born in La Ceiba and after working on the docks for the fruit companies for many years he moved to Roatán, where he lives in a simple wooden one-room house and devotes himself to wood carving and painting. His home itself is a work of art and reflects his unique vision. His front yard is a veritable sculpture garden, scattered with carvings of angels, turtles, fish, mermaids, or whatever other creature the wood suggests to him. He paints his visions of angels and guardian spirits who watch over different aspects of our daily lives: a bewinged, androgynous angel stands watch over a flower garden; a protector angel is vigilant as a reclining figure rests in a field after a day's work. Another series of paintings depicts figures standing at windows looking out upon all of creation: sun, moon, stars, and the spinning blue and green Earth. One especially endearing canvas shows the artist's vision of paradise, in which a figure rests beneath a flowering tree in a wide, green meadow in the top half of the painting. Below is a mythical figure bathed in light in the center of a garden. Melvin sells his work to people who stop at his house for whatever price comes to mind. His disregard for the market, his profoundly mystical vision and his devotion to his art make him a unique naïf artist.

The work of William Lewis (a.k.a. Guillermo Yuscarán [1940–]) occupies a unique niche in contemporary Honduran art. A Californian by birth, with a doctorate degree in history from the University of California, Lewis first went to Honduras in 1972, after living in Spain and Venezuela, to teach history at the American School in Tegucigalpa, but soon realized that he wanted to devote himself full time to writing and painting. He was inspired by what he perceived as the deeply painful yet beautiful mysteries of the Honduran soul as well as the loving and humorous side of the Honduran character. He has published eleven books since then, including poetry, fiction, and an acclaimed biography of artist José Antonio Velásquez. He also is a prolific painter whose work might best be described as tropical naïf dreamscapes, in which intriguing scenes of plazas, beaches, and markets glow with luminous primary colors and clear, bold shapes. A surrealistic touch has parrots, toucans, and fish commingle with statuesque female figures, small blue dinosaurs, and the ever-present blue dog. His work is in private collections in the United States, Mexico, and Latin America. Numerous Honduran collectors have acquired his paintings and some can be seen in public venues throughout the country such as the Hotel San Martín in Tegucigalpa and the Church of San Francisco in Santa Lucía. He makes his home on the North Coast, in Tela and also in Santa Lucía, a picturesque hill town a short distance from Tegucigalpa. In 2002 the Santa Lucía Cultural Center, which he was instrumental in founding, was named after him. A permanent exhibit of his paintings is housed at the center.

Honduran Women Artists

The life and work of Teresa Fortín (1885–1982) is illustrative of the cultural barriers and expectations that defined women's role in the arts in the first half of the twentieth century as well as the power of the creative spirit and what one can accomplish despite cultural and social restrictions.[5] Teresa was born in Tegucigalpa into a well-to-do entrepreneurial family. She worked as an elementary school teacher in Valle de Angeles in the 1920s and during that time began painting. In 1933 the Ministry of Education sponsored an exhibit of her work at the National Library and the art community was impressed. She then studied with Max Euceda and briefly with Pablo Zelaya Sierra before his untimely death. She was invited to give classes at a private art academy and in the next few years showed her work in thirteen different exhibits. In 1942 she was commissioned to work on the restoration of José Miguel Gómez's paintings of the four evangelists in the Cathedral of Tegucigalpa and that same year, at the height of her success, was awarded a scholarship to study in Paris, but her father would not allow her to go, insisting that, since Teresa's mother had died some years before, it was her duty to stay home and care for him. He felt that art was not a proper profession for a woman and discouraged her from pursuing her love of painting. Respecting the family ties and traditions so ingrained in her, she took care of him until his death in 1951. She continued to paint, despite her family's disapproval, living alone in impoverished conditions. She worked tirelessly, oblivious of financial remuneration, donating her paintings to churches, schools, libraries, and government agencies. Some of her work is realistic, some is impressionistic and during the last decade of her life she turned to a naïf style. Among her most notable achievements is a series of twenty paintings called "Recuerdos" (Memories) that were exhibited in the Galería Nuevo Continente in 1978. They are scenes recalled from the 1920s and 1930s that portray family life, rural landscapes, political strife, and the effect of civil war in the countryside. Twenty additional canvasses were added to the series for the exhibit "Mi vida" (My Life) in 1980. Earlier that same year her painting "El Futuro, El Pueblo Feliz" (The Future, Happy People) was exhibited in Washington, DC in honor of International Women's Year. In 1981, 500 signatures were collected among the Honduran art community to petition to give her the prestigious Pablo Zelaya Sierra Art Award.

Art with a Social Conscience

Many of the Honduran artists who have chosen to stay in Honduras to live and work share a passionate interest in the social and political realities of their country. In 1974, under the leadership of Virgilio Guardiola (1947–), a group of young painters that included Luis H. Padilla (1947–), Dino Falconi (1950), Aníbal Cruz (1943–), César Rendón (1941–), Ezequiel Padilla (1944–), Felipe Burchard (1946–), Lutgardo Molina (1948–), Mario Mejía (1946–) and others, formed the collective "Taller la Merced." They shared studio space in a "liberated" historic building in downtown Tegucigalpa in the Plaza la Merced, along with an experimental theater troupe, the literary collective "Tahuanka" and a student political action group. The predominant style among the members was a vigorous expressionism that unequivocally denounced social injustice, class privilege, and military violence. They exhibited their work throughout the country and participated in a variety of cultural events of a sociopolitical nature, sometimes creating the sets, for example, for plays performed by the experimental theater group or for readings by the "Tahuanka" poets. Until they were evicted in 1976, these groups worked together to produce art that addressed such immediate concerns as land reform, workers' rights, and the increasing militarization of the government. The collective reformed in 1982 under the name "Taller Dante Lazzaroni" and was joined by Rony Castillo (1944–) and Dagoberto Posadas (1959–) among others. They were inspired to employ their artistic talents to denounce the now frightening militarization of their country and the violent tactics used to repress peasant and worker organizations as well as criticism of the government. An example of what took place during the period that Hondurans call "the dirty war" was the unearthing in 1982 of a mass grave in "La Montañita," on the outskirts of Tegucigalpa, where the bodies of a number of young people who had spoken out against the military were buried. At this time the United States had significantly increased its military presence in Honduras as part of its support of the Nicaraguan Contras. The presence of U.S. personnel and American dollars at the Palmerola Military Base near Comayagua occasioned an increase in gambling, prostitution, and AIDS. These were all themes that dominated the work of these Honduran artists for nearly two decades. Their work from this period is powerful, laced with anger, frustration, and irony. In Dagoberto Posadas' "Visiones del desaparecido" (The Disappeared's Visions) a human figure bound with ropes howls in agony and rage, surrounded by vicious dogs, ghoulish men and helmeted skeletons. The muddied reds, yellows, and greens bring the viewer into an inferno of physical and psychological pain that causes repulsion and indignation. Ezequiel Padilla's "Palmerola Souvenirs" points sarcastically at the cultural costs of war. The gaily colored canvas is dominated by a female figure with a bare midriff wearing tight orange shorts, high heels, and hot pink stockings. Behind her a harlequin-suited musician plays a pink cello as three helicopters hover above him in a square of bright blue. A faceless androgynous figure dressed in red and blue completes this grotesque trio. The background is composed of irregularly shaped panels that suggest the artificial decor of a nightclub or bar.

With the end of the Contra War and the return of civilian government in the 1990s, some of these artists went on to explore other themes and techniques. Mario Mejía's "Cansancio campesino" (The Tired Farmworker), for example, is a portrait of the physically exhausting effort of plowing dry, rock-strewn fields with a team of oxen. It is at once a paean to the enduring strength of the Honduran *campesino* and a lament for his life of suffering. The barbed wire in the foreground and the subtle insinuation of cracked glass suggest a level of social critique, but it is integrated into the movement and color of the composition to imply compassion more than anger. Ezequiel Padilla, on the other hand, continues to express rage and indignation as he denounces injustice, corruption, hunger, unemployment, and greed.

Art and the Market

Although it is clear that works of this nature have significant social and cultural value; and even though many of the works of these artists demonstrate an impressive mastery of color and technique, their is little market for art that is so unsettling, which makes it all the more admirable that so many Honduran artists of the 1960s, 1970s, and 1980s devoted so much of their time and talent to nonlucrative projects. Some artists openly, even contemptuously, resist the lure of the market. Ezequiel Padilla, Aníbal Cruz, and Virgilio Guardiola once formed what they referred to as "Los Artistas de lo no Vendible" (The Coterie of the Unsellable).

Teresa Fortín's experience with the market was difficult in part because she was a woman, but male artists also commonly complain that it is extremely difficult to make a living as an artist in Honduras. Art teachers are poorly paid and the market for fine art has until recently been limited. In the past artists have looked to the government or to wealthy patrons to purchase their work. The relatively recent phenomena of Hondurans investing in the work of Honduran artists and of Honduran artists enjoying international recognition have allowed some individuals to devote themselves full time to their art. The colorful landscapes and picturesque street scenes of Carlos Garay (1943–), for example, are in great demand and have made him one of Honduras' best-known and most popular painters.

There are now a number of galleries where local artists show their work, not only in the major cities of Tegucigalpa and San Pedro Sula but also in many smaller towns such as Valle de Angeles, Santa Lucia, and Ojojona, where there is a growing awareness that cultural tourism holds economic promise for the future. Galería Portales in Tegucigalpa, for example, holds regular exhibits of national and international artists and Waves of Art Gallery in West End on Roatán exhibits and sells the work of local artists.

The young artists of today face many of the same challenges and choices as their predecessors. Honduras continues to be a country where poverty, illiteracy, social inequalities, and inadequate public assistance affect the quality of life of the majority of its citizens, and it is as important today as ever for artists to determine what role that reality will play in their art. Honduras is at the same time a participant in the ever-evolving global economy and global culture. Honduran artists now participate in regional and international exhibitions such as the Central American Biennale and the Venice Biennale and international collectors seek out the works of renowned Honduran artists such as Luis H. Padilla and Virgilio Guardiola.

In some cases, artists themselves have organized groups and conferences and sought alternatives when local support is unavailable. With small budgets, they organize exhibits, produce publications, and stimulate a grassroots dynamic. A recent positive development has been the creation of cultural centers in towns throughout the country. These centers are funded by the Ministry of Culture and provide a space where local communities can hold a variety of events such as art exhibits, festivals, lectures, and workshops.

ARTISTS AND TRENDS TODAY

Although their struggles, influences, and experiences may be similar, there is great stylistic as well as thematic variety in the work of young artists today. Honduran painters have mastered the internationally recognized techniques of impressionism, cubism, surrealism, realism and neorealism, abstract expressionism, and neofiguratism and have found original and visually exciting ways to employ them in pictorial representations of the Honduran experience.

Many young artists today are working with materials and techniques that require sophisticated technology, large venues, and/or interaction with the public. The most exciting and innovative art of today is rarely seen in the traditional form of paintings on canvas. It has become commonplace for art critics, museums, and artists themselves to refer to the field as the visual arts, thereby allowing for a wide range of forms, techniques, materials, and conceptualizations as well as for collaboration with other disciplines such as theater, dance, and education. Installations, graffiti, photography, performance, video art, and digital art in original combinations are being explored, mostly by young artists still studying or recently graduated from the National School of Fine Arts in Tegucigalpa or from art institutes abroad, sometimes individually but often collectively. Their work tends to be what we might call the contemporary Central American version of socially conscious or *engagé* art: It embodies a complex and far-from-complacent examination of their surroundings and questions the cultural symbols we use and that use or manipulate us. In contrast to or possibly as a reaction to the nationalistic and denunciatory urgency of *engagé* artists of previous generations, particularly from the 1960s to the 1980s, the work of many of these contemporary artists projects more detachment and less messianic passion, more individualism and less ideology. The themes explored are the urgent realities of our times: social injustice, ecological degradation, immigration, consumerism, violence, gender inequality, and cultural imperialism. Their themes and techniques work together to create aesthetic experiences that tend to move the spectator on an energetic rather than a rational level. The size, the message, and the dynamic and interactive nature of much of this work make it public, relevant, dynamic—and unsellable. But, given that so much of this art reaches out to the larger community and is so often prophetic or didactic or critical, it has sought and found support outside the collector/gallery marketplace. Public funding for the arts, which many Hondurans believe should be a dedicated line in the government budget, continues to be scarce and precarious. Friendly foreign embassies, nonprofit organizations and private businesses are now the most generous sources of funding for the arts in Honduras, which in turn has generated the need for expertise in self-promotion and grant-writing. This professionalization of art, some would say commercialization, has spawned a number of local nonprofit associations that promote the arts by organizing shows and providing exhibition space, securing funding for projects, and generating new and exciting ways for artists to work together and reach out to the community.

Perhaps the most active and successful of these associations is Women in the Arts (Mujeres en las Artes "Leticia de Oyuela" [MUA]). Founded in 1995 to be a forum for women artists and to provide a space where women could exhibit their work, MUA has evolved into a working group dedicated to developing policies and strategies oriented toward the enrichment and promotion of Honduran culture in the most inclusive sense. Under the direction of América Mejía and Bayardo Blandino, MUA strives to bring together individuals, government, private business, and nonprofit cultural groups to generate and promote progressive and innovative art. In its initial phase, MUA exhibited the work of a number of well-known as well as promising new female artists, including Patricia Cervantes' photographs of Honduran women, sculptures in glass, wood, and metal by Regina Zelaya and an installation by Xenia Mejía. MUA's more recent projects promote artistic collaboration and interaction with the public. MUA has initiated, for example, an ambitious plan to sponsor annual interdisciplinary arts festivals in the historic downtown center of Tegucigalpa that have included mobile art and photography exhibits, street theater, live radio interviews, and workshops open to the public. MUA's projects in the old downtown were partly motivated by a desire to bring attention and resources to areas severely damaged by Hurricane Mitch in 1998. Additionally, as the capital grows, its center of commerce and social life has shifted away from the historic downtown area and there is a growing consciousness of the value of the old buildings and neighborhoods. In 2003–2004, MUA focused its attention on Barrio Abajo, one of Tegucigalpa's oldest neighborhoods, and developed a series of activities, performances, and workshops designed to foster a sense of pride and community among local artists and neighborhood residents. Anthropologist and poet Rebeca Becerra interviewed residents and also compiled an oral history of the neighborhood that was published along with historic photographs and a wealth of description and anecdote that are a reminder of the rich human heritage of this section of the city. Several elderly residents delved into their memories to retell, for example, stories of the burning of the national police headquarters in 1957. It was a two-story wooden building with cells on the first floor where juvenile delinquents, drunks, and petty criminals were jailed. It also housed the Boys' Correctional Institute of Tegucigalpa, where street kids were taken in and taught either woodworking or shoemaking. They were subject to strict discipline but not punished; in fact it was considered a privilege to be there: They were given uniforms to wear and marched along with the police in the annual September 15 parade. The fire that burned the building to the ground, taking with it all the inmates and destroying the equipment in the workshops, was started during an aborted *coup* when government troops loyal to President Ramón Villeda Morales and followers of Colonel Armando Velásquez Cerrato battled in the streets. "Street kids" continue to be a presence in the city, but now they are gangs called *maras* that have sown terror in the hearts of many residents. Government has lately adopted a hard-line policy of dealing with these youth, creating dangerously overcrowded prison conditions. The socially involved cultural projects out on the streets among the city's residents do not necessarily offer solutions to the country's urban problems, but they unquestionably demonstrate artists' engagement with their reality and willingness to be involved with their communities on the grassroots level.

MUA also has been instrumental in promoting the participation of Honduran artists in international venues. It organized the Bienal de Artes Visuales de Honduras 2008, a biannual event that lays the foundation for Honduran artists to participate in the regional art biennale that the seven Central American countries initiated in 1998 (Bienal de Pintura del Istmo Centroamericano) which was subsequently renamed the Bienal de Artes Visuales to reflect the widespread changes that have taken place in the use of techniques and materials. This has become the most important contemporary art event in the region, where the latest trends in the visual arts are displayed for and discussed by the public and evaluated by judges from outside the region. Artists representing the seven countries can appreciate each other's work and benefit from critical and theoretical dialogue. There has been some criticism that this event encourages Honduran artists to mimic or borrow concepts and techniques that are stylish or trendy but not autochthonous and not relevant to their reality. Other critics argue that for Honduran art to evolve and flourish it must not be isolated from global trends but rather be aware and informed in order to respond to the challenges of globalization from a position of strength and be an actor on the world stage.

These two points of view reflect what has long been a fundamental division or difference in the stance of Honduran intellectuals regarding their cultural identity: the desire to celebrate that which is local and somehow authentically Honduran and the urge to be players in a larger field. Regardless of what may be the predominant point of view within the intellectual and academic communities at any given time, Honduran artists have always and probably will continue to evolve in both of these directions. It seems that many of the new generation of visual artists are firmly rooted in the reality of Honduras and explicitly conscious of forging their role as both observers and actors whose artistic expression questions, defies, criticizes, and/or celebrates this reality but is never complacent in representing it. It may be appropriate here to mention that while historically the pictorial and visual art of Honduran women has either been absent or has received little or no attention or critical recognition, some of today's most original and significant work is being done by women. Two whose work is particularly noteworthy are Regina Aguilar and Xenia Mejía.

Xenia Mejía (1958–) has studied in Brazil, Belgium, and Germany and is one of the most internationally visible of contemporary artists of Honduras. She has been invited to participate and won recognition in numerous international exhibits, including the Venice Biennale. Her work typically employs easily accessible materials and often centers on the lives of women from developing countries. Her installation "Memorias" (Memories), for example, consisted of the faces of children printed on tortillas lying on *comales* (flat, round, rustic metal pans used for warming tortillas), scattered on a worn cement floor. An image of a grate was projected onto a row of baby bottles partially filled with milk that sat atop a shelf on the wall above the *comales*. The installation's power is derived from the silent hope and vulnerability of the children's faces and the suggestion of barriers, incarceration, and abandonment. Her mixed media on paper titled "Homenaje Póstumo" (Posthumous Homage) consists of twenty-four panels and was inspired by the damage done to Honduras both by hurricanes and by escalating violence, which are conveyed by images of telephone poles, buildings, streets and screaming human faces executed in reds, browns, and blacks. Xenia represented Honduras at the Venice Biennale for the second time in 2007 with her installation of twenty-four painted panels from the series titled "Perfil de Ciudad" (City Profile). Employing a hot palette of reds, blacks, and yellows and impressionistically executed human figures that communicate a desperate, edgy energy, her urban profile is one of chaos and disintegration.

Regina Aguilar (1954–) studied sculpture and glass arts in Germany, Belgium, France, and Brazil and graduated from the Massachusetts College of Art in Boston. Her sculptures, installations, and video art have been shown in numerous individual and collective exhibits throughout the world and have been recognized for their technical excellence and originality at the Venice

Biennale, the Sao Paulo Bienal, and other prestigious art venues. She lived and worked abroad until 1991, when she returned to Honduras and settled in the historic mining town of San Juancito in the hill country about an hour's drive northeast of Tegucigalpa. San Juancito was a prosperous town during the first half of the twentieth century when the Rosario Mining Company owned and operated gold and silver mines in the vicinity. After the company closed its operation in 1954, the town's population declined, many of the services that the company supported such as telephones and transportation were closed down or reduced and unemployment rose dramatically. Regina bought a property in the quiet town in 1991 and installed her art studio. When she needed assistants she began to train and employ local craftspeople in glass and metal work. Her commitment to the community has grown over the years and now includes a variety of projects and activities that contribute to the economic and cultural life of the community. She has trained San Juancito residents in the arts and crafts of making hand-made paper from natural materials that they fashion into such products as cards and lampshades. They create a variety of glass items including vases, tableware, and jewelry and there is a metal shop that receives commissions to make light fixtures and furniture. Her interest in the arts and education inspired her to open a school where artists from around the world have come to San Juancito to teach classes in ceramics, painting, drawing, and digital art to the local children. Regina also initiated and organizes the annual Festival Cultural de San Juancito. In 2008, she celebrated her eighth successful gathering of artists, musicians, mimes, dancers, actors, and chefs to celebrate Honduran culture.

In the midst of her teaching and cultural promotion in the community Regina continues to produce her own art of stunning originality. Her work is characterized by intriguing combinations of dense and translucent materials such as stone and glass and by the juxtaposition of abstract and figurative elements. Her video installation "La Flor de la Inocencia" (The Flower of Innocence), that she prepared for the I Bienal de Artes Visuales de Honduras in 2006, is a translucent glass sculpture that resembles a lotus blossom. The edges of the petals are jagged and reminiscent of the broken glass commonly found atop security fences throughout Central America as a deterrent to thieves or intruders. A deep red light pours through the lower petals, suggesting both violence and passion. The title of the piece makes it impossible for the spectator not to associate the sculptural elements with both violated virginity and human resistance and durability. The piece has a disquieting beauty and dynamism. In 2004, her video "Central America Now" won second place at the IV Bienal de Artes Visuales del Istmo Centroamericano in Panama. Like her sculptures, it juxtaposes soft and harsh, tenderness and violence. The youth gangs and violence that have become such a presence throughout the region are shown beside the police violence that is used to combat it. It is a work of art of deep social engagement that offers no solutions but rather opens the viewer to the complexities of human violence and human community.

There are many young artists today; it remains to be seen which ones will have the technical expertise, the vision and the dedication to continue to pursue a career in the visual arts. Among those who show promise are Adán Vallecillo, Johanna Montero Matamoros, Hugo Ochoa, and Roque Galo. Continuing the tradition of forming collectives for mutual support and sharing, groups such as "La Cuartería" (The Neighborhood), "El Círculo" (The Circle) and "Manicomio" (Insane Asylum) have formed in the last decade, "Manicomio" being perhaps the most radical and innovative. Its members, Leonardo González, Fernando Cortés, Gabriel Núñez, and Dina Lagos, were all students at the National School of Fine Arts when they issued a manifesto in 1999 protesting what they considered to be its outdated and irrelevant pedagogical practices. Central to their philosophy is a rejection of the notions that art consists of objects to be preserved, owned, and revered and that the identity of the individual artist is of primary importance. They profess a belief in art as experience, as performance and as collective creation in dialogue with the spectator.

NOTES

1. The most complete histories of Honduran painting are Leticia de Oyuela. *La batalla pictórica: síntesis de la historia de la pintura hondureña* and J. Evaristo López and Longino Becerra, *Honduras: 40 pintores.*

2. Archaeologists Gloria Lara Pinto and George Hasemann contributed greatly to expanding the frontiers of research in Honduras. See for example Lara Pinto, "La investigación arqueológica en Honduras: lecciones aprendidas para una futura proyección," *Revista pueblos y fronteras digital,* 2006:2. www.pueblosyfronteras.unam.mx.

3. Leticia de Oyuela's *José Miguel Gómez, pintor criollo* is an interdisciplinary approach to the life, work, and times of this talented artist that offers insight into the complex social structures and relationships operative at this time in history. It includes relevant historical documents and full-color reproductions of his masterpieces.

4. Guillermo Yuscarán's excellent biography, *Velásquez, the Man and His Art,* is a portrait of the man, the artist and his context.

5. See Leticia de Oyuela's *Confidente de soledad: vida íntima de Teresa V. Fortín* for a brief biography and a selection of the artist's work.

8

The Performing Arts

TRADITIONAL RITUALS AND DANCES

ALTHOUGH SOME SCHOLARS have asserted that the dramatic arts in Honduras originated in the Mayan center of Copán, in the form of ritual ball games and other ceremonies of a practical, spiritual, or bellicose nature, there is as yet insufficient information available from archaeological research to allow an accurate description or interpretation of these performances.[1] However, one can still witness, albeit in modified form, anonymous religious reenactments of the passion of Christ and the lives of saints as well as ceremonial dances, processions, and rituals that reveal a blending of Christian and indigenous beliefs and practices. These include The Mystery of the Passion (El Misterio de la Pasión); The Dance of Moors and Christians (Baile de Moros y Cristianos); The Story of Charlemagne, also called The Ribbon Dance (La Historia de Carlomagno o El Baile de las Tiras); The Tragedy of St. Sebastian, also called the Dance of the Devils (La Tragedia de San Sebastián o El Baile de los Diablitos); and El Guancasco (The Guancasco).

The Mystery of the Passion

The most common representation of the passion of Christ is the *Via Crucis* or Stations of the Cross, enacted on Good Friday, in which the actors, playing the roles of Christ, Roman soldiers, Pontius Pilate, and so on, are accompanied by a procession as they stop at the twelve stations and reenact the various scenes of the crucifixion. The actors' lines are taken from the Bible or are paraphrases of scripture with which the public is familiar. In Ojojona, a small town twenty miles from Tegucigalpa, a local *cofradía* or fraternal organization affiliated with the Catholic Church organizes an annual dramatization of the *Via Crucis*.

Comayagua, located fifty miles north of Tegucigalpa is known for its elaborate celebration of Holy Week, which begins on Palm Sunday with the procession of The Lord of the Little Donkey (El Señor de la Burrita), in which a life-size statue of Jesus astride a donkey is led through the streets of the city, accompanied by music, singing, and the waving of olive branches. On Holy Thursday the Last Supper is reenacted at the Church of San Francisco and in the evening a procession featuring participants carrying thousands of candles accompanies the suffering, blindfolded Christ through the streets for the entire night, finally ending their march at the cathedral at dawn. For Good Friday, twenty-four colorful sawdust carpets are created on the streets over which the procession passes as it makes its way to the cathedral, where the crucifixion is reenacted. A burial procession follows in which thirteen small girls dressed as angels and crowds of the faithful, carrying candles, accompany the pallbearers to the cathedral. On Easter morning, statues of the Virgin, Mary Magdalene, and the Apostles, John and Peter, search the streets for the Resurrected Christ. Finally Mary and Jesus find one another and reenter the cathedral, where mass is celebrated.

The Dance of Moors and Christians

This ancient ritual, which is performed in many parts of Latin America, is rooted in the basic idea that two social groups are in conflict. Originally, the opposing sides were Christians and Moors, the prototypical infidels, although the groups that do battle today are towns, neighborhoods, or simply actors and dancers that represent the two sides. In Comayagua, for example, two neighborhoods, Barrio Abajo and Barrio Arriba, act out the dance of conquest, known there as The Tragedy of St. Sebastian or The Dance of the Devils. In anticipation of the confrontation, each side stakes out its territory. The spoken monologues and dialogues occupy a minimal portion of the drama, which is mainly a ritualized battle in the form of dance with musical accompaniment. The actors wear masks and stage their dance at the entrance of the church.

The Story of Charlemagne or The Ribbon Dance

Every community's representation of the battle between Moors and Christians is unique and reflects its own history and idiosyncrasies. A vibrant and unique example of this is the Garífuna version, known as The Story of Charlemagne or The Ribbon Dance. An elaborate rendition of this drama is presented annually in the North Coast town of Trujillo, where the Garífuna neighborhoods of Cristales and Río Negro collaborate to form the two battalions. A woman, the "*generala*," or general, directs each battalion and trains the musicians, choreographs the dances, and supervises communication with the opposing camp. The battalions are composed of approximately 100 women who wear beautiful and elaborate hats decorated with flowers. On the day of the ritual the women are organized in military formation; each battalion is directed by its *generala* and an admiral. The admirals ride horses and are the only male participants. The Christian admiral rides a white horse and dresses in pink and blue while the admiral of the Moors has a dark-colored steed and wears red and yellow. Each battalion is preceded by its own band and has two marshals who carry pistols, a keeper of a large wooden key and five young girls who carry trays laden with flowers. Each side chooses its queen from among the participants, as the symbolic conflict is resolved through a series of choreographed encounters, culminating in a final battle that integrates dialogue in its representation. The predominance of women in this ritual drama, the beautifully executed dance rhythms and the use of both drums and saxophones are examples of the incorporation of native culture into this drama of medieval European origin.

El Guancasco

The *guancasco* was a form of ritual pilgrimage practiced among the Lenca people of western Honduras in pre-Hispanic times. According to colonial Spanish chroniclers there were approximately 500 Lenca communities that represented four different linguistic groups at the time of the conquest. Wars between and among the groups were common and served the purposes of capturing slaves and extending territory. On occasion, times of peace were determined when communities that shared the same language came together to trade such products as salt and cacao. With the influence of the Spanish Catholic Church and the introduction of the concept of patron saints and their corresponding images, the *guancasco* evolved: Religious associations or *cofradías* from neighboring towns now carry the image of their town's patron saint to "visit" each other's churches. These are reciprocal visits and occur during the visiting town's patron saint celebration and are accompanied by festivities such as music, folk dances, and the preparation of special foods. Each year the neighboring towns of Gracias and Mexicapa, for example, hold their *guancasco*. The image of St. Sebastian, the patron saint of Gracias, visits Mexicapa between December 12 and 16 and stays for nine days. Between January 20 and 25, St. Lucia, the patron saint of Mexicapa, vists Gracias and stays for nine days. These pilgrimages are also sometimes referred to as *paisanazgos*, a more general term for encounters between two towns. The religious and political leaders of the communities, with the participation of the citizens, organize the *paisanazgos*. The purpose of these reciprocal encounters is to reaffirm ties of friendship or to reconcile differences. In the towns of Ojojona and Lepaterique, for example, festivals in honor of the patron saints of each village open and close the *paisanazgos* and a representation of "Moors and Christians" is part of the tradition.

La Toreada de la Danta

In a few Tolupán communities in the department of Yoro, residents annually reenact a ritualized battle between hunters and tapirs. The tapir, or *danta,* is a large, herbivorous mammal endemic to Central America. The adult weighs between 500 and 850 pounds and typically reaches a height of four feet and measures six feet from its prehensile proboscis to its pig-like tail. They are solitary animals that live in dense tropical forests and are now in danger of extinction although they once were an important source of food for indigenous peoples throughout Central America. Tapirs are known to charge wildly when threatened, so hunting them can be dangerous.

As part of their annual celebration in honor of the town's patron saint, San Sebastián, the residents of Agalteca, Yoro stage the ritual tapir battle in the central plaza. The celebration begins on January 20, the day of St. Sebastian, with the playing at dawn of traditional drums, *toncontín.* Later in the day a Catholic mass is celebrated and various sacraments are administered, including baptism, Holy Communion, and confirmation. A tapir costume is constructed using reeds, sticks, and branches covered with sackcloth and the plaza is decorated with branches and foliage stuck in mounds of earth. Bonfires illuminate the ritual, which is enacted in the early evening hours. Hunters on horseback attack the tapir, which fights back, trying to knock off the riders' hats. Ostensibly a hunting ritual, this duel between man and beast also represents the historical invasion of Tolupán territory by men on horseback and the rejection of their presence by the native inhabitants.

POPULAR AND FOLK DANCES

According to a recent inventory of traditional folkways sponsored by the Ministry of Culture, Arts and Sports there are well over 100 traditional folk dances performed informally and by amateur dance troupes throughout Honduras.[2,3] David Flores has seen most of these dances performed and describes them in his detailed survey, *Evolución histórica de la danza folklórica hondureña* (History and Evolution of Honduran Folk Dance). In addition to his research, teaching, and choreography, Flores directs the dance troupe "Zots," which performs folk dances in venues throughout the country. According to Flores, *mestizo* folk dances fall into several broad categories:

courtship dances; dances that imitate birds and animals; dances that represent customs and work such as harvesting and cooking; children's dances; and dances to enjoy at parties or fiestas. Indigenous and Garífuna dances correspond to these same categories but additionally may be inspired by a desire to communicate with the ancestors or with the spirit world. The Lenca area, in particular the department of Choluteca and the municipalities of Intibucá and Valle, has a rich folk dance tradition.

Flores asserts that the quintessential Honduran folk rhythm is that which accompanies the dance called the *xique* or *xixique*, an onomotopoeic word that mimics the sound of sandals scraping the ground. It has numerous variations but essentially is an energetic and rapid dance that some say resembles the Spanish *jota*. *Las Escobas* (The Brooms) is a dance with religious and political roots in which the dancers carry brooms decorated with ribbons and flowers, symbolizing the sweeping of the temple on August 8, the Feast of the Immaculate Conception, when the saint is honored and the traditional staff of power changes hands in the community. *Amor en Puyitas* (Young Love) is a courtship dance popular in the department of Santa Bárbara in which a male dancer carries a red bandana in his right hand as he asks a woman to dance. In *La Aguatera* (The Water Carrier), a flirtatious courtship dance from the department of Olancho, the men call and gesture provocatively to the women who bow their heads shyly and respond coquettishly to their choreographic advances.

One of the most popular dances in Honduras today has its origins in the traditional Garífuna *punta*, a combination of music and rhythmic movement originally performed by elders at wakes or mourning ceremonies and as a courtship dance.[4] Traditional punta music is played with drums, maracas, and conch shells. Its complex rhythm consists of one drum playing 2/4 or 4/4 time; dancers move to the beat of a second drum playing 6/8 time while the women sing in 4/4 time. The singing that accompanies traditional punta music takes the form of the African call-and-answer style whereby a soloist sings a phrase and the chorus repeats or answers it. But the young people today who dance punta not only in Honduras (especially on the North Coast) but throughout Central America and in many U.S. cities probably have no idea of the origins of the music and dance that has become popular in bars and night clubs. Acoustic and electric instruments have been added to create what is now known as "punta rock." The musicians in the past were always men; today there are some female musicians and even a Honduran all-female punta band. Traditional Garífuna women wear modest skirts and dance with self-assured dignity; young female punta dancers today tend to wear short skirts and provocative clothing to emphasize the dance's sexuality. It is fast and high in energy, danced with the feet, hips, and buttocks. A competitive element often enters the dance as the drummers play faster and faster, challenging the dancers to keep up with them. A number of popular Honduran bands such as La Banda Blanca, Los Gatos Bravos, and La Tribu Lenca play punta music.

Stylized or choreographed versions of traditional folk dances are performed by local and national troupes. The Ballet Folklórico Zots (Zots Folkloric Ballet), directed by Flores, has an impressive repertoire, largely based on Flores' research of his country's folk dances. The *Ballet Folklórico Garífuna* (Garífuna Folkloric Ballet) has been performing in Honduras and internationally since 1976.

CLASSICAL DANCE

Dance as a discipline of the performing arts came into being in Honduras in 1958 when Mercedes Agurcia (1903–1980) founded the Teatro Infantil de Honduras (Children's Theater of Honduras). Although her forte was theater, children were taught dance as well and her school later became the Escuela Nacional de Ballet (National School of Ballet). After her death in 1980 the school was named Escuela Nacional de Danza Merceditas Agurcia after its beloved founder.

In the early 1960s, Judith Entner de Suárez (also known as Judith Burwell), a graduate of the Boston Conservatory, opened the Escuela de Ballet IHCI (Ballet School of the Honduran Institute of International Culture). Because of her excellent classical ballet and modern dance training and her dedicated and disciplined approach to teaching, she was able to train a number of young dancers who went on to become professional dancers, choreographers, and teachers, including César Guifarro and Claudia and Lourdes Zelaya. Her company performed classical ballets and choreographed versions of Honduran folk dances for more than fifteen years in the Manuel Bonilla National Theater in Tegucigalpa, until she returned to the United States in 1979. She was also instrumental in starting a dance program at the National University in 1979, which continues to this day. The first director of the university program was Leslie Bryan, who combined her teaching and choreography skills to present original dance-theater productions inspired by themes from Honduran history such as *William Walker,* based on the life of the notorious nineteenth century filibusterer and staged at the colonial fort at Trujillo, where Walker was executed in 1860. Alma Caballero, Claudia Matute and Norma Zambrano have also directed the university program.

Today a number of academies, some government-sponsored, others private or affiliated with nonprofit organizations offer instruction in classical ballet and modern dance. Although the majority of these academies are concentrated in Honduras' most populated urban centers, Tegucigalpa and San Pedro

Sula, there are a number of cultural centers in smaller towns such as Santa Rosa de Copán and Juticalpa that offer dance instruction and theater groups often incorporate dance in their training. In addition to training in classical ballet and the various forms of modern dance, students learn stylized versions of popular folk dances.

CONTEMPORARY INNOVATIONS IN DANCE

Performance artists who have chosen to experiment with technique, theme, and/or venue, typically working outside the traditional boundaries of the established genres, often include dance and movement in their work. The group Danza Libre (Dance Free) formed in the late 1990s with the artistic agenda of exploring new avenues of expression, uses dance to raise awareness of issues of cultural significance. One of the group's early productions was "Con ojos de mujer" (With a Woman's Eyes), performed at the Manuel Bonilla National Theater in 1998 and sponsored by MUA. It combined music, declamation, and movement to interpret poems by Honduran women writers.

Isadora Paz and Lempira Jaen form a unique duo they call "Danzabra Artescénica." They perform original works of their own choreography that have poetic, metaphysical, and philosophical dimensions. Two of their recent creations are "4Elemental" (2005), which they describe as a journey into and with the four elements, the four cardinal directions, and the four seasons of the year to find our place in the creation of the universe; and "Pluma de Plomo," (Lead Feather, 2007), a meditation on the polarities of fate and chance, power and fragility. They have won national and international recognition for the quality and originality of their performances.

CONTEMPORARY THEATER

The dramatic arts have flourished in Honduras in recent years. The number and quality of contemporary theater groups are impressive and reflect the desire of so many Honduran artists to take their message to the street and to involve the public in their performances.

The most long-lived of these troupes is Teatro La Fragua (The Forge Theater), which was started by the Jesuit priest Father Jack Warner in 1979 in Olanchito and later moved to El Progreso, a rapidly growing urban area east of San Pedro Sula where many of Honduras' *maquiladoras* are located. The troupe incorporates methods common to the *commedia dell' arte* and finds inspiration in a broad range of national and international dramatists such as the *pastorelas* of Padre José Trinidad Reyes, Honduran writer and intellectual of the nineteenth century and Chicano playwright Luis Valdéz. Their repertoire includes works they call "el evangelio en vivo" (the living gospel), which they usually perform in churches; works of historical significance such as "Requiem por el Padre Las Casas" (Requiem for Father Las Casas, a sixteenth-century Spanish priest known for his defense of the indigenous population) and "Romero de las Américas" (Romero of the Americas, Father Oscar Romero, Catholic archbishop of San Salvador who was killed in 1980 for his defense of the poor); and Honduran and Latin American legends and tales. The performance of these stories began shortly after Hurricane Mitch in 1998 when Teatro La Fragua toured the local schools as a way of contributing to the spiritual and cultural reconstruction of the city. Their motivation was to instill a love of reading in school children and to provide an alternative to the influence of video games and electronic media that has become so prevalent among Honduran youth. They bring their performances to schools in poor neighborhoods that operate with minimal resources. The company is supported by the Jesuit Order and by contributions from individual donors.

In 1989, the Centro Cultural Hibueras, an independent nonprofit entity was founded in Santa Bárbara by playwright Candelario Reyes. The center has grown and now includes programs in the areas of health, education, arts and culture, and conflict resolution, all with the goal of creating a culture of peace among the least privileged members of Honduran society. One of the Center's most successful projects has been the biannual Festival de Teatro por la Paz (Theater Festival for Peace). Since 1982 this event has brought together amateur and professional troupes, playwrights, theorists, and the general public to share ideas, performances, and techniques. The "teatro popular" (people's theater) movement, inspired by the ideas of Paolo Freire, engages rural communities, particularly children, in the collective creation of performances that address their sociopolitical concerns. This practice is often referred to as the "Teatro de la Basura" (Theater of Trash) because costumes and props are typically made from inexpensive and found materials. The festival has become very popular and it was estimated that some 25,000 people attended the four-day event in 2006.

The Asociación Cultural Arte Acción (The Art in Action Cultural Association) is a collective that came into being in 1998 as a result of Hurricane Mitch. It was formed in the Amarateca Valley on the outskirts of Tegucigalpa as a kind of artistic brigade that desired to lift people's spirits in the wake of the disaster through the use of theater, dance, puppets, stilts, music, and art that they performed in streets, plazas, and homeless shelters. The artists subsequently acquired nonprofit status and have received financial support from an impressive list of sources including The Humanist Institute for Development Cooperation (HIVOS), Children at Risk of Holland, UNICEF, the International Development Bank, and Christian Aid. Arte Acción, as the name implies, is a diverse group with a combined artistic and social agenda. The group consists of actors, musicians, dancers, and circus performers with expertise in traditional and audiovisual arts. Group members collaborate with educators and social workers to design arts projects with social impact in both rural and urban areas. Projects include "No nos roben la alegría" (They Won't Take Away Our Joy) with young people from La Joya, a town just outside of Tegucigalpa that was hit hard by Hurricane Mitch; "Detalles Cotidianos" (Everyday Details), a combined circus–theater production about peaceful co-existence and the prevention of juvenile violence. "Detalles Cotidianos" was financed through a World Bank fund that supports innovative efforts to address violence. Another theater production that deals with violence, "Huellas" (Footprints), was performed at the Manuel Bonilla National Theater in Tegucigalpa and toured Central America, Holland, and Cuba.

The independent Grupo Teatral Bambú (Bambú Theater Group), founded in 1990, presents the works of Honduran as well as international playwrights. This group works collectively, creates improvisational performances, and is especially interested in children's theater. The group's members organize an annual arts festival in Honduras, which has expanded to include a diverse representation of writers and visual and performance artists from Latin America and Europe; they participate in the annual Festival Centroamericano de las Artes Escénicas (Central American Festival of Performance Arts); and they have performed throughout Central America and in the United States in a variety of venues including theaters, schools, and public parks and plazas. A sampling of their performances includes *La SIDA o la vida, la historia de Colacha Cruz* (AIDS or Life, the Story of Colacha Cruz) by Honduras' most respected playwright, Rafael Murillo Selva; *La tortilla sin voltear* (The Tortilla Face Up) by Ecuadorian José María Romero, a play for young adults that turns machismo and traditional gender roles upside down; and *El invento* (The Invention), a participatory comedy for children by U.S. playwright Brad Gromelski that has the audience helping the actors prevent a spy from destroying the invention that brings happiness to all children.

Other recent theater activities reflect Honduran society's growing awareness and acceptance of its own diversity. Teatro Laboratorio de Honduras (Theater Laboratory of Honduras), directed by Tito Estrada, takes actors onto the streets of Tegucigalpa with mime and improvisational theater that calls attention to such volatile topics as AIDS, government corruption, and gender discrimination. MUA has sponsored a number of creative projects that include performance art such as "Estatuas Vivientes" (Living Statues) in the historic Barrio Abajo neighborhood of Tegucigalpa and "Ventanas a la Memoria," written by Eduardo Bähr and directed by Sandra Herrera, a play written with the collaboration of local residents of Santa Rosa de Copán that recreates the town's singularity through the oral testimonies of its inhabitants. A women's theater group from Nacaome recently performed "Retratos," by Amanda Castro, a play that celebrates Honduran women and their history and is an example of the courage and conviction of feminist writers to bring their creative projects to the public.

CHILDREN'S THEATER

Mercedes Agurcia's Teatro Infantil de Honduras awakened interest in children's theater in Honduras. Some of her productions were based on classic children's stories such as Little Red Riding Hood and Sleeping Beauty, whereas others were her original creations. She worked with elementary and also secondary school students and was able to create imaginative sets and costumes with very little in the way of funding. Youthful musicians provided musical accompaniment and the plays were broadcast on the radio and staged at the Manuel Bonilla National Theater. Some of Agurcia's successors in writing, directing, and promoting children's theater are Isidro España, Rubén Berríos, and Mirian Sevilla Rojas.

España's love for the theater was inspired by his experiences as a student of Mercedes Agurcia in the Teatro Infantil. He studied theater at the National University, has acted in and directed numerous plays, and is the author of *Clementina Suárez Vive* (Clementina Suárez Lives, 1969), among other works. He publishes a children's magazine, *Tin Marín*, and tirelessly promotes children's theater. He is currently the director of the Teatro Infantil, carrying on the work of his beloved teacher.

Berríos is known primarily as the author of numerous children's books and as a pioneer in the field of children's literature in Honduras, but he has also written children's theater and was instrumental in organizing the annual Festival de Teatro Infantil (Festival of Children's Theater), which has showcased works by and for children since 1994.

A unique, innovative, and controversial figure in children's theater is Mirian Sevilla Rojas (1955–), who works as a librarian in a large, public elementary school in a poor neighborhood of Danlí, a city approximately sixty miles south of Tegucigalpa with a population of 300,000. After studying theater in Guatemala, Mirian returned to Danlí and started the Grupo Teatral Danlidense (Theater Group of Danlí) in 1981; in 1985 she created the Teatro Infantil (Children's Theater) and the Teatro de Títeres (Puppet Theater) in the Escuela Manuel de Adalid y Gamero, where she is the librarian. After work and on weekends she devotes her time to writing songs, poems, stories, plays for children, and plays for adults; designing and fabricating stage sets and costumes, often with her own limited resources; and rehearsing her plays with her casts of children and adults. Her theater group for adults performs her original works for an adult audience, while her young people's troupe performs for both adults and children. Her plays for adults all have a social theme, as evidenced by their titles: *Un juicio oral y público* (*An Oral and Public Indictment*) deals with domestic violence; and *La censura de los condenados* (*The Censure of the Condemned*) is about the victims of AIDS.

Her plays by and for young people are equally realistic, breaking with the tradition of a light-hearted, fanciful, or evasive children's literature and theater. In 2005, Mirian published a collection of twelve original plays she had written for her students. They are plays acted by children for an adult audience and have been staged in Danlí, Tegucigalpa, and San Pedro Sula and have been presented at international festivals. Honduran actor and theater critic Mario Jaén has called her approach "teatro de valores" or theater of values, because she openly and graphically portrays painful and far from pleasant aspects of Honduran society. Among her themes are gangs, violence, drugs, and the destruction of the environment. *Niños y niñas de la calle* (*Homeless Boys and Girls*) depicts the daily challenges, fears, and hopes of young children on their own in the streets of urban Honduras. She calls attention to their suffering, exposes the government's indifference to their situation and reminds us of the violation of human rights implicit in the damaged lives of children with no access to education or social services, lives that could be saved if society were more humane. The play takes place on a busy urban street with the constant sounds of traffic in the background throughout the play. The characters are a young girl who sells chewing gum, a shoeshine boy, a boy addicted to sniffing glue and a girl infested with lice. Through dialogue, songs, and monologues the characters convey not only the desperation of their precarious situation but also their compassion for one another, their sensitivity, and their intelligence.

When Mirian started her Teatro Infantil in 1985, many of the children's parents and the residents of Danlí expressed their concern that children should not be exposed to such crude realities. But she believes that only by becoming aware of their country's problems will today's children grow up to become tomorrow's moral leaders. The children themselves are proud of their work and Danlí has come to recognize the worth of Mirian Sevilla Rojas. A new municipal theater was recently named in her honor.

FILM

Cinema is perhaps the least developed of the arts in Honduras. There are no schools or institutes that offer the technical training necessary and the cost and access to equipment makes it prohibitive to all but a few. Those individuals who have managed to make films have studied abroad, been resourceful regarding financing and extremely dedicated. The first Honduran film, *Mi amigo Angel* (*My Friend Angel*) was independently produced in 1964 by Sami Kafati, who is recognized as the father of Honduran cinema. Kafati made the thirty-minute film at the age of twenty-six, shortly before leaving to study film in Rome. He subsequently worked in Chile and Honduras in the fields of publicity and documentary film. In the 1980s he began filming what would be Honduras' first feature-length film, *No hay tierra sin dueño* (*All Land Has Its Owner*). Working on the North Coast with Honduran actors and crew, he filmed in black and white on a limited budget but with the good will and cooperation of a sometimes-volunteer company. In 2003 filmmaker Katia Lara produced the documentary *Corazón abierto* (*Open Heart*), which details the life of Kafati and the story of the making of the film. Kafati died in 1996 before he had completed the editing of the film, but friends and family finished the task and it debuted in 2002.

Katia Lara studied cinema in Argentina, where she filmed her first short, *De larga distancia* (*Long Distance Call*), about a Honduran student in a foreign country who receives a telephone call from home informing her of the destruction caused by Hurricane Mitch. Her latest short, *Gas de pimienta* (*Pepper Gas*) portrays the dilemma of a young Honduran woman preparing to emigrate to the United States who, upon losing her visa, must come to terms with her reasons for wanting to leave her country. Upon returning to Honduras in 2001 Lara became a founding member of the Asociación de Cineastas de Honduras (Filmmakers Association of Honduras) and also of Terco Producciones, a collective that works in the field of audiovisual arts. They stage concerts, produce documentary films, and provide audiovisual assistance for cultural events.

The next feature-length, nondocumentary film produced by a Honduran filmmaker in Honduras was *Anita, la cazadora de insectos* (*Anita the Insect Hunter*), which debuted in 2001. The film is based on the homonymous short story by Honduran writer Roberto Castillo. The screenplay, which diverts significantly from the original, is by Hispano Durón, who also directed the film, which tells the story of Anita, a model child who grows up to have severe emotional problems and becomes incapable of adjusting to the demands of her social-climbing family.

The most recent Honduran film is *Almas de media noche* (*Midnight Souls*, 2007), written and directed by Juan Carlos Fanconi, an intriguing blend of mystery, terror, Lenca religious beliefs, and contemporary Honduran life. The plot involves a group of journalism students who travel to northern Honduras to investigate the death of a journalist and experience a blending of past and present.

The Asociación Cultural Arte Acción, as part of its mission to bring hope and solutions to communities suffering from violence, poverty and natural disasters, has collaborated with young filmmaker Mayra Alvarado to make the film *Un día en la vida de mi vida* (*A Day in the Life of My Life*, 2007) about Carlos, a sixteen-year-old from Amarateca, a town forty-five minutes from Tegucigalpa that has been virtually taken over by gangs who terrorize the local population. Carlos cares for his sick mother and depends on the generosity of his neighbors to survive. He gives in to the temptation to steal a pair of tennis shoes and suffers violent consequences. The film offers three different endings and invites the audience to craft a solution to Carlos' dilemma.

Gangs and gang violence are topics of great interest and concern among Hondurans. Filmmaker and screenwriter Oscar Estrada, who also works with Arte Acción and is an associate producer for May I Speak Freely Media, a project that produces media on human rights issues in Honduras, recently produced the documentary *El Porvenir*, about the 2003 slaying of sixty-nine individuals, most of them gang members, at the El Porvenir penal institution in La Ceiba. Evidence suggests that it was a premeditated massacre organized by prison officials. The film addresses not only the specific El Porvenir tragedy but also the phenomenon of gang violence, its origins and possible solutions. It has been screened in numerous cities throughout the United States.[5]

MUSIC[6]

Classical Music

Although Honduran music always has been and continues to be a popular art form and a source of local entertainment and creative expression, there is also an appreciation for classical, European, and international music among Hondurans. In the early nineteenth century Father José Trinidad Reyes is said to have brought the first piano to the country and in 1884 Father Yanuario Girón (1827–?) founded the country's first school of music, in Tegucigalpa. Manuel Adalid y Gamero (1872–1947) of Danlí was a professional organist and talented musician and composer. He composed and recorded several original pieces, among them "Suita Tropical" (Tropical Suite), that was performed in Philadelphia and New York and "Remembranzas Hondureñas" (Honduran Memories) and invented the "*orquestrófono*," an organ modified to produce symphonic quality sound. He founded the Orquesta Eólica in Danlí and directed the nation's official military band. Humberto Cano (1906–1987) achieved international recognition as a virtuoso violinist. And German-born Carlos Hartling (1869–1920) devoted his career to teaching classical music to generations of Honduran students and directing several orchestras. He organized the first military band in the country, the Band of the Supreme Powers (Banda de los Supremos Poderes) and composed the music for the Honduran

National Anthem, which became official in 1915. The poet Augusto Coello (1884–1941) wrote the words.

Among contemporary classical musicians Sergio Rodríguez, a native of San Pedro Sula, is one of the most accomplished and internationally known. He studied violin at the Victoriano López Music School in his home town and later in the United States and has performed with the Vermont Symphony Orchestra, the Baton Rouge Symphony Orchestra, the New England Philharmonic, and other orchestras at home and abroad. In Honduras he directed the National University Chamber Orchestra and the National Symphony Orchestra of Honduras and in 1995 he founded the National Youth Chamber Orchestra in Tegucigalpa. He continues to teach, compose and perform in both the United States and Honduras. In his musical compositions, which include chamber music, children's musicals, and arrangements of Honduran music, he is inspired by the rhythms of traditional folk songs and native dances.

The National Conservatory of Music (Conservatorio Nacional de Música) opened in Tegucigalpa in 1936 under the direction of Francisco Díaz Zelaya. Today it offers instruction in a variety of string, wind and percussion instruments as well as music theory. A number of other schools, both public and private, operate in Tegucigalpa, San Pedro Sula, and other cities. These schools have trained the numerous musicians who perform in the National Philharmonic Orchestra (Orquesta Filarmónica Nacional) as well as other orchestras, bands, quartets, and trios and who are the teachers of ongoing generations of trained musicians.

Honduran Popular Music

Music is unquestionably one of the most popular art forms in Honduras today. Bands playing everything from hard rock to punta to traditional folk music perform at large and small venues every day around the country. There are still bands that play traditional country-style music with guitar and marimba, such as the Ensemble de Marimba from Santa Rosa de Copán, but they are mostly in rural areas and enjoy limited local fame. The following is a sampling of the best-known and most popular groups and individuals composing and performing today.

Khaos takes pride in being Honduras' first authentic hard rock band. Junior Mejía, Marcelo Alvarado, Max Urso, and Issa Molina got together in the early 1980s in San Pedro Sula and performed locally and in neighboring El Salvador until they disbanded in 1985. They have one album, Forjado en Rocka (Forged in Rock).

Rafael Murillo Selva founded Rascaniguas in 1982 as an experiment in combining music and theater. Originally an eclectic group of actors, musicians, and artists, it later became a musical group that performs many of its own compositions. Some of the group's repertoire is influenced by autochthonous rhythms of Honduras such as the Garífuna punta and parranda. The band also performs original pieces, many by group member David Herrera. The band's interpretations of jazz are typically infused with a soft Latin-Caribbean rhythm. The composition of the group has changed over the years but it continues to be one of Honduras' most popular and professional musical groups, performing at home as well as abroad.

Mario Ernesto Castro, known as Mario de Mezapa, was born in Mezapa in the department of Atlántida in 1948. His fifth-grade teacher gave him a guitar and since then he has been writing and singing songs about rural life, local legends, the trials and tribulations of the working class and the struggle for social justice, in particular the agrarian reform laws. As a young man he moved to San Pedro Sula to find work and subsequently became involved in labor organizations. He soon became a popular performer at rallies, demonstrations, and popular festivals and today is considered the "singer-songwriter of the common people." He performs solo and accompanies himself on the guitar, although he also often has back-up from other musicians performing at the events. His CDs, Retorno al campo (Return to the Countryside) and Junto al pueblo (With the People), celebrate the strength and imagination of rural Honduras.

The Garífuna musical tradition, which has its roots in communal and spiritual rituals and ceremonies, has grown, evolved, assimilated other traditions, and influenced non-Garífuna musicians. One of Honduras' most vibrant and talented Garífuna musicians is Aurelio Martínez, who was born into a musical family from Plaplaya, a small indigenous and Garífuna community in the Río Plátano Biosphere Reserve. At an early age he could play the guitar and drums and has devoted himself to composing original songs that combine modern and traditional rhythms and blend Latin and African acoustic instruments with vocals. He is one of the original members of the Garífuna All Star Band, whose members hail from Belize, Guatemala, and Honduras. Martínez is recognized for his efforts to preserve as well as modernize the parranda, a musical tradition that dates from the nineteenth century, when the acoustic guitar was first incorporated into Garífuna music. His album Garífuna Soul is an example of how he has reworked and updated parranda. Another Honduran member of the Garífuna All Stars is Evangelisto Centeno, known as Lugua, from Triunfo de la Cruz, a Garífuna village near Tela on the North Coast. And in February 2008 Honduras celebrated when Garífuna singer Jireh Wilson was awarded the first prize for best performance in the category of folk music at the prestigious music festival of Viña del Mar, Chile. She sang "Ay este amor" (Oh This Love) with the group Percusión Garífuna.

Pez Luna is a group of accomplished musicians who primarily play acoustic guitar, flute, cello, and percussion. Their original compositions include romantic ballads, flamenco jazz, and entirely original arrangements. They play in a variety of locations but are suited to intimate venues such as Café La Caramba in Tegucigalpa.

Another talented and original group is El Sol Caracol, which performs a fusion of many styles and rhythms including rock, reggae, salsa, calypso, milonga, and punta, which they call "rock del Caribe" (Caribbean rock). Their first album, Planeta Sol (Planet Sun), released in 2002, was recorded in La Ceiba at Costa Norte records. The song "El Compa" (slang for friend or companion) became an international success and a promotional video was directed by Hispano Durón and produced by Latino Estudio. The composition of the group has changed but they continue to experiment with their unique blend of sounds and rhythms.

Singer songwriters abound in Honduras. Most perform solo with guitar accompaniment. A few of the most talented and popular are Nordestal Yeco, Polache, and Karla Lara. Their themes range from love ballads to social protest, but they all share the conviction that while music and song are fun and entertaining, they can also lift the spirit and create a sense of community and cultural identity. Polache is popular among young listeners for his characteristically Honduran use of Spanish. One of his songs is "Hablo Catracho pero Español" (The Honduran I Speak Is Spanish). Karla Lara has worked in the Ministry of Culture to promote community involvement in the arts and Nordestal Yeco is one of the creators of the Web page "Trovadicta," which publishes information about musicians and musical events, critiques of concerts and comments by musicians and music lovers.

One singer songwriter stands out not only for his talent as a lyricist and performer, but for his luminous presence in the world of Honduran culture. Born in the coastal city of La Ceiba, Guillermo Anderson studied music and theater at the University of California, Santa Cruz and worked with Chicano playwright Luis Valdez and his Teatro Chicano Campesino. After singing and playing his way around Europe he returned to La Ceiba where he and Jesús Lesmes formed "Colectivartes" and organized numerous workshops, exhibits, concerts, and musical theater productions. His devotion to music as an essential expression of Honduras' spirit and character has inspired the creation of songs whose themes include the gifts of the natural environment and our responsibility to care for them, the strength and beauty of Honduran women and the joys and sorrows of Honduran daily life. "En mi país" (In My Country) has become a sort of alternative national anthem and "Encarguitos" overflows with a nostalgic appreciation for the traditional foods of Honduras, while the CD El tesoro que tenés (The Treasure You Have) celebrates the natural resources of Honduras and reminds its listeners to embrace who they are and protect and preserve their land, their culture, and their heritage. With enormous good will and generosity of spirit, Guillermo Anderson continues to perform throughout Honduras and internationally, both solo accompanying himself on the guitar and with his band that backs him up with a fusion of traditional Garífuna and Caribbean rhythms.

NOTES

1. Alma Caballero made this suggestion in *Escritos sobre el teatro centroamericano, vol. I: Honduras hasta el 2002.* Tegucigalpa: UNAH, 2002, the first complete and systematic study of the history of the dramatic arts in Honduras. Much of the information on drama in this chapter is based on Caballero's work, with the exception of the discussion of the most recently formed theater groups. Commentary on Teatro la Fragua, Mirian Sevilla Rojas, Arte Acción et al. is based on personal interviews by the author and various Web sites.

2. The dances discussed here are mestizo; additional dances are described in the sections devoted to each of the indigenous groups of Honduras.

3. Estrada, Tito A. "El censo de la cultura y las artes contemporáneas de Honduras." Tegucigalpa: Ministerio de Cultura: 2007.

4. Wendy Griffin describes *punta* in an article in *Honduras This Week,* "Popular Punta Music Readily Available at Punta Shops," October 26, 1998, available online.

5. In 2008 Estrada toured several U.S. cities to promote his film, along with Adrienne Pine, whose book *Working Hard, Drinking Hard: On Violence and Survival in Honduras.* Berkeley: University of California Press, 2008, documents violence in Honduras.

6. A complete history of Honduran music has not been published to date. The información on mestizo and contemporary music is from a wide range of sources including *Cancionero,* a songbook published by the Centro de Comunicación y Capacitación para el Desarrollo, nd; various articles in *Honduras This Week,* available online; and the Web sites of the musicians. Traditional instruments and indigenous music are discussed in the sections devoted to the various indigenous groups.

Glossary

Achiote   Also known as annatto, a tropical shrub (*Bixa orellana*) whose seeds produce a reddish substance used in coloring and flavoring food.

Atol   Beverage made from ground corn.

Bajareque   Material used in the construction of traditional houses, usually in the countryside, made from mud and water.

Campesino   Spanish word for a person who lives in a rural area and farms the land.

Catracho   Nickname for a Honduran.

Chicha   Homemade fermented beverage made from sugar cane, pineapple, or corn.

Cofradía   An association whose members are affiliated with the Catholic Church and often pay homage to a particular patron saint.

Compadrazgo   A system that links parents, children, and godparents in a social or economic relationship.

Criollo   A person of Spanish descent born in the New World.

Fútbol   Soccer.

Guancasco   Ritual pilgrimage of indigenous origin.

Guaro   Honduran rum.

Guayabera   A traditional man's button-down shirt, typically decorated with embroidery.

Ladino   Mestizo or westernized; nonindigenous.

Lempira   Honduran monetary unit from 1926 to the present; also a Lenca chief who resisted the Spanish invasion in the sixteenth century.

Mano vuelta   Indigenous custom of reciprocating in kind after being assisted by friends or family members.

Maquiladora   A factory or assembly plant operated under preferential tariff programs.

Mara   Youth gang.

Marimba   Musical instrument similar to the xylophone.

Mestizaje   The blending of Spanish and indigenous cultures.

Nacatamal   A Honduran-style tamal, made from cornmeal, stuffed with meat and/or vegetables, wrapped in a banana leaf and steamed.

Paisanazgo   Ritual encounters between communities.

Parranda   Traditional Garífuna rhythm.

Pastorela   A traditional dramatic form of medieval European origin, presented during the Christmas season.

Punta   Traditional Garífuna dance, now popular outside the Garífuna community.

Bibliography

Alvarado, Elvia. *Don't Be Afraid, Gringo: A Honduran Woman Speaks from the Heart.* Medea Benjamin, trans. San Francisco: The Institute for Food and Development Policy, 1987.

Andrews, E. Wyllys, and William L. Fash, eds., *Copán: The History of an Ancient Maya Kingdom.* Santa Fe, NM: School of American Research Press, 2004.

Ardón Mejía, Mario. "Las manifestaciones artísticas populares tradicionales en Honduras." *Visiones del sector cultural en Centroamérica.* San José, Costa Rica: AECI, 2000.

Argueta, Mario and Edgardo Quiñónez. *Historia de Honduras.* Tegucigalpa: Escuela Superior del Profesorado "Francisco Morazán," 1986.

Brett, Edward T. "The Impact of Religion in Central America." *The Americas*, 4 (1993): 297–344.

Caballero, Alma. *Escritos sobre el teatro centroamericano, vol. I: Honduras hasta el 2000.* Tegucigalpa: Universidad Nacional Autónoma de Honduras, 2002.

Cárdenas Amador, Galel. ed. *Primer simposio de literatura hondureña.* Tegucigalpa: Universidad Nacional Autónoma de Honduras, 1991.

Carías, Claudia Marcela, et al. *Tradición oral indígena de Yamarangüila.* Tegucigalpa: Guaymuras, 1988.

Carney, James Guadalupe. *To Be a Revolutionary, The Explosive Account of an American Priest, Missing in Honduras.* New York: Harper and Row, 1984.

Carr, Archie. *High Jungles and Low.* Gainesville: University of Florida Press, 1953.

Castegnara de Foletti, Alessandra. *Viaje por el universo artesanal de Honduras.* Tegucigalpa: Instituto Hondureño de Antropología e Historia, 2002.

Chapman, Anne. *Masters of Animals: Oral Traditions of the Tolupan Indians, Honduras.* Philadelphia: Gordon and Breach, 1992.

————. *Los hijos del copal y la candela: ritos agrarios y tradición oral de los lencas de Honduras.* Mexico: Universidad Nacional Autónoma de México, c. 1969.

Coates, Anthony G. *Central America: A Natural and Cultural History.* New Haven, CT: Yale University Press, 1997.

Cohen, Milton. "The Ethnomedicine of Garífuna (Black Caribes) of Rio Tinto, Honduras." *Anthropological Quarterly,* 57 (1984).

Conzemius, Eduard. *Miskitos y Sumus de Honduras y Nicaragua.* Managua: Fundación Vida, 2004.

Cox, Harvey. *Fire from Heaven: The Rise of Pentecostal Spirituality and the Reshaping of Religion in the Twenty-first Century.* Boston: Addison-Wesley Publishing Co., 1995.

Davidson, William V. "El Padre Subirana y las tierras concedidas a los indios hondureños en el siglo XIX." *América Indígena* 44, 3 (1984): 447–459.

Dennie, Steve. *Tío Archie: Archie Cameron and the Story of Honduras Conference of the Church of the United Brethren in Christ.* Huntington, IN: Healthy Ministry Resources, 2001.

Dow, James W. "The Growth of Protestant Religions in Mexico and Central America." Paper presented at the annual meeting of the Society for the Scientific Study of Religion, Norfolk, VA, October 2003.

Durón, Rómulo E. *Honduras literaria.* Tegucigalpa: Ministerio de Educación, 1896, 1899. 2 vols.

England, Sarah. "Negotiating Race and Place in the Garífuna Diaspora: Identity Formation and Transnational Grassroots Politics in New York City and Honduras." *Identities,* 6 (1999): 5–53.

Estrada, Tito A. *El censo de las artes contemporáneas de Honduras.* Tegucigalpa: Ministerio de Cultura, 2007.

Euraque, Darío A. *Conversaciones históricas con el mestizaje y su identidad nacional en Honduras.* San Pedro Sula: Centro Editorial, 2004.

————. *Reinterpreting the Banana Republic: Region and State in Honduras.* Chapel Hill, NC: University of North Carolina Press, 1996.

Flores, David. *Evolución histórica de la danza folklórica hondureña.* Tegucigalpa: Ediciones Zots, 2003.

Flores, Lázaro and Wendy Griffin. *Dioses, héroes y hombres en el universo mítico pech.* San Salvador: Universidad José Simeón Cañas, 1991.

Flores, Oscar R. *La toreada de la danta en Agalteca (un rito tolupán).* Tegucigalpa: Editora Casablanca, 2005.

Funes, José Antonio. *Froylán Turcios y el modernismo en Honduras.* Tegucigalpa: Litografía López, 2006.

Galatea, Revista de creación y de cultura. Tegucigalpa, 1999.

Galvao de Andrade Coelho, Ruy. *Los negros caribes de Honduras,* Tegucigalpa: Guaymuras, 1981.

García Buchard, Ethel. "Evangelizar a los indios de la frontera de Honduras: una ardua tarea (siglos XVII–XIX)." *Intercambio. Journal of CIICLA* (Centro de Investigación de Identidad y Cultura), Universidad de Costa Rica I:1 (2002).

Gold, Janet. *Clementina Suárez, Her Life and Poetry*. Gainesville: University Press of Florida, 1985.

———. *Volver a imaginarlas: retratos de escritoras centroamericanas*. Tegucigalpa: Guaymuras, 1998.

Gollin, James D. *Honduras: Adventures in Nature*. Emeryville, CA: Avalon Travel Publishing, 2001.

González, José. *Diccionario de autores hondureños*. Tegucigalpa: Editores Unidos, 1987.

Gonzalez, Nancie L. *Sojourners of the Caribbean: Ethnogenesis and Ethnohistory of the Garífuna*. Urbana: University of Illinois Press, 1988.

Greene, Oliver N., Jr. "Ethnicity, Modernity, and Retention in the Garífuna Punta." *Black Music Research Journal*, 22 (2002): 189–216.

Griffin, Wendy. *Los garífunas de Honduras: cultura, lucha y derechos bajo el Convenio 169 de la OIT*. Trujillo, Honduras: Comité de Emergencia Garífuna, 2005.

Guardiola Cubas, Esteban. *Historia de la Universidad de Honduras en la primera centuria de su fundación*. Tegucigalpa: Talleres Tipográficos Nacionales, 1952.

Herranz, Anastasio. *Estado, Sociedad y Lenguaje*. Tegucigalpa: Guaymuras, 1996.

Honduras This Week. On-line edition. www.hondurasthisweek.com.

Kerns, Virginia. *Women and the Ancestors: Black Carib Kinship and the Ancestors*, 2nd. ed. Urbana: University of Illinois Press, 1997.

Lanza, Rigoberto de Jesús et al. *Los Pech: una cultura olvidada*. Tegucigalpa: Guaymuras, 2003.

Lara Pinto, Gloria. "La investigación arqueológica en Honduras: lecciones aprendidas para una futura proyección," *Revista pueblos y fronteras digital*, 2006:2. www.pueblosyfronteras.unam.mx.

LiterArte (Journal of Culture and Criticism). Tegucigalpa, 1998.

López, Evaristo and Longino Becerra. *Honduras: 40 pintores*. Tegucigalpa: Editorial Baktún, 1989.

López García, Víctor Virgilio. *Lamumehan garífuna/Clamor garífuna*. n.d.

López Lazo, José D. *Voces de la literatura hondureña actual*. Tegucigalpa: Universidad Nacional Autónoma de Honduras, 1994.

Luna Mejía, Manuel. *Indice general de poesía hondureña*. Mexico: Editora Latinoamericana, 1961.

Martin, David. *The Explosion of Protestantism in Latin America*. Oxford: Basil Blackwell, 1990.

Martínez, José Francisco. *Literatura hondureña y su proceso generacional*. Tegucigalpa: Universidad Nacional Autónoma de Honduras, 1987.

McKittrick, Alison. "Arte Rupestre en Honduras." In *Arte Rupestre de México Oriental y de Centro América*, edited by Martin Künne and Matthias Strecker, 163–182. Berlin: Gebr. Mann Verlag, 2003.

McSweeney, Kendra. A demographic profile of the Tawahka Amerindians of Honduras. *The Geographical Review* (2002).

Meyer, Harvey K. *Historical Dictionary of Honduras*. Metuchen, NJ: The Scarecrow Press, 1976.

Muñoz Tabora, Jesús. *Folklore de Honduras*. Tegucigalpa: Secretaría de Cultura y Turismo,1984.

Muñóz, Willy O. *Antología de cuentistas hondureñas*. Tegucigalpa: Guaymuras, 2003.

Murillo Selva Rendón, Rafael. *Loubavagu o El otro lado lejano*. Tegucigalpa: Litografía López, 1998.

Newson, Linda. *The Cost of Conquest: Indian Decline in Honduras Under Spanish Rule*. Boulder, CO: Westview Press, 1986.

Olsen, Carolyn. *Loss of Innocence: An Ethnography of Sandy Bay, Roatán, Bay Islands, Honduras*. E-book. Xlibris Corp., 2006.

Oyuela, Leticia. *La batalla pictórica: síntesis de la historia de la pintura hondureña*. Tegucigalpa: Banco Atlántida, 1995.

———. *Confidente de soledad: vida íntima de Teresa V. Fortín*. Tegucigalpa: Credomatic, 1997.

———. *Fe, riqueza y poder: una antología crítica de documentos para la historia de Honduras*. Tegucigalpa: Instituto Hondureño de Cultura Hispánica, 1992.

———. *José Miguel Gómez, pintor criollo*. Tegucigalpa: Banco Atlántida, 1992.

———. *Senderos del mestizaje*. Choluteca, Honduras: Ediciones Subirana, 2005.

Paredes, Rigoberto and Manuel Salinas Paguada, eds. *Literatura hondureña*. Tegucigalpa: Editores Unidos, 1987.

Pawlikowski, Barbara. *Man on a Mission: On the Road with Father Emil Cook and Mission Honduras International*. Skokie, IL: Acta Publications, 2007.

Peckenham, Nancy and Street, Annie, eds. *Honduras: Portrait of a Captive Nation*. New York: Praeger, 1985.

Pine, Adrienne. *Working Hard, Drinking Hard: On Violence and Survival in Honduras*. Berkeley: University of California Press, 2008.

Pineda de Gálvez, Adaluz. *Honduras: mujer y poesía (Antología de poesía escrita por mujeres 1865–1998)*. Tegucigalpa: Guardabarranco, 1998.

Rápalo Flores, Oscar. "Diagnóstico de la artesanía de Honduras." Tegucigalpa: UNESCO and IHAH, 2004.

Revista Ixbalam: Estudios culturales y literatura. Tegucigalpa. 2004–2006.

Revista de la Universidad Pedagógica Nacional Francisco Morazán. Tegucigalpa, 2000–2008.

Rivas, Ramón. *Pueblos indígenas y garífuna de Honduras*. Tegucigalpa: Guaymuras, 1993.

Salinas, Iris Milady. *Arquitectura de los grupos étnicos de Honduras*. 2nd ed. Tegucigalpa: Guaymuras, 2002.

Salinas Paguada, Manuel. *Cultura hondureña contemporánea*. Tegucigalpa: Universidad Nacional Autónoma de Honduras, 1991.

Schulz, Donald E and Deborah Sundloff Schulz. *The U.S., Honduras and the Crisis in Central America*. Boulder, CO: Westview Press, 1994.

Sosa, Roberto, *Prosa armada*. Tegucigalpa: Guaymuras, 1981.

———. Ed. *Diálogo de sombras*. Tegucigalpa: Editorial Guaymuras, 1993.

———. Ed. *Documentos para la historia de Honduras*. Tegucigalpa: Honduras: Imagen y Palabra, Vol. I, 1999, Vol. II, 2002, Vol. III, 2004.

Squier, Ephraim George. *Notes on Central America, Particularly the States of Honduras and El Salvador.* New York: Harper and Brothers,1855.

Stephens, John Lloyd. *Incidents of Travel in Guatemala, Chiapas and the Yucatan,.* New York: Dover Publications, 1969. Originally published 1841.

Stoll, David. *Is Latin America Turning Protestant? The Politics of Evangelical Growth.* Berkeley and Los Angeles: University of California Press, 1990.

Stone, Doris. *Pre-Columbian Man Finds Central America: The Archaeological Bridge.* Cambridge, MA: Peabody Museum Press, 1972.

Suazo, E. Salvador. *Uraga: la tradición oral del pueblo garífuna.* Tegucigalpa: CEDEC, 1992.

Thorne, Eva. "Land rights and Garífuna Identity." *NACLA Reports on the Americas,* 38 (2004): 21–25.

Umaña, Helen. *Literatura hondureña contemporánea.* Tegucigalpa: Editorial Guaymuras, 1986.

———. *Narradoras hondureñas.* Tegucigalpa: Editorial Guaymuras, 1990.

———. *Ensayos sobre literatura hondureña.* Tegucigalpa: Editorial Guaymuras, 1992.

———. *Panorama crítico del cuento hondureño (1881–1999).* Guatemala: Letra negra, 1999.

———. *La novela hondureña.* Guatemala: Letra Negra, 2003.

———. *La palabra iluminada: el discurso poético en Honduras.* Guatemala: Letra Negra, 2006.

Valle, Rafael Heliodoro. *Historia de la cultura hondureña.* Tegucigalpa: Universidad Nacional Autónoma de Honduras, 1981.

Wallace, David Rains. *The Monkey's Bridge: Mysteries of Evolution in Central America.* San Francisco, CA: Sierra Club Books, 1997.

Woodward, Ralph Lee. *Central America: A Nation Divided.* New York: Oxford University Press, 1985.

Wells, William V. *Explorations and Adventures in Honduras.* New York: Harper and Brothers, 1857.

Yaxkin. Journal of the Honduran Institute of Anthropology and History.

Yuscarán, Guillermo (William Lewis). *Conociendo a la gente garífuna/The Garífuna Story.* Santa Lucia, Honduras: Nuevo Sol Publications, 1990.

———. *Velásquez, the Man and His Art.* Santa Lucia, Honduras: Nuevo Sol Publications, 1994.

———. *Gringos in Honduras.* Santa Lucia, Honduras: Nuevo Sol Publications, 1995.

Index

Lagos, Dina, 135
Laínez, Daniel, 88
Languages, 3, 8, 14–15. *See also* Chortí;
    Garífuna; Lenca; Pech; Tawahka;
    Tolupán
Lara, Karla, 152
Lara, Katia, 148
Lara Pinto, Gloria, 135 n. 2
Lazo, Sotero, 120
Leather craft. *See* Artisanry
Lempira, 12; and national identity, 74
Lenca: agriculture of, 38; artisanry of,
    38–39, 110–12; Catholic Church
    and, 41, 51–52, 58; contact with
    Chorotega, 11; cooperatives of,
    38–39; folk dances of, 141–42;
    history of, 36–37; houses of, 30–31;
    language of, 15, 36–37;
    Mesoamerican influence on, 13; and
    national identity, 5; political
    organizations of, 37; portrayal of in
    film, 148; traditional beliefs and
    rituals of, 36–37, 38–39, 139–40
León Gómez, Alfredo, 86
Lesmes, Jesús, 152
Lewis, William. *See* Yuscarán, Guillermo
Liberation Theology. *See* Theology of
    Liberation
Lindsay, Jim, 95
Literacy, 79–81; NGOs and, 101
Literary criticism, 101, 106
Literary history, 105–6
Literary journals, 80, 85–86, 104, 105
Literary workshops, 98, 104
Lobo, Edmundo, 101
Lobo, Raquel, 97
Logan, Elisa (Elizeth García), 98
López García, Víctor Virgilio, 45
López Rodezno, Arturo, 122–23
Lugua (Evangelisto Centeno), 151
Luna Mejía, Manuel, 106

Madrid, Salvador, 104
Maquiladora, 6, 143

Maras (gangs), 7, 132, 149
Martínez, Aurelio, 151
Martínez, Cipriano, 35
Martínez, Jorge, 74
Martínez, José Francisco, 106
Martínez, Vidal Antonio, 102
Matute, Claudia, 142
McKittrick, Alison, 116, 118
McLaughlin, Edward V., 95
Medina, Sara de, 97
Mejía, América, 131
Mejía, Junior, 150
Mejía, Mario, 127–28
Mejía, Medardo, 100
Mejía Medina, Waldina, 98, 104
Mejía, Xenia, 131, 133
Meléndez, Crisanto, 50
Méndez, Luis, 104
Mesoamerican Biological Corridor, 26
Mestizaje, 5, 13, 51
Metalwork. *See* Artisanry
Mezapa, Mario de (Mario Ernesto
    Castro), 151
Migration: current, 3; of Garífuna,
    44–45; among Lenca, 36, 38; Pech,
    27; prehistoric, 12
Militarism, 90; concern with in art, 128;
    denunciation of in literature, 90–91,
    94–96
Mining, 4–5
Ministry of Culture, Arts and Sports,
    109
Miralda, Adolfo, 88
Miranda, José Luis, 65
Miskito: agriculture of, 20–21; artisanry
    of, 109–10, 112–13; cosmogony of,
    18–19, 21–22; dances, 23; gender
    roles of, 20; history of, 18–19;
    housing, 21; language, 14, 20; music,
    23; oral tradition, 23; political
    organizations of, 51–54; religions of,
    19–21; traditional beliefs, 21–22
Missionaries, 28. *See also* Catholic
    Church; Moravian Church

About the Author

JANET N. GOLD is Professor of Latin American literature at the University of New Hampshire in Durham, NH. She is the author of several books and essays on Central American literature and culture.

CEN

972.83 G618
Gold, Janet N.
Culture and customs of Honduras /

CENTRAL LIBRARY
05/15